Corporate China 2.0

CW01572650

Qiao Liu

Corporate China 2.0

The Great Shakeup

palgrave
macmillan

Qiao Liu
Guanghua School of Management
Peking University
Beijing, China

ISBN 978-1-137-60372-2 (Softcover)   ISBN 978-1-137-55089-7 (eBook)
DOI 10.1057/9781137550897

Library of Congress Control Number: 2016957719

Cover illustration: Cover image © zhangkun / Getty Images

Printed on acid-free paper

This Palgrave Macmillan imprint is published by Springer Nature
The registered company is Nature America Inc.
The registered company address is: 1 New York Plaza, New York, NY 10004, U.S.A.

I don't know why we are here, but I'm pretty sure that it is not in order to enjoy ourselves.

—*Ludwig Wittgenstein*

Acknowledgments

This book grew out of my own research, teaching, and consulting experiences at different institutions in China over the past 15 years. I have benefited tremendously from suggestions, comments, encouragement, and support from many people, even long before I began this project in 2015. It is impossible to thank them all individually. Still, there are a few without whom this book would never have been written. Although I take full ownership of any remaining errors in the book, I would like to extend my gratitude to them.

I am grateful to my coauthors, with whom I have spent the best part of my academic life, for stimulating conversations, constructive debates, and, more importantly, inspiration and friendship. Part of the book has drawn on our collaborative works. I owe both personal and intellectual debts to many more than I can possibly acknowledge. I wish to thank in particular Douglas Arner, Chong-en Bai, Hongbin Cai, Bradford Cornell, Michael Darby, Qiang Kang, Paul Lejot, the late Joe Lu, Wei Luo, Rong Qi, Alan Siu, Frank Song, Xiaoquan Wang, Keith Wong, Nianhan Xu, Miaojie Yu, Yuande Zhu, and Lynne Zucker.

I owe many of the ideas in this book to the stimulating intellectual environment at the institutions that have employed me: Guanghua School of Management at Peking University, Faculty of Business and Economics at the University of Hong Kong, and McKinsey's Asian Corporate Finance and Strategy Practice. I have benefited enormously from interactions with colleagues and former colleagues. Several of my friends and students have assisted with research for this book, shared research or archive material with me, or provided helpful comments on draft chapters. To list all of them would greatly lengthen the book. However, there are some individuals who have been especially helpful and deserve special mention: Sherry Bai, Yuyu Chen, Zhiwu Chen, Joseph Fan, Helen Huang, Guohua Jiang, Li Jin, Jiang Luo, Dragon Tang, Qing Wang, Wei Xiong, Lin Xu, Se Yan, Joy Yang, Renxiong Zeng, Hong Zhang, Zheng Zhang, Ying Zheng, Xianmin Zhou, and Ning Zhu.

My gratitude also goes out to Siline Cen, Jingyi Liu, Yixiao Qing, and Yong Wei for their outstanding research assistance throughout my research career. Xiaoquan Wang, who was also my invaluable coauthor on some of the work summarized in this book, provided excellent research assistance throughout its development.

Equally important, I would like to thank numerous students I have taught at Guanghua School of Management at Peking University, the University of Hong Kong, and other places in the past 15 years. Part of the book had been used in my MBA course Corporate Finance at Guanghua, which has drawn more than 70 students each year since 2010. The materials contained in this book have also been used in my EMBA course Corporate Investment and Value Creation. More than two thousand EMBA students at Guanghua, from Class 68 to Class 108, have taken this mandatory course. I have also used part of this book in my Advanced Financial Management course in the Guanghua-Kellogg Joint EMBA program. Almost all of Guanghua's EMBA students are corporate founders or executives with rich business experiences and deep insights about the Chinese economy and Chinese companies. I benefit tremendously from the interactions with them in the classroom, at the dinner table, and during late-night hangouts.

Several organizations provided me with generous support during different stages of this book's preparation. I acknowledge the support of the National Science Fund for Distinguished Young Scholar (#71325004) and the Ministry of Education ChangJiang Scholar Special Professorship Scheme. I am also grateful to the New Finance Center at Peking University, Phoenix Finance, and PetroChina for generous research grants.

I also want to extend my thanks to the Palgrave Macmillan team. In particular, I thank Jacob Dreyer and Rachel Krause, my editors at Palgrave Macmillan, for their patience, encouragement, and support throughout the project. I thank Marcus Ballenger and the other staff members of Palgrave Macmillan for great skills and care in producing the final version of this book.

The book and the research underlying it would not have been possible without the strong support of my family, who have put up with my work. I want to thank my parents, who taught me how to stand firmly on sound principles. Finally, I want to thank my two sons, Alan and Nick, for providing a wonderful distraction from my research and writing. I hope that one day they will find reading the book enjoyable, and understand the reasons I was always away.

Qiao Liu
Beijing, April 2016

CONTENTS

ABOUT THE AUTHOR

Qiao Liu is Professor of Finance and Associate Dean for EMBA in the Guanghua School of Management at Peking University. He is the winner of the National Science Foundation Distinguished Young Talent Award and the Ministry of Education "ChangJiang Scholar" Special Term Professor. Before he joined Guanghua in 2010, Qiao Liu worked as a tenured professor in the Faculty of Business and Economics at the University of Hong Kong. He also worked as a corporate finance expert at McKinsey & Company's Asia-Pacific Corporate Finance and Strategy Practice from December 2001 to July 2003. Qiao Liu has published dozens of academic articles in leading journals including *Journal of Financial Economics, Journal of Financial and Quantitative Analysis, Journal of Accounting Research, Management Science, and Economic Journal.* He is a co-editor of *Asia's debt capital markets: prospects and strategies for development* (Springer, 2006). His book *Finance in Asia: Institutions, Market, and Regulation* (with Paul Lejot and Douglas Arner) was published by Routledge in 2013. Qiao Liu holds a PhD in economics from UCLA.

Qiao Liu has a wide range of business experiences. He has conducted numerous consulting projects for leading Chinese firms and MNCs. He is the founder of Huaxinhui (TrustWorks), a platform advising Chinese local governments on financing issues. He pioneers the practice of compiling balance sheets and income statements of local governments, and providing them with market-based credit ratings. Qiao Liu is also co-founder of Oasis International Medical Group, a private healthcare company based in Beijing.

LIST OF FIGURES

LIST OF TABLES

Introduction: A New Game in Town

I always count myself as a lucky one. Born in 1970, by the end of the first ten years of my life, China's paramount leader Deng Xiaoping initiated the economic reform and open-door policies. In the second ten years of my life, an entrepreneurial wave redefined the Chinese economy. The household responsibility system was introduced, which unleashed millions of individuals' productivity. Millions of township and village enterprises (TVEs) were established. China's private sector took off—Zhang Ruimin, Liu Chuangzhi, Ren Zhengfei, and Lu Guanqiu, with little business experience, respectively set up Haier, Legend (later changed to Lenovo), Huawei, and Wanxiang during the 1980s. After a short period of political turmoil and economic stagnation, Deng Xiaoping's "southern China tour" in 1992 heralded a new round of economic reform as well as China's second entrepreneurial wave—this time, many well-educated people left academics or government to start their own businesses.[1] During the 1990s, the Chinese government also began reforming the state-owned enterprises (SOEs) and opened stock exchanges in Shanghai and Shenzhen.

By the time I reached my 30s, China joined the World Trade Organization (WTO) in 2001, opening up to international business. Many internet pioneers had ridden the technological innovation wave and set up their own internet companies. Most failed. But the few who survived flourished and later developed into China's IT giants such as Alibaba, Tencent, Baidu. dom, and JD.com. In the first decade of the twenty-first century, while international trade skyrocketed, China also welcomed its property market boom that lasted for more than ten years. The soaring property price profoundly changed the structure of the Chinese economy, as well as the behavioral pattern of local governments. While the boom had contributed significantly to China's GDP growth, it also planted the seeds of various risk factors that are now threatening China's long-term prosperity.

As I approached my 40s, I settled down in Beijing in 2010. China became the world's second largest economy and overtook the USA to become the world's largest manufacturer, accounting for almost a quarter of the world's total manufacturing value-added.

Unlike my parents, whose lives had been filled with vicissitudes associated with economic stagnation due to ideological conflicts and political instability, I enjoyed an extraordinary increase in living standards in the first four decades of my existence. I experienced first-hand how the market-oriented development approach had delivered required growth to turn the Middle Kingdom into a most dynamic economy. Over the past three and a half decades, China has maintained a double-digit GDP growth rate every year. The whole country was like a huge construction site—skyscrapers were rising and cranes loomed large everywhere. Between 2011 and 2013, China used more cement than the USA had used in the entire twentieth century (6.5 gig tons vs. 4.5 gig tons).[2] The results, of course, were also impressive. Since economic reforms began in the late 1970s, China has lifted 620 million people, half of its population, out of poverty.[3]

Along the way, I also felt the excitement due to the surge of Chinese companies. Now, China boasts of more than 20 percent of the world's largest companies (by sales), based on the 2015 list of the *Fortune* Global 500 companies. China has become the world's largest automobile and home appliances maker, as well as the largest consumer. In the meantime, wealth has grown explosively. In Beijing alone, there are 101 billionaires, according to Forbes' 2015 China rich list.[4] Across the shopping malls or outlets in Paris, London, and New York shuttle Chinese tourists with various dialects, talking on their iPhones, carrying their Chanel bags, and wearing their Prada shoes. Like a dream, things that had taken more than 300 years to happen in the western world became a reality in China in just slightly more than 30 years. China has developed so fast economically that many of us have started taking long-term growth for granted.

Over time, other ways of looking at the Chinese economy and Chinese companies have emerged. As I approach my 46th birthday, something seems to have gone wrong. Many of the factors that have led to China's mysterious economic rise are no longer working their magic: the once abundant labor force is aging and no longer cheap, the forces of globalization are in retreat, credit-fueled investments have resulted in a pile-up of corporate debt and overcapacity everywhere, and the once strong faith in long-term prosperity by Chinese entrepreneurs and corporate founders is eroding. The underlying rate of economic growth is beginning to slow. In 2015, China's national output grew only 6.9 percent, below 7 percent for the first time since 1991. Skepticism about the sustainability of China's economic growth is mounting. It has become a consensus among policymakers and corporate executives that China desperately needs to accomplish the transition of its economic growth model from investment-led to consumption- and services-driven before it gets too late.

The ongoing economic transition poses many challenges for those national champions in China's corporate sector. The structural problems, which have long been camouflaged by rapid economic growth, are surging onto the scene. The investment spree that lasted for 35 years has created many corporate behemoths. However, most of them are debt-laden and fail to deliver reasonable returns. For example, even though China has become the world's largest auto maker, the profit harnessed by its home-grown brands is less than 5 percent.[5] Out of 98 *Fortune* Global 500 companies from mainland China in 2015, 12 reported net losses; one of them, Sinosteel, even failed to honor its debt. As the world's largest manufacturer, most Chinese manufacturing firms compete fiercely in the low-end segments of the value chain. China-made products can hardly escape the perception that China is still about cheapness and copycats. On top of all this, some variant of the same question has been repeatedly raised: Does China have great brands and great companies? Indeed, the world is yet to see the birth of some truly great Chinese companies.

Companies, the "little republic" as Peter Drucker calls them,[6] are micro-foundations of an economy. Only when the micro-foundations exhibit a strong capability of creating value can the aggregate economy grow in a healthy and sustainable way. Recall the growth identity: *Growth rate = Investment rate × Return on Invested Capital (ROIC)*, which says that both investment rate and ROIC can drive growth. Nevertheless, China's ongoing economic transformation calls for a shift of the growth driver from investment rate to ROIC. Only in this way can the Chinese economy accomplish its long overdue metamorphosis (from quantity growth to quality growth). To raise ROIC at the aggregate economy level, the micro-units of the Chinese economy—Chinese companies—need to put value creation far ahead of aggressive pursuit of operation scale.

The Chinese economy is now faced with the onset of a seemingly permanent slowdown. Pessimists are already predicting a long period of stagnation, reminiscent of Japan's lost decade. Will it happen? What should we do to prevent it from happening? Intense worries make people rush to economists for answers. Unfortunately, most economists are still busy debating what macroeconomic policies might be appropriate to absorb excess capacity and inventory and lower overriding corporate debt. For the few who have coined the term "the supply side structural reform," they are also failing horribly because they only create an ambiguous term that leads to no meaningful and implementable policy suggestions. It may even mislead people's discussions about the real issues. No matter how the narratives change, the nature of the structural problems facing China has been the same: The Chinese economy needs to improve its capital efficiency because economic growth thriving on a massive use of debt simply cannot be sustained. When the economy goes underperforms, people tend to hold lower respect for economists, for reasons—there has been a huge gap between what they do and what people expect them to do.

As an economist myself, I try to provide an intellectual framework to understand what has been going on. To me, the answer is extremely simple and straightforward—China needs to breed a large number of great companies that can maintain high ROIC for a long enough time. Only with such companies around every corner can micro-foundations of the Chinese economy be fixed and enduring growth be achieved. Of course, my narrative immediately leads to many unanswered questions: Why are there big but few great companies in China? Why is it important to have great companies? What external or internal factors are constraining the surge of great companies in China? What rules can make Chinese companies truly great? How can we fix the foundations of the Chinese economy to ensure its sustainable growth?

I will address all these questions in this book.

The Surge of Corporate China

The surge of corporate China did not happen until the late 1990s. In 20 years, the number of *Fortune* Global 500 firms from mainland China has increased from 2 in 1996 to 98 in 2015. If I include the companies located in Taiwan and Hong Kong, the number is 106.[7] This is a great achievement China has accomplished during the first stage of its reform era and, by all means, marvelous. Several features characterize mainland China's *Fortune* Global 500 companies. First, the majority of them are state owned. Out of the 98 mainland companies on the 2015 *Fortune* Global 500 list, only ten are private. The three largest companies in China, Sinopec, PetroChina, and State Grid, which are also among the world's ten largest companies by sales, are all central government-controlled SOEs. Second, 60 percent of China's large firms come from the financial services and resources sectors. Among the ten most profitable companies in the world, four are from China and all of them are the state-owned banks dubbed "Big 4." Third, 12 out of mainland China's 98 *Fortune* Global 500 companies reported net losses in 2015—these corporate behemoths are very big but not that profitable.

In Chap. 1 of this book, I explore the structural factors that account for the quick surge of Chinese companies: investment-led growth model, government policies, and external environment in their favor. The economic expansion in China has been driven by fixed-asset investments. The rapidly expanding economy experiencing a persistent investment boom has strong demand for production factors such as resources and capital, which are still monopolized by the state. Strong demand, together with state monopoly, gave birth to big state-owned companies in the resources and financial services sectors.

In the mid-1990s, China shifted the focus of reform to the urban areas. To promote operating efficiency of the state-owned enterprises (SOEs), the government has adopted the so-called grasp the big and let go of the small strategy to consolidate SOEs through mergers, acquisitions, divestitures, and, oftentimes, outright shutdowns. The SOEs' reform facilitated the surge of a number of large companies. Nowadays, the central government only directly controls slightly more than 100 SOEs, half of which have been listed as *Fortune* Global 500 companies.

China's WTO accession in 2001 is another facilitator. During the first decade of the twenty-first century, annual export growth rate had been over 20 percent in most years, and total exports accounted for over 30 percent of China's GDP, thanks to the lower tariff rates. The Chinese economy and Chinese firms are beneficiaries of global trade liberalization. Strong exports also led to a pile-up of foreign exchange reserves, which once reached $4 trillion. The deep base of foreign exchange reserves allowed the Chinese firms, state-owned or private, to aggressively pursue foreign targets through cross-border acquisitions. For example, Geely, a privately owned auto maker in Zhejiang, acquired Volvo in 2011 and became one of the *Fortune* Global 500 companies in 2012.

However, not all big companies are great. Firm size captured by sales is not the measure of firm value. Chalco[8] reported a net loss of $1.76 billion in 2015. Sinosteel and many other government-controlled steel and iron groups are on the brink of bankruptcy. These large companies surely contribute to GDP, but they do not generate much value.

To sustain future growth, it is important for China to strike a new balance between investment rate and ROIC. While maintaining a 50 percent of fixed-asset investment to GDP ratio becomes increasingly impossible, improving firm-level ROIC seems the only way out. Based on the four different combinations of the values (high or low) of the two variables driving growth, I conjure up in Chap. 1 four potential end scenarios of the Chinese economy.[9] Whether China can successfully escape the worst scenario—"the mid-income trap"—which corresponds to a permanent economic stagnation resulting from a combination of low investment rate and low ROIC, hinges on whether the aggregate ROIC could be significantly improved. Enhancing ROIC at the aggregate level calls for the micro-foundations of the Chinese economy, Chinese companies, to improve their capital efficiency significantly.

In Chap. 2, I provide a corporate finance version of the definition of great companies, "Great companies are those that can maintain higher return on invested capital (ROIC) for a long enough time." This definition is analogous to those raised in *Built to Last* and *Creative Destruction* in the sense that they all emphasize an indispensable feature of the great companies: Great companies have to first create value consistently and persistently. In my narrative, the greatness of a company derives from its business model innovation, and is embodied in its sustainably high ROIC.

Does ROIC apply to Chinese companies? As an empirical economist, I resort to the large data on China's listed companies and techniques developed in the empirical finance literature. I find, in Chap. 3, that trading strategies designed around ROIC can generate alpha—the secret source of value in capital market investment. Specifically, a hedge strategy with a long position of stocks with higher ROIC and a short position of stocks with lower ROIC can generate a risk-adjusted abnormal return as high as 20 percent. In addition, I show that investing in the top quintile of the listed companies (by ROIC) can generate an annualized return as high as 13.2 percent from 1998 to 2012, which is on par with China's nominal GDP growth over the same time period. While ROIC indicates a firm's fundamentals, I find that the average ROIC of the universe of China's listed companies during 1998–2012 was only 3 percent, far smaller than that of their US counterparts. Clearly, there is a paucity of quality companies (i.e., companies with high ROIC) in China.

WHY ARE THERE BIG BUT FEW GREAT COMPANIES IN CHINA?

What factors, external or internal, are preventing the Chinese companies from putting value ahead of operation scale? Chapter 4 of the book explores two external factors: the investment-led growth model and weak institutional infrastructure.

Several features characterize China's economic rise, among which high investment rate stands out. With persistently high investment rate, the economy has strong demand for resources and capital. However, the resources and finance industries are still dominated by SOEs. Because of the moral hazard problems and the soft budget constraints faced by SOEs, investments by SOEs are not as efficient as those by private firms. In Chap. 4, I analyze the cross-ownership distribution of ROIC and find that SOEs on average have ROIC 4 to 6 percentage points lower than that of non-SOEs.[10] In the meantime, China's state-dominated financial system allocates most banks lending to the state sector, which squeezes the private companies and makes it difficult for them to grow bigger. As such, we see many large SOEs but very few companies with high ROIC in China. The very factors that make the Chinese companies big are also the factors that prevent them from being truly great. The spirit is vividly epitomized in the lyrics of Lou Reed's "A Perfect Day," "*You are going to reap just what you sow.*"

China has been practicing a financial repression policy during its reform era. This is reflected in the following aspects: The financial system is dominated by the state-run banks; the interest rates are regulated; and the barriers of entry to finance are extremely high for private capital. The state-owned banks are incentivized to allocate disproportionate amounts of funds to SOEs, which gives birth to large firms, but not great firms. The problem can be best illustrated by applying the following principle: ROIC ≥ WACC, where WACC is shorthand for weighted average cost of capital. An investment generates value if and only if this inequality holds. Due to inefficient financial intermediation, WACC perceived by SOEs and local governments is likely lower than the market rate or the rate applied to private companies. Perceiving a much lower WACC, SOEs and local governments likely over-invest, while more efficient private firms may under-invest.

Another fundamental problem associated with China's institutional infrastructure is the lack of an open and integrated domestic market. As discussed in Chap. 4, during China's reform era, China has been sufficiently open to the outside world. But the domestic market is still segmented, due to the political tournament based on economic performance. Regional competition leads to regional protectionism, which significantly increases the cost of cross-region transactions. Without a level playing field, market competition likely only creates winners that are better at seeking rents than generating value.

Over the past three and a half decades, China invested heavily in infrastructures such as expressways, high-speed railways, and airports. It is now time for China to invest in its institutional infrastructure.

Poor corporate governance practice is an internal factor explaining the lack of great companies in China. I attack this issue in Chap. 5. Corporate governance problems arise because of agency problems. In general, the corporate governance mechanisms used by Chinese firms are not effective enough to resolve very sophisticated and twisted agency problems among Chinese companies. There is plenty of evidence showing that poor governance is associated with lower ROIC. Clearly, to have great companies, improving corporate governance practices is a must. Drawing from my own research, I zero in on the weakest link in Chinese firms' governance practices—the widespread use of pyramidal ownership structure. I provide robust evidence that obsession with building corporate pyramids could be very effective in forging corporate colossuses, but does not help improve ROIC at all.

The myth on diversification is another internal factor explaining the lack of great Chinese companies. Diversification has been a popular strategic choice for many Chinese Companies. Does diversification lead to higher ROIC? Thanks to the recent explosion in data availability and computing power, I can use the data on the Chinese listed companies to address this issue. Chapter 6 provides empirical results and two prominent case examples (Kunlun Energy and China Resources Enterprise (CRE) respectively) to showcase the value effect of diversification. My analysis shows that there is a negative correlation between firm-level ROIC and the extent of diversification, suggesting that value-minded companies in general should stay focused. Of course, diversification may still work for companies with superior organizational capital and management skills (i.e., General Electric) or companies with unusually talented founders who have broader vision and sharp minds on technology and business model innovation (i.e., Alphabet and Alibaba). But it does not apply to an average Chinese company. The case analysis of both Kunlun Energy and CRE yields the same conclusion:

Staying focused generates more value. Misconceived corporate strategy should be held responsible for the abundance of big companies but the lack of great companies in China.

How Can Corporate China Rise to Greatness?

How can the Chinese companies rise to greatness? To cultivate great companies, China needs to first lay down solid institutional foundations. Chapter 7 points out that the enabling institutions should have three building blocks: redefining the economic role of the government, enhancing the efficiency of financial intermediation, and seeding a culture of innovation and entrepreneurship. What roles should the government play in economic development? I attack this issue head on. I admit that the heavy involvement of the government in economic affairs has been one important contributing factor to China's economic success in the first stage of its reform era. State planning and government spending have built the infrastructure indispensable for China's industrialization and economic takeoff. The state involvement even set the stage for innovation. For example, the rise of China's e-commerce had benefited tremendously from the telecommunication network, the highway system, and the high-speed railways built by the state. In addition, the state has committed large amounts of resources to drive innovations in many crucial areas, which private companies alone cannot commit.

However, it is important to bear in mind that China is entering a new stage of economic development, during which capital efficiency and business model innovations are much more important. Governments at all levels should thus adjust their roles and make efforts to transform themselves from participants in economic activities to rule-setters and public service providers, whose main responsibility is to develop and maintain level playing fields.

On the second point, deregulating interest rate and allowing private capital to enter the financial services sector are the key to rejuvenating the financial system in China. Only when capital can be allocated more efficiently can firm-level ROIC be improved. As such, China needs a new generation of financial system, which I call "Finance 2.0." The new finance should channel the funds from savers to end-users in simple, direct, and effective ways.

The Chinese economy has benefited tremendously from unleashing individuals' creativity, to which China's reform experiences in the 1980s and 1990s attest. The most feasible source of future economic growth is the improvement of total factor productivity. To achieve this, China needs to create a fair, equitable, and transparent business atmosphere, protect and acknowledge the seemingly trivial attempts by numerous individuals, seed the culture of innovation, and inspire entrepreneurship.

Great companies are created by great minds. China's great companies will surely arise from those who are brave enough to disrupt the incumbents through technology and business model innovations, hold deep respect for the market and customers, and aim at creating long-term value rather than short-term gains. In Chap. 8, I discuss four promising candidates that have lined up to join the small elite club of truly great companies: Huawei Technologies, Alibaba Group, Xiaomi.dom, and SF Express. They have very different business models and compete in different industries. Huawei is a telecommunication equipment provider and is now also involved in consumer business; Alibaba is the world's leading e-commerce platform with a wide range of investments in almost everything; although it sells more than 60 million smartphones every year, Xiaomi perceives itself as a mobile internet company; and SF Express is China's leading private delivery company. Despite the fact that the four have very different corporate culture and provide differentiated products and services, they share one thing in common: Their business models and business practices can be traced back to one unifying theme—creating value by aggressively pursuing higher ROIC.

I hope that the end result of this book is that it provides an intellectual framework, strongly supported by both empirical and anecdotal evidence, which can help the Chinese companies rise to greatness. In Chap. 9, I summarize findings in the book by highlighting eight must-does.

China Now

At one time, the rise of the Chinese economy seemed unstoppable. Now the old growth model, which relies heavily on state planning and huge investment in infrastructure and property, and thrives on a massive use of debt provided by the state-dominated financial system, is running out of steam. The success of China's economic transformation hinges on whether its micro-foundations can be fixed. Much can be gained if we can draw the right lessons from the past economic success in China and start to tackle the structural problems that have shackled the Chinese people's entrepreneurial spirit. I lay down the challenges that confront us in this book, with the hope that our collective efforts can help us overcome their constraints.

Finally, despite all the suspicions people have held about the Chinese economy, the picture is not all gloom. There are plenty of reasons to be hopeful. Although the annual GDP growth rate has dropped to below 7 percent, it still represents more economic output than the 14 percent in 2007 simply because the economy has become much larger. More importantly, over time, we are seeing the rise of new breeds of companies in China. Those highly disruptive ones are more aggressively using new technologies such as mobile internet to challenge inefficient incumbents. They are global in outlook, more willing to take risks, and more skilled in capital market maneuvering. They can take full advantage of the potentials of new technology and deliver not only better manufacturing goods but also increasingly sophisticated quality services. They are the hope of China's great companies.

In November 2012, I flew to Lima, the capital city of Peru, to attend the annual meeting of the Partnership in International Management (PIM), a consortium of leading international business schools. On behalf of the Guanghua School of Management at Peking University, I joined the discussions with representatives from more than 50 business schools around the world on a wide range of issues, mostly on the new challenges facing business schools and business education. It was the first time that I had been to Latin America. To me, Latin America is an exotic and mysterious continent epitomized in Gabriel Garcia Marquez's *One Hundred Years of Solitude*. Although I knew that the town of Macondo in the novel is a metaphor for Colombia, not Peru, walking on the streets of Lima and passing by those storied buildings, I still felt strongly a sense of magical realism. Peru had just experienced an average of 6 percent of GDP growth over the past five years. It seemed that the country was pulling out of years of turmoil and stagnation and economic growth issues were what the current Peruvian government was most concerned with.

China and the Chinese firms were the most popular topics at the 2012 PIM annual conference. Participants were curious to know how to account for the rise of the Chinese economy and what the rise implied for the rest of the world. The surge of the Chinese economy has stemmed from the entrepreneurial spirit by the corporate executives and founders which had been unleashed due to China's reform and open-up polices. Their success and failure stories have gradually become the subjects of business research and case materials used in business school teaching, and enlighten entrepreneurs and business leaders elsewhere. After three and a half decades of economic development, China has transformed from an impoverished country to the world's second largest economy.

During my short stay in Lima, I had a chance to catch a glimpse of Peru's storied history. I was told that slavery was not abolished in Peru until the 1870s. And the precondition for the abolishment of slavery, as raised by slave owners, was that they could use "coolies" from China as substitutes.

Nowadays, walking on the streets of Lima, one can easily spot advertising boards of Chinese companies such as Huawei Technologies and Dongfeng Automobile. One can feel that local people do hold respect for Chinese companies. This is a big difference between the past and the present for China. Indeed, what can really bring to a nation widespread respect are great products, great companies, great thinkers, and great ideas. While Chinese companies have successfully achieved their first Long March and risen rapidly on a global scale, I expect that those with a broader vision and more entrepreneurial spirit will continue to power ahead and become world-class companies. I am hopeful that this will happen!

NOTES

1. For example, Chen Dongsheng of Taikang Life Insurance and Guo Guangchang of Fosun Group.
2. See http://www.gatesnotes.com/About-Bill-Gates/Concrete-in-China.
3. *The Economist*, "Just a little bit richer," April 4, 2015.
4. Billionaires refer to households with wealth over $1 billion (approximately RMB 6.4 billion).
5. See Chap. 2 of the book for more discussion on China's auto industry.
6. Cited in "The Company: A short history of an evolutionary idea" by John Micklethwait and Adrian Wooldridge in 2003.
7. *Fortune* magazine ranks the world's 500 largest companies based on their total sales in the previous year.
8. Shorthand for Aluminum Corporation of China Limited.
9. See Fig. 1.2 of Chap. 1.
10. See Liu and Siu (2011).

CHAPTER 1

The Improbable Surge of Corporate China

In 1984, Liu Chuanzhi, a research scientist from the Institute of Computing Technology at the Chinese Academy of Science (CAS), decided to venture into the business world. With the help of ten other colleagues, he set up a technology company in Zhongguancun, a district where most national research institutes are located.[1] They managed to put together RMB 200,000 as the initial investment. Liu's goal was humble—he wanted to develop a system to speed up typing Chinese characters on computers and, if possible, make some money. It was probably beyond Liu's wildest dreams that his small company would one day develop into one of China's most successful technology companies. The company, later known as Lenovo, was ranked as the world's 231st largest company (by sales) by *Fortune* magazine in 2015. It not only boasts of the world's largest PC market share, but has also developed a solid footing in areas such as smartphones, tablets, Big Data, cloud computing, private equity, venture investment, and agriculture. Lenovo was a fully homegrown company prior to its acquisition of IBM's PC unit in 2005. As of 2015, both overseas assets and sales had exceeded 50 percent and non-Chinese executives account for more than half of Lenovo's senior executives. Lenovo has been widely viewed as the most market-oriented and most international company in China.[2]

In 1980s, Ren Zhengfei, a former army officer in his 40s, relocated to Shenzhen to explore his luck. After a few failed attempts, he founded Huawei Technologies in 1988. In less than 30 years, Huawei has become the world's leading information and telecommunication equipment provider, exporting products and services to more than 150

© The Editor(s) (if applicable) and The Author(s) 2016
Q. Liu, *Corporate China 2.0*, DOI 10.1057/978-1-137-55089-7_1

countries. In 2014, Huawei's total sales exceeded RMB 288 billion and its net profit stood at RMB 27.9 billion. Huawei now has sales significantly larger than traditional champions in this field such as Ericsson, Alcatel-Lucent, and Siemens. Huawei is also the world's third largest smartphone producer, with more than 9 percent of the global market share as of the third quarter of 2015.

On January 20, 2012, Sany Group, a company headquartered in Changsha, the capital city of Hunan Province, announced its €360 million acquisition of Putzmeister—a German engineering machinery manufacturer and a giant in the industry. When Liang Wengen founded Sany in 1994, owning the "elephant" (Putzmeister's nickname) was just a dream for Mr. Liang. In less than 20 years, Sany owned the elephant, and has also obtained access to Putzmeister's cutting-edge technologies and distribution channels across the world.

In May 2013, China's largest meat processor, Shuanghui International Holdings Ltd., struck a $4.7 billion deal to acquire Smithfield Foods Inc. in the USA. The deal marked the largest takeover of an American firm by a Chinese company. Set up in 1936, Smithfield Foods Inc., together with four other companies, controls 73 percent of the US pork-processing industry. While the revenue of Shuanghui was RMB 39.7 billion in 2012, Smithfield had reported revenue twice the size of Shuanghui (approximately RMB 80.3 billion in 2012). The acquisition greatly boosted Shuanghui's operation scale, laying a solid foundation for its later initial public offering (IPO) in Hong Kong. As the demand for pork keeps rising in China, Shuanghui is emerging as a porcine empire.

In April 2010, in a small rented office in Beijing, Lei Jun, together with his six partners, announced the founding of Xiaomi.com. Lei Jun had been a successful businessman before he founded Xiaomi. He took Kingsoft, a software developer, to IPO status. He also founded Joyo, an e-commerce platform that was acquired by Amazon. Founding Xiaomi, Lei Jun aimed to get into the high-end smartphone market. One year later, Xiaomi.com launched its first-generation millet phone with a retail price set at RMB 1999. Relying on internet sales and word-of-mouth buzz, Xiaomi's sales rose quickly. It sold more than 60 million handsets in 2014, making it the world's sixth largest mobile phone producer. To Lei Jun, millet phone is not just a simple device. It is a gadget encompassing software, internet services, and hardware. From the outset, Xiaomi.com has successfully managed to develop an ecosystem that not only houses apps but also sells a wide range of items from content, to software, to services. With its newest round of fund-raising in late 2014, Xiaomi.com was valued at $45 billion, easily making it one of the world's most valuable startups, and one of the ten largest internet companies (by estimated market value) in the world.

Over the past three and half decades, stories like Lenovo, Huawei, Sany, Shuanghui, and Xiaomi have abounded in China. Corporate China is surging. Along with the improbable surge of corporate China is the fast growth of the Chinese economy. Since the Chinese government kick-started the economic reform in 1978, China has managed to maintain an average GDP growth rate of over 9 percent. In 2010, China overtook Japan to become the world's second largest economy; in 2012, China surpassed the USA to become the world's largest manufacturer. In 1990, China produced less than 3 percent of the world's total manufacturing output (by value). This share has now increased to nearly a quarter. Take the aluminum industry as one example. In 1990, Chinese aluminum producers made up only 4 percent of global production; by 2014, their share had increased to 52 percent.[3] Along the way, China has also become the world's largest luxury goods consumer. Walking on the streets of Beijing, Shanghai, Shenzhen, and many coastal cities, one can easily feel the excitement of Chinese citizens. Many of them seem to be in an optimistic hurry, talking on iPhones, carrying their Rimowa suitcases, wearing their Prada shoes and Piaget watches. Although GDP growth has slowed down in recent years and many have lost faith in the narrative of China continuing to be the world's manufacturing and export center, China still remains one of the world's most powerful growth engines.

FROM ZERO TO 106

Every year, *Fortune* magazine publishes a list of the world's 500 largest companies, the *Fortune* Global 500. This vintage product of the magazine is greatly valued by the Chinese media as well as Chinese companies. To many, appearing on this list is tantamount to becoming a well-respected world-class company. For corporate China, the real breakthrough came along in 1996 when two Chinese companies entered the list for the first time. Since then, the number of China's *Fortune* Global 500 companies has been increasing. On the 2015 list, there are in total 106 Chinese companies, compared to 128 in the USA.[4] Since 2011, China has claimed more *Fortune* Global 500 companies than Germany and Japan, second only to the USA. Over the past 35 years, Chinese firms have successfully transformed themselves from following the practice and standards of companies like GE, Toyota, and Shell to setting their own practice and standards.

Fortune ranks the global companies according to their total sales. The threshold for the 2015 list is close to US$24 billion, approximately RMB 154 billion (US$1 = RMB 6.4). More than one hundred companies report sales over RMB 150 billion in 2015—the surge of corporate China could not be more obvious. To a greater extent, this surge symbolizes China's economic success in the past 35 years. In 2015, ranking among the ten largest companies in the world by revenue are three Chinese state-owned manufacturing firms: Sinopec, PetroChina, and State Grid Corporation of China.

Figure 1.1 presents the dynamic distribution of *Fortune* Global 500 companies in the USA and mainland China from 1996 to 2015. Here, to be consistent across time, I only report the mainland Chinese firms by excluding companies in Taiwan and Hong Kong. Given the trend demonstrated in this Figure, China will very likely catch up with the USA, in terms of the number of *Fortune* Global 500 companies, by 2020.

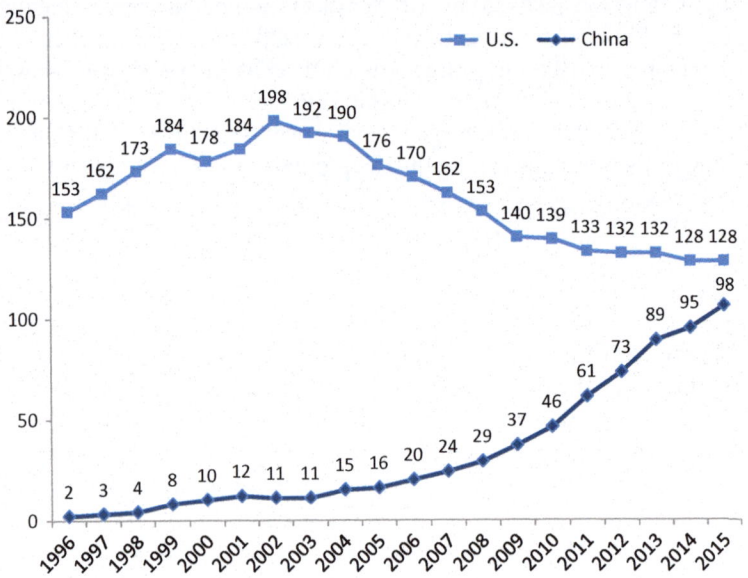

Fig. 1.1 *Fortune* Global 500 companies: USA versus mainland China
Source: Collected and calculated by the author

Back in 1978, when China was forced to start its economic reform, China did not even have a company in the modern sense. All the so-called companies were the Soviet Union type of work units designed to fulfill the tasks assigned to them by the planning agencies at different levels. By then, China's central bank, the People's Bank of China (PBOC), under the supervision of the Finance Ministry, also functioned as a commercial bank. PBOC spun off its commercial functions and formed the Industrial and Commercial Bank of China (ICBC hereafter) in the early 1980s. ICBC has since then grown into one of the largest finical intermediaries in the world. In 2015, ICBC is the world's 18th largest company by revenue, the largest bank, and overall, the most profitable company, beating Apple and Exxon.

Transforming from simple production units under the planned economy to profit-driven and market-minded firms, corporate China successfully completed its first metamorphosis. Studying the quick and improbable rise of corporate China is engrossing as it poses many fascinating, and often troubling, questions: How do millions of Chinese firms, often on a large scale, conduct business in the absence of well-developed institutional infrastructure such as effective law enforcement and the protection of property rights? What is behind corporate China's improbable surge? What does the surge of corporate China imply for China and the rest of the world? How are those corporate giants going to evolve? How many of these corporate giants that emerged during the past three and a half decades are truly great companies, and what made these companies great?

BEHIND THE IMPROBABLE SURGE

To understand the quick and improbable rise of the Chinese firms, we need to place the corporate stories in the context of China's fast economic growth in the past three and a half decades. China has been a stable contributor to the global economic growth. China's economic boom has led to an unprecedented surge of productivity and prosperity that has lifted hundreds of millions from poverty, pushed the country to the forefront of global manufacturing and trade, and unleashed sweeping transformations of employment, education, urbanization, consumption, healthcare, inequality, ownership, and many other dimensions of economic and social life in the world's most populous nation. While China's strong economic growth momentum plays an important role in catalyzing the birth of corporate giants, the approach China has taken to grow its economy also helps explain the quick surge of corporate China.

The Investment Feast

Hangzhou Bay Bridge, spanning the Hangzhou Bay on the East China Sea and crossing the Qiantang River, is one of the longest ocean-crossing bridges in the world. Opened to the public in May 2008, the 36-kilometer-long bridge cuts the trip between Ningbo and Shanghai from 400 kilometers to 180 kilometers and the ground time from more than 4 hours to about 2 hours. The total project cost of the six-lane, two-direction bridge with cable-stayed design was RMB 11.8 billion. Part of this amount was funded by loans from China's state-owned banks and regional banks (close to 60 percent). The rest was provided by private companies in Ningbo. The bridge, although expensive by any standard, greatly boosts economic integration and development in the Yangtze River Delta, the most economically developed area in China.

Investments like Hangzhou Bay Bridge were by no means rare in China over the past 35 years. The cranes looming over vast construction sites have been most foreigners' first impression of China. China today, for example, with less than 6 percent of the world's water resources and just 9 percent of the world's arable land, can produce in one year 50 billion T-shirts, 10 billion pairs of shoes, 800 million metric tons of crude steel (50 percent of global supply), 2.4 gigatons of cement (nearly 60 percent of world production), close to 4 trillion metric tons of coal (burning almost as much coal as the rest of the world combined), more than 23 million vehicles (more than a quarter of global supply), and 62,000 industrial patent applications (1.5 times that in the USA). China is also the world's largest producer of ships, speed trains, robots, tunnels, bridges, highways, electricity, chemical fiber, machine tools, cell phones, computers, bicycles, motorcycles, air-conditioners, refrigerators, washing machines, furniture, textiles, clothing, footwear, toys, fertilizers, agricultural crops, pork, fish, eggs, cotton, copper, aluminum, books, magazines, television shows, and college students. China produces one-third of world agricultural products and supplies nearly 50 percent of global industrial goods. Currently, China builds the square-foot equivalent of Rome every two weeks.

A large academic literature has been devoted to the understanding of China's economic ascendance. Fixed-asset investment has been singled out as one of the most important and reliable pillars of China's growth. Fixed-asset investment accounts for more than 40 percent of China's GDP in the past 40 years, and the ratio of fixed-asset investment to GDP even reached 50 percent in recent years. In a comparison, between 1970 and 2009, fixed-asset investment accounted for only 23 percent of GDP in India, and less than 30 percent in most of the East Asian economies including South Korea, Singapore, Taiwan, and Hong Kong.[5] The Chinese growth model can be characterized as an investment-led growth model.

In hindsight, an investment-led growth model was a natural choice for China. Traditionally, saving ratio in China has stayed at a high level. It was relatively easier for China's less sophisticated financial system to channel savings into investment.[6] Throughout China's reform era, the central government relegated economic decision-making power to local governments. Local politicians hence retain significant autonomy in economic matters. Under this regime, provincial and municipal political leaders are assessed and promoted primarily based on measurable objectives such as GDP growth. The political tournaments based on economic growth provide local politicians with strong incentives to promote growth through investments, especially investments in transportation, urban infrastructure, fancy public buildings, squares, and heavy-industrial and chemical projects.[7]

Economies experiencing a persistent investment boom tend to exhibit extremely strong demand for factors such as energy, capital, and commodities. Now China is the world's largest consumer of steel, coal, and oil. Countries like Australia and Angola had experienced economic boom simply by digging materials out of the ground and shipping them to China. Another example may help. Although the Chinese economy is only two-thirds of the size of the US economy, China has more money supply (measured by M2, which includes cash, deposits in current and saving accounts, money market securities, mutual funds and other time deposits.) than does the USA. All of these reflect strong demand for production factors in the Chinese economy, resulting from China's investment-led growth strategy. Strong demand for factors also provides a solid foundation for companies operating in those industries to scale up their operation. The composition of China's *Fortune* Global 500 companies reveals this vividly.

A careful examination of China's *Fortune* Global 500 companies reveals at least two interesting findings. First, most of China's *Fortune* Global 500 companies are in banking, energy, steel, metal products, railways, and building materials. This distribution pattern is consistent with China's investment-led growth strategy. Second, the names of most companies begin with "China" or province names, suggesting that the majority of China's largest companies are either central government-controlled SOEs or local government-controlled SOEs. Out of 98 mainland companies on the 2015 *Fortune* Global 500 list, only 10 companies are private. On the one hand, this reflects the absolute dominance of the state in China's factor markets; on the other, it demonstrates how China's investment-led growth strategy helps nurture large companies in the industries providing production factors.

China's investment-led growth model is also reflected in the structure of China's young stock market. Out of the 300 component companies constituting the Shanghai and Shenzhen 300 Index, a widely used index to capture the overall stock market performance, firms in finance, energy, and raw materials account for over 60 percent of total market value; for the Standard & Poor's 500 companies, the market capitalization of companies from the same three sectors is only 30 percent of the total market value. In the US stock market, the three largest sectors are, respectively, information technology, healthcare, and consumer goods, which collectively account for more than 50 percent of the market value. These three sectors only account for 23 percent of China's total market capitalization. Such a structure is consistent with the features of China's investment-led growth model.

Table 1.1 presents the ten largest listed companies in the US stock market and China's A-share market, respectively, and reveals several differences. First, in terms of composition, the US companies are more diverse. Five out of the ten largest companies in the USA, including the top three,

Table 1.1   Top 10 listed companies in the USA and China's A-share market

Rank	US companies	Market cap. ($ billion)	Chinese A-share firms	Market cap. ($ billion)
1	Apple	649.8	ICBC	252.1
2	Google	435.2	PetroChina	244.3
3	Microsoft	353.9	China Construction Bank	214.6
4	Berkshire Hathaway	351.4	Bank of China	180
5	Exxon Mobil	312.1	Agricultural Bank of China	161.3
6	Wells Fargo	269.9	China Life Insurance	118.9
7	Johnson & Johnson	265.6	Sinopec	94.8
8	Facebook	264.1	Ping An Insurance	88.6
9	GE	255.1	Bank of Communication	73.1
10	Amazon.com	251.2	CMBC	71

Note: The data are as of September 17, 2015. I do not include Alibaba and Tencent as they are listed in the NYSE and Hong Kong Stock Exchange.

Source: Author's calculation

are in information technology; Johnson & Johnson is in consumer goods; Exxon and Mobil is in energy; although GE has a diversified portfolio, it is more like an industrial company; and only Wells Fargo and Berkshire Hathaway are in finance. In stark contrast, eight out of the top ten companies are either commercial banks or insurance companies in China. The other two, PetroChina and Sinopec, are energy companies. Second, all of the top ten companies in China are from sectors providing factors, reflecting the nature of the Chinese economy—an investment-led and fast-growing economy has inherently a huge demand for production factors (e.g., funds, energy, raw materials, etc.), and hence spurs the rapid growth of firms in those sectors.

Take the Chinese banking sector as an example. Conventional wisdom in economics is that a moderate degree of financial repression is useful to accelerate an economy's industrialization. Through financial repression, scarce financial resources can be allocated to producers based on the national industrial policy.[8] Capital formation is more likely to occur in the industries favored by the state. In doing so, the government has incentive to constrain the development of the financial system. Over the past 35 years, the Chinese government has also adopted a policy of financial repression to boost economic development, as reflected in the dominance of the state in the financial sectors. Interest rate regulation and strict control on the entry of private capital into finance are behind the financial repression policy implemented in China.

To cope with the thrust of the 2008–2009 global financial crisis, the Chinese government embraced a package of aggressive fiscal and monetary policies to stimulate the economy. As a result, China's financial assets rose considerably. Now, the money supply in China, as captured by M2, has exceeded 200 percent of China's GDP. As of June 2014, the total amount of debt in the corporate sector had increased to 125 percent of China's GDP, compared to less than 70 percent in the USA. Because of financial repression, China's financial assets are mainly concentrated in the state-controlled banking sector, and the interest rate spread remains tightly controlled by the regulatory authorities. A quick rise in financial assets is naturally accompanied by the surge of the banking sector. The 16 listed banks in China's A-share markets contribute to close to 60 percent of total profits made by all the listed companies (more than 2700 as of September 2015).

Similar stories have also been observed in China's oil and natural gas industry. Investment-led growth strategy leads to a strong demand for oil and natural gas. In 2012, China surpassed the USA to become the world's largest consumer of energy. Sinopec, PetroChina, and CNOOC, the three central government-controlled SOEs, dominate the energy sector and have experienced a considerable increase in their sales. On the 2015 *Fortune* Global 500 list, both Sinopec and PetroChina are ranked among the world's top five largest companies. Both had reported sales exceeding US$400 billion.

The investment-driven economic growth model has spurred China's strong demand for energy, capital, and commodities. This, together with the state dominance in the factor markets, results in a large number of corporate giants owned by the state and concentrated in the banking, energy, and raw materials sectors.

Biased Policies

Aside from an investment-led growth model, a series of policies and regulations implemented by the Chinese governments are also favorable for companies, especially state-controlled companies, to grow in size.

China's economic reforms started in rural areas. Throughout the 1980s, the government adopted loose regulations and gave farmers a larger degree of freedom. Scarce financial resources were also distributed in rural areas. China's rural areas achieved rapid development, lifting millions of people out of poverty. The government encouraged farmers and urban residents with entrepreneurial spirit to set up township and village enterprises and private enterprises, which made poor peasants more productive workers and greatly accelerated China's industrialization.

In 1992, the 14th Party Congress made it clear that China would practice a "socialist market economy," which for the first time indicated that China would not take a hostile attitude toward the private companies. In 1997, the 15th Party Congress announced that the private sector was an important component of the economy. In the same year, China began large-scale consolidation and privatization of SOEs. In 2002, Jiang Zemin, China's president and the Chinese Communist Party's (CCP) general secretary by then, called to expand the communist party membership to include private business owners, which greatly improved the atmosphere for private business in China. As ideological barriers fell, small businesses flourished.

However, as Yasheng Huang, a management professor at the Sloan School of Management of MIT, points out, beginning in the 1990s the

Chinese government gradually shifted its reform emphasis from rural areas to cities and from the private sector to the state sector.[9] To spur the development of cities and SOEs, governments tightened up preferential policies and loose environment extended to rural areas in 1980s, and diverted financial resources and fixed-asset investments to SOEs and the public sector. As a result, more vigorous bottom-up and more market-oriented approaches were replaced by top-down and government-led approaches. Over time, China's center of economic gravity shifted to the cities. The impact was subtle but was felt with the passage of time. The state sector powered ahead as more resources were allocated to the sector. Government spending also skyrocketed and was largely diverted to the construction of urban infrastructure. The pace and scale of forces at work favored the rise of large companies, especially in the state-controlled industries.

It would be an empirical challenge to formally test Huang's hypothesis on the state capitalism emerging in China since the 1990s. However, anecdotes abound. Take China's *Fortune* Global 500 companies as an example. We observe a real breakthrough for China in 1996, when two Chinese SOEs broke onto the list. The Chinese firms have since then powered ahead. The number of *Fortune* Global 500 companies exceeds 100 in less than 20 years. The trajectory coincided with the shift of China's center of economic gravity.

At the 16th Party Congress which was convened in 2002, the senior leaders made clear that improving the efficiency level of SOEs was one of the top priorities in the next stage of China's economic reform. Under the slogan "Bigger and Stronger," a series of policies and regulations were put in place to facilitate SOE reform and make SOEs bigger and stronger. The guidelines are straightforward. As put forward at the third Plenary Session of the 16th CCP Central Committee in 2004, China would proactively pursue multiple forms of ownership structure, through asset restructurings, mergers and acquisitions, and, under certain conditions, bankruptcies, to accelerate the adjustments of the pattern and structure of the state economy. It was clearly stated that for SOEs, absolute controlling ownership by the state would not be necessary. It would only apply to a handful of industries concerning the state security or the implementation of national strategies. By promoting market competition, the superior would survive and the inferior would be eliminated.

In December 2006, the watchdog of China's central government-controlled SOEs, the State-owned Assets Supervision and Administration Commission (SASAC), for the first time, specified industries and sectors in which SOEs must play a dominant role. In unspecified industries, non-profitable SOEs should exit by 2008; and by 2010, the number of central government-controlled SOEs should drop to 80–100, of which 30–50 should be developed into large groups with world-class competitiveness.

Like the central government, the local governments also took proactive steps to boost the scale of the companies in their jurisdiction. China's local governments have developed a strong propensity for economic growth, given that local GDP growth rate has been used as the most important measurable indicator to evaluate local politicians' performance.

The iron and steel industry is one example that shows how mergers and acquisitions enabled by local governments help generate a large number of corporate behemoths. In September 2009, under the auspices of the Shandong provincial government, Shandong Iron & Steel Group Co., Ltd. (a loss-making SOE) and Rizhao Iron & Steel Co., Ltd. (a profitable private firm) signed a merger agreement. Although the deal was in fact an acquisition initiated by a loss-making SOE on a profitable private company, it was favored and, hence, orchestrated by the local government— the merger has resulted in a company in Shandong that is large enough to enter the *Fortune* Global 500 list. One interesting fact behind this episode is that Shandong Iron & Steel Group was by itself a product of a series of government-initiated mergers and acquisitions. It was formally formed in March 2008 by merging Jinan Steel and Laiwu Steel, two local government-controlled SOEs. After the merger, Shandong Iron & Steel emerged as one of the premier players in the industry with total assets of RMB 85 billion and a capacity exceeding 30 million tons per year. Since its acquisition of Rizhao Iron & Steel, the combined entity has expanded its capacity to 40 million tons per year. This, combined with a 10 million ton capacity under construction in Rizhao, easily escalates Shandong Iron & Steel to one the largest iron and steel manufacturers in the world.

Similar stories are everywhere in the iron and steel industry. In May 2010, the SASAC approved the restructuring plan between Anshan Iron and Steel Group and Pangang Iron and Steel Group, two central SOEs reporting directly to the SASAC. According to the plan, a new Anshan Iron and Steel Group would be formed, which would be composed of the old Anshan Iron and Steel Group and Pangang Iron and Steel Group. After the merger, the new entity would boast a capacity of over 54 million tons per year.

Almost at the same time, Baoshan Iron and Steel, a company located in Shanghai, announced its acquisitions of Baotou Iron and Steel and Ningbo Iron and Steel, expanding its capacity to 49.3 million tons. Wuhan Iron and Steel was able to produce 40 million tons per year after its acquisition of Liuzhou Iron & Steel. Hebei Iron and Steel, one of China's *Fortune Global 500* companies, reached a capacity of 40 million tons as well, after several within-province mergers and acquisitions initiated by the Hebei provincial government. In China's iron and steel industry, government-initiated restructurings are not rare. One direct consequence is the emergence of a number of outsized state-owned groups. In 2014, out of China's 500 largest companies (by sales), companies from the iron and steel industry occupied 58 seats.

But size is not equivalent to profitability. This is especially true in China's iron and steel industry, where the overcapacity problem has been severe as the economy slows down. In 2012, out of China's ten publicly listed companies that had experienced the heaviest loss, five were from the iron and steel industry. Among them, Anshan Iron and Steel's net loss reached RMB 4.157 billion; Ma'anshan Iron and Steel Group suffered a loss of RMB 3.863 billion; Shandong Iron & Steel Group's loss amounted to RMB 3.836 billion; Anyang Iron and Steel Group lost RMB 3.498 billion; and, finally, Valin Steel reported a loss of RMB 3.254 billion.

The local governments' strong propensity to promote large companies in their jurisdictions results in many corporate giants. However, it also worsens the overcapacity problem in many manufacturing sectors. In 2012, the average utilization rate in China's iron and steel, cement, electrolytic aluminum, flat glass, and ship manufacturing were reported at 72, 73.7, 71.9, 73.1, and 75 percent. The conventional view is that an industry can be seen to have excess capacity as long as its utilization rate is below 75 percent.

Favorable External Environment

Another structural factor driving the rapid surge of corporate China is the favorable external environment that Chinese firms have been facing in the past 35 years. Globalization and trade liberalization have created tremendous opportunities for the Chinese firms to break into foreign markets and achieve rapid growth. Besides fixed-asset investment and consumption, export has long been viewed as one reliable growth engine. During the first decade of the twenty-first century, annual export growth rate had been over 20 percent in most years, and total exports accounted for over 30 percent of GDP. The Chinese economy and Chinese firms are beneficiaries of global trade liberalization.

Trade liberalization has lowered tariff rates faced by China's exporting firms, especially after China's WTO accession in 2001, which significantly boosted China's total exports. Trade liberalization and China's entry into WTO have also considerably lowered import tariffs. While foreign investments and commodities swarm into the Chinese market, to ward off eroding profit margin, corporate China has resorted to technological innovation, partnership with more competitive global players, and upgrading products and services. Such corporate dynamism has not only strengthened Chinese firms' competitiveness but also greatly expanded their geographical reach and business scope.

Building on the strong exporting momentum, China's foreign exchange reserves have piled up, reaching over US$3.5 trillion as of 2014. The impact of the enormous foreign reserves is particularly evident, as reflected in many attempts made by the Chinese firms to exploit cross-border transaction opportunities. In 2011, Geely Automobile launched a bid for Volvo and eventually closed the deal. Before the transaction, Geely's total revenue was only RMB 40 billion. With its acquisition of Volvo, it total sales, based on the consolidated financial statements, skyrocketed to RMB 150 billion, large enough to push Geely onto the *Fortune* Global 500 list in 2012.

The advancement of globalization and trade liberalization is vividly reflected in the dynamism of both import and export tariff rates corporate China had experienced before and after the 2001 WTO accession. In one of my research papers coauthored with colleagues at Peking University,[10] we computed average tariff rates at the three-digit industry level from 1997 to 2008 in China.[11] Specifically, we computed volume-weighted average import and export tariff rates in every three-digit industry in China based on the import and export tariff rates at the product level. We found that China's average import tariff rates (the tariff rates faced by foreign companies) dropped from 17 percent in 1997 to 8 percent in 2008. Likewise, average export tariff rates facing Chinese firms also decreased after 2001, suggesting that, on average, the tariff rates imposed by foreign governments on imported Chinese products dropped as well.

Notably, tariff rates are only one dimension that captures the ease of international trades. Factors such as non-tariff trade barrier may also affect the cross-border movements of products and services. However, it is difficult to quantify non-tariff barrier and its impact on trade. In general, there exists a very strong positive correlation between tariff rates and non-tariff barrier. The analysis thus shows that Chinese firms have indeed faced a relatively friendly external environment, starting from the 1990s and lasting until now, with China's 2001 WTO accession being one key milestone. Against this backdrop, some Chinese firms have broken away from the limitations of the old system and become strong competitors in the global market. Take Huawei as an example. In 2014, Huawei hired 32,000 non-Chinese employees, accounting for 20 percent of its employee base. The revenue from overseas markets contributed to more than 62 percent of Huawei's total revenue.[12]

In his bestseller *How Asia Works?* Joe Studwell, an *Economist* journalist based in Asia, elaborates on the importance of international trade in spurring Asian corporate giants. Studwell, in his narrative of the industrialization process of major Asian economies, observes that Asian economies, including Japan, South Korea, and now China, began their industrialization in manufacturing, and postulates that this was due to two reasons. First, unlike the service sectors, manufacturing relies more on machines and equipments, rather than high-skilled workers and managerial proficiencies. It is therefore easier for Asian economies to take off, especially in the earlier stages of their economic development, by overcoming obstacles caused by a lack of adequate education and professional skills in the workforce. In contrast, service sectors hinge more on human capital, which poses an insurmountable challenge for developing economies, especially in the early stages of industrialization.

Second, Studwell points out that a more fundamental reason explaining the importance of manufacturing to Asian economies' industrialization process lies in the fact that it is easier to promote international trade in manufacturing. In international trade, opening up services sectors is accompanied by free flows of people across borders, especially from low-income countries to high-income countries. Even for people who are most supportive of free trade and globalization, free flows of personnel could be a concern.

Choosing to focus on manufacturing, Asian companies tapped into the international markets. They started from low ends of the value chain, and gradually moved up. Along the way, they continued to expand their scale and sharpen their competitiveness. Eventually, some Asian companies emerged as giants in their own industries. This narrative easily explains the success of Sony, Hyundai, Samsung, and HTC. The same corporate dynamism has also been experienced by many Chinese companies during their development over the past 30 plus years. The seemingly improbable surge of corporate China can be partially accounted for by the explosive growth in international trade and the export-led strategy the Chinese government had adopted to drive the economy.

Still at the Party

I routinely take research trips to different parts of China. Over the past five years, I have visited dozens of municipal cities and interviewed many mayors and high-ranking government officials. What impresses me most is these officials' penchant for having several large companies—one or two *Fortune* Global 500 companies the best—in their jurisdiction. When introducing their plans for local development, almost every mayor enthusiastically talks about the current capital-intensive projects, fancy plazas, and highway networks and how much they would contribute to local GDP and local glamor. More than occasionally, the term *Fortune* Global 500 slips out of their mouths. How many are already there? How many more may show up on the list in the coming years? Who are they? How close are they currently?

Indeed, possessing a few large companies helps boost fiscal revenue and local employment; having well-known companies increases local visibility among more than 300 municipal cities in China. Chinese mayors strongly believe that having several corporate giants is one of the "commanding heights" for them to excel in the political tournament based on measurable economic results such as GDP and fiscal income growth.

In November 2011, I was invited to present my research on corporate China at a high-end business forum in Beijing. The theme of the forum was corporate China's strategies over the next five years, overlapping with the time period during which China's 12th five-year plan would be implemented. At the panel I attended, I was arranged to be seated next to the board chairman of one of the largest SOEs in China. He is a strong man and well known for his toughness in business circles. The discussions had centered on the megatrends in the Chinese economy and how companies should adapt to these structural breaks. Many viewpoints were raised from various perspectives. Some stressed the decisive role of innovation; and some argued for the virtues of diversification. When my turn came, I briefly talked about the key thesis of this book: It is time for the Chinese firms to shift their strategic focus from pursuing size to cultivating competitive business models to achieve higher return on invested capital (ROIC). Not surprisingly, reactions from the audience were lukewarm.

The chairman was invited to deliver the concluding speech. He stood up. Holding the microphone tightly, he said in a terse but infectious tone: "What is corporate strategy? It is the direction a company is heading! It is the goal that a corporate leader must set and achieve. China's 12th five year plan offers a grand opportunity for us to expand our business scale and scope. Regardless of what could happen, I told my CFO one and only one thing—manage to secure another RMB 150 billion worth of bank loans over the next five years. Don't hesitate! It is time for development. With this amount of loans, through investments and acquisitions, we can further expand our production capacity. We may even double our sales in three to four years. If we can do this, we can make our way to the *Fortune* Global 500 list and our company can have real influence in the global market. Ask about our corporate strategy? Simple, make our company bigger. In doing so, we can push our company into the list of the world's top 500 companies very soon. Remember that China has, up to this point, no companies among the world's top 500 in this area!"

The audience reacted to his emotional speech with thunderous applause. Out of excitement, his face became flushed, and his breath grew somewhat heavier. Sitting next to him, all of sudden I felt a bit at a loss. I truly believed what I just said. But at that very moment, I felt that my remarks were disconnected from the audience. They were expecting something much more positive about surging corporate China. While the chairman delivered this message, I did the opposite by overemphasizing the weaknesses of those corporate behemoths.

CORPORATE CHINA IN THE NEXT TEN YEARS

From zero to 106, corporate China has achieved a successful first long march. In the next 10–15 years, will everything remain the same? The surge of corporate China largely resulted from China's fast growth in the past 35 years. However, skepticism over China's growth momentum is now mounting. In 2015, China's GDP growth rate has dropped to below 7 percent, the first time since the early 1990s. Many have started to talk about the odds that the Chinese economy will soon experience a hard landing. Is Chinese economic growth over? Indeed, the Chinese economy is now facing several headwinds that are in the process of slowing down its growth. They include overcapacity in many industries, over-reliance on the property market, an aging population, a weak social safety net, environmental issues, inequality, political uncertainty, and the overhang of corporate and government debts. In the meantime, one should see the buildup of positive forces powering the Chinese economy ahead. They include opportunities due to China's continued urbanization,[13] a more educated labor force, and a surging middle class with stronger demand for consumption. The future of China's economic growth hinges on which forces discussed above dominate.

What could happen to corporate China if the Chinese economy were to fail to return to its normal growth rate? What are the challenges facing the Chinese firms? China's economic success shares many commonalities with that of Japan and Asian Tigers decades ago. It is a story about high savings and high investment, export-led strategy, generally disciplined fiscal and monetary policies, well-managed (manipulative) exchange rates, abundant cheap labor, continuing gains in productivity and, ultimately, political tournament based on economic growth. However, coming to the second decade of the twenty-first century, the various factors supporting China's fast economic growth are eroding.

Investment-led growth strategy has led to a high level of corporate debt. The consultancy McKinsey & Company estimates that as of June 2014, the total amount of corporate debt in China reached 125 percent of its GDP. In stark contrast, the corporate debt-to-GDP ratio in the USA was only 67 percent.[14] Let us assume that the average cost of debt for Chinese companies is 8 percent. This suggests that every year, 10 percent of China's GDP will be used to pay for interest expenses. The corporate debt problem is severe. Another consequence of high fixed-asset investment is the overcapacity issue in many industries, as I discuss earlier in this chapter.

Going forward, continuing to rely on investment may not be feasible. Meanwhile, the ever-increasing labor cost and aging population signal the end of demographic dividend in China. Weak European and American economies dampen the importance of exports, and even make exports increasingly irrelevant to the Chinese economy. While political tournaments based on economic growth provide local bureaucrats with discretion and capacity to spur local economic growth, resources have been misallocated everywhere, resulting in a large amount of local government debts. Based on a survey conducted by the National Audit Office in 2013, the total amount of local government debt had reached RMB 18 trillion as of June 2013. However, it is widely believed that the actual amount of local government debt is much higher—somewhere between RMB 20 and 30 trillion.

Without any doubt, the Chinese economy is entering into a new stage characterized by slower economic growth and numerous pending structural challenges. The economic dynamism in China is inevitably generating profound implications for corporate China. The dynamism of corporate China will ultimately be shaped by a mixture of economics, institutions, and technology, among which economics is arguably the most relevant. The future of China's corporate sectors largely hinges on the prospects of the Chinese economy.

A 2 × 2 Matrix

Let me first tease out the possible end scenarios of the Chinese economy in the next 10 years. First, let us go back to the well-known identity:

Growth = Investment Rate × Return on Invested Capital

This identity applies to both the corporate sector and national economies. Take national economy as an example. This identity suggests that both investment and investment efficiency (measured by ROIC) could be drivers of economic growth. The future of the Chinese economy depends on its respective performance on investment rate and investment efficiency.

China's economic growth in the past 35 years is largely driven by investment rate. Of course, in the early stage of China's industrialization process, ROIC was also maintained at a relatively higher level due to the following two forces. First, capital was scarce in China and the capital-to-labor ratio was at a low level. The marginal return of capital thus tended to be higher. Second, China's industrialization was accompanied by the swarm of a large number of farmers to cities. These farm workers enjoyed a much improved productivity, which led to higher return on investment.

However, the delicate balance between investment rate and investment efficiency, which we saw in the first stage of Chinese economic reform, could be easily broken. High investment rate can hardly be sustained mainly because of widespread overcapacity and heavy corporate debt. China has completed its industrialization and in 2014, for the first time, the contribution of the tertiary industries to GDP exceeded that of the secondary industries. The rule of diminished return of capital in economics starts to take its toll. As a result, we are seeing a declining ROIC in China. China needs to strike a new balance between investment rate and investment efficiency. The way the future balance is achieved will surely play a decisive role in shaping the future of China.

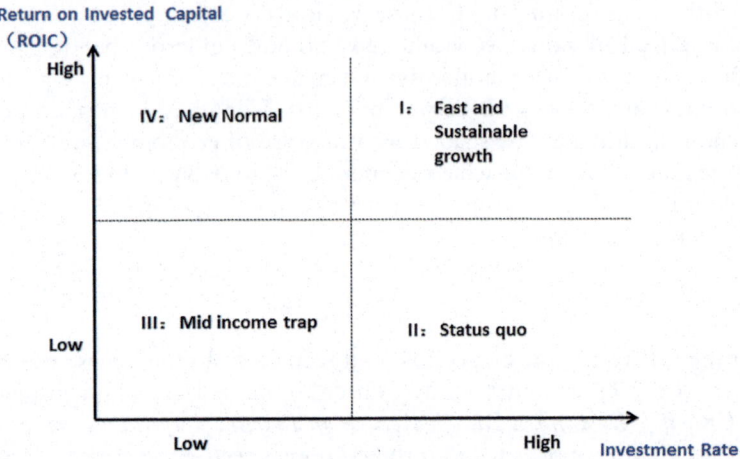

Fig. 1.2   The four end scenarios of the Chinese economy

Figure 1.2 presents four possible end scenarios of the Chinese economy formed based on the levels (high or low) of the two factors driving economic growth: investment rate and ROIC.

Scenario I, the northeast area, is characterized by high investment rate and high ROIC. With such a combination, China will continue to grow at rates enjoyed in the past 35 years, and, more importantly, the quality of growth will remain at a high level. Clearly, scenario I is the best scenario for the future Chinese economy. The odds? Probably zero. Otherwise, the Chinese government would not be so determined to reinitiate a new round of economic reforms to address structural problems deeply rooted in the economy. China will have to find a new growth engine.

Scenario II, the southwest area, is characterized by high investment rate and low ROIC. It is the status quo, under which investment rate will remain at a high level (e.g., the fixed-asset investment-to-GDP ratio will be kept at 40–50 percent), and China fails to significantly improve its investment efficiency. If this happens, China can probably still maintain a high level of GDP growth rate through aggressive fiscal policy and loose monetary policy (e.g., interest rate cut, and the Chinese version of quantitative easing). But the quality of growth will be very poor due to low investment efficiency. If this scenario lasts, the overcapacity and corporate debt problems will worsen and become harder to address in the future. Although Scenario II is less favorable, the chance that the Chinese economy will end up with this scenario is quite high.

Scenario III is the least favored one. A combination of low levels of investment rate and investment efficiency will surely lead to a much slower GDP growth, together with very poor quality of economic growth. If this happens, China will be caught in the mid-income trap and will not be able to escape from economic stagnation. In this case, the Chinese companies could lose confidence and stop investing. The aging population with close to 300 million elderly people may prefer not to spend. The Chinese economy will face significant barriers to growth. The only feasible way out might be government spending. Yet, extra government spending will merely lead to further misallocation of resources, and cannot rejuvenate economic growth. If the GDP growth rate drops to below 3 percent, the per capita GDP in China may stay below $12,000 for a very long time.

Finally, it is time to discuss Scenario IV, a combination of a high level of investment efficiency and a relatively low level of investment rate. If the ROIC can go back to the levels in the early stage of China's industrialization process, through innovations in technology and business models, more private investment, and enhancement of institutional infrastructure, the Chinese economy can still grow at a moderate rate (e.g., 5–6 percent per year). More important, the quality of growth can be greatly improved as a result of improving investment efficiency. This is the "new normal" that China's president Xi Jinping has proposed. It is also the most realistic scenario China's policy-makers should make every effort to achieve.

Among the four possible end scenarios, "new normal" presents itself as one feasible and acceptable state of the future Chinese economy. Going forward, maintaining an investment-to-GDP ratio as high as 50 percent is no longer feasible. The Chinese government can still use aggressive fiscal policy combined with loose monetary policy to stimulate economy growth. But no amount of policy stimulus can return the Chinese economy to the rates enjoyed in the first decade of this century. The source of China's future growth can only be further improvement in productivity. In fact, despite the rapid growth of the last three and a half decades, China's productivity is still only 13 percent of the US level, which suggests that China still has plenty of room for productivity growth through further economic reforms. Even if China can replicate its extraordinary growth performance for another two decades, its productivity would still be only around 40 percent of the frontier productivity level.[15] The future of the Chinese economy largely hinges on the other growth driver—ROIC.

Rise to Greatness: Corporate China's Value Redemption

The surge of corporate China is the consequence of the country's fast-growing economy and the approach it chose to grow the economy. For the economy, continuing to expand at the old rates is an illusion. While people prefer to stick to illusions, and put their faith in the policy-makers' magic hands, this time is different. The Chinese economy has slowed down. In order for it to escape the mid-income trap, China has to maintain a moderate rate of growth, and the source of growth has to be ROIC rather than investment rate. If we still trust policy-makers' magic wands, we hope that they can sort out ways to strike a new balance between investment rate and ROIC in China. But are there such magic ways?

Government spending may boost GDP, but it will tax already over-stretched finance in China, as well as crowd out investments in the private sector. China needs a large number of firms with higher levels of ROIC, which, in aggregate, will increase the overall efficiency of the Chinese economy. This inevitably calls for a change in mindsets of Chinese corporate executives; the ultimate goal of firm operations is to generate value rather than growing scale.

As the Chinese economy is entering a new period, heavily indebted Chinese companies need to overhaul their corporate strategies. Pursuing size will no longer be the best response to the changing business environment. Chinese companies need to work on their investment efficiency. After successfully completing the very difficult first "Long March,"[16] Chinese firms are now facing an even more challenging second "Long March." The theme of the second "Long March" is how to transform the Chinese economy from big to brilliant. The success or failure of the second "Long March" will directly decide whether or not China can successfully transform its economy from investment-led to efficiency-driven; and whether or not China can avoid plunging into the "mid-income trap."

The journey has just begun.

NOTES

1. Zhongguanchun has since developed into China's innovation and entrepreneurship center, where most of China's high-tech companies cluster. It has been called "China's answer to Silicon Valley."

2. See "Paper tiger, roaring dragon" (*The Economist*, September 12, 2015b) for more on China's surging private sector, which deserves more credit for China's economic rise.

3. For more on the massive scale and profit prospects of the Chinese firms, see McKinsey Global Institute's report (2015b), "The new global competition for corporate profit."

4. Here, we also count the companies in Hong Kong and Taiwan.

5. See, for example, Liu et al. (2013).

6. There are many explanations for China's high saving rate. Lack of a social safety net is one popular explanation. China's less sophisticated financial system results in fewer investment vehicles for households, which also leads to a higher saving rate. The Confucian value rooted in the Chinese tradition calls for a frugal lifestyle, which also helps explain Chinese people's propensity for depositing money in banks. A recent academic paper by Wei and Zhang (2011) suggests that an imbalance in sex ratio could be one important driver of China's high saving rate.

7. See, for example, Maskin et al. (2000), Li and Zhou (2005), Xu (2011), and Liu and Siu (2011).

8. See "Fault Lines" by Raghuram G. Rajan, Princeton University Press (2010).

9. See "Capitalism with Chinese Characteristics" (Yasheng Huang), Cambridge University Press (2010).

10. See Cai et al. (2013).

11. Ibid.

12. See Huawei's 2014 annual report, available at http://www.huawei.com. cn.

13. Just over 50 percent of China's population are now living in cities. It is estimated that by 2030, the urban population will reach 70 percent. This implies that in 15 years, more than 300 million people will migrate from the countryside to cities.

14. Source: McKinsey Global Institute Analysis.

15. See Zhu (2012).

16. Originally, 'the Long March' refers to a military retreat undertaken by the Red Army of the Communist Party of China to evade the chase of the Kuomintang army from October 1934 to October 1935. This military retreat was vital for the survival of the Red Army and also made its leader Mao Zedong a living legend. 'The Long March' has since been used to describe an arduous but great journey.

CHAPTER 2

What's In A Great Company?

In September 2014, Alibaba Group, the Chinese e-commerce juggernaut, announced its initial public offering (IPO) at the New York Stock Exchange (NYSE). With the IPO price at $68 per share and a total amount of offering at $25 billion, Alibaba's IPO has been one of the largest in the American history. Into November of 2014, Alibaba's market capitalization at one time even exceeded $300 billion, overtaking Facebook, Amazon, and even GE for a short while. The IPO debut and subsequent market performance of Alibaba, a company that was not founded until 1999, awed the world.

Is Alibaba a great company? Fifteen years of corporate history might not be enough to answer such a question. While the world hailed the ascent of Alibaba, a fact going unnoticed by most people is that Alibaba actually does not yet belong to the *Fortune* Global 500 club. Although Alibaba is the largest online and mobile commerce platform in the world, with gross merchandise value (GMV) exceeding RMB 3 trillion (approximately $468 billion) in 2015, only a small percentage of Alibaba's GMV can translate into revenue, thanks to its marketplace business model. In 2015, Alibaba's reported revenue is only slightly more than RMB 76 billion (approximately $11.8 billion), far lower than the revenue threshold required to be included on the *Fortune* Global 500 list in 2014 (approximately $24 billion).

Although it does not belong to the army of the 106 *Fortune* Global 500 companies from China,[1] nobody denies that Alibaba is probably the best known Chinese company outside China. Much larger *Fortune* Global 500

© The Editor(s) (if applicable) and The Author(s) 2016
Q. Liu, *Corporate China 2.0*, DOI 10.1057/978-1-137-55089-7_2

companies such as COSCO, Datang, Shenhua, and Ansteel most likely are unknown by ordinary investors living outside China. In fact, being a *Fortune* Global 500 company does not guarantee any brand premium or stock market premium. Now, China boasts of more than 20 percent of *Fortune* Global 500 companies in the world, and produces 80 percent of air-conditioners, 70 percent of mobile phones, 60 percent of shoes, and a quarter of passenger cars in the entire world. Still, there is a paucity of internationally recognized Chinese brands and Chinese companies. In China, companies like Alibaba are rare. Here come the questions: If size does not count, then what is in a great company? Why are there so many big companies but very few great companies in China?

One Character Difference

In the Chinese language, there is only one character difference between "big" (大) and "great" (伟大). However, there are significant differences in their implications. For example, 12 out of China's 106 *Fortune* Global 500 companies on the 2015 list were unprofitable. While Sinopec, PetroChina, and State Grid are among the ten largest companies in the world, their profitability and return to shareholders are hardly satisfactory.

As Chinese companies rapidly expand their global market share, few exhibit strong competitiveness in high-end manufacturing. They also fail to grab a bigger share of high-margin marketing and customer service. Moreover, Chinese companies are now facing fiercer competition from outside of China—the rising labor costs have forced manufacturers such as Samsung, Microsoft, Toyota to relocate their production bases in Vietnam, Cambodia, Myanmar, Philippines, and Bangladesh. "Made in China" is seemingly losing glamor.

Beginning in the second decade of this century, we are seeing signs of the recovery of manufacturing in the USA as well. Shale gas, with strong potential for commercial use, may drive down the cost of energy, and reshape the global energy industry. Innovation in manufacturing abounds. 3-D printing technology, automation, driverless vehicles, immune engineering, reusable rockets, and many other technologies have been adopted or are close to being commercially used to improve productivity, suggesting the arrival of a new era of high-end manufacturing.

Take China's automobile industry as an example. China has emerged as the world's largest automotive market with over 20 million vehicles sold every year. SAIC Motor, China FAW Group, Dongfeng Motor Group,

Beijing Automotive Group, Guangzhou Automotive Industry Group, and Geely are all on the 2015 *Fortune* Global 500 list, accounting for 20 percent of the *Fortune* Global 500 companies in automotive. SAIC Motor reported total sales of over $100 billion in 2014, making it one of the largest auto makers in the world. Still, the Chinese auto players have not demonstrated core competence—global players such as Daimler-Benz, Volkswagen, Toyota, and BMW dominate bestselling brands, R&D, and key auto parts such as engines.

These multinational companies tightly control high-end segments of the automotive value chain. Foreign auto parts suppliers nurtured by the global giants also take the lion's share of profits through direct investment or setting up joint ventures with local firms. While homegrown auto brands own over one-third of China's auto market share, they harness less than 5 percent of the profit. The rest has been taken by joint auto ventures selling foreign brands.[2] China has large auto companies, but none of them could be viewed as great auto makers.

Rambling around Bund in Shanghai, what first grabs one's attention are fancy shopping malls with displays of luxury brands such as Giorgio Armani, Dolce & Gabbana, Prada, and Patek Philippe. China's surging middle class are fans of those brands. While China had surpassed the USA to become the world's largest luxury goods consumer in 2012, one can hardly name a homegrown luxury brand.

An academic paper by three scholars from the USA examines the distribution of Apple's profit within its global value network.[3] The findings are appalling. In 2010, for every sold iPhone set, Apple locked in 58.5 percent of the total value added. Immediately behind Apple were plastics and metal suppliers, who took in 21.9 percent of the value. South Korea, as the major screen and electronic components supplier, got 4.7 percent. In the order from high to low, others shared the value of an iPhone set as follows: unclassified components (4.4 percent), non-Chinese labors (3.5 percent), non-Apple American employees (2.4 percent), and mainland Chinese labors (1.8 percent). Almost all iPhone sets are assembled in China by Foxcom, a Taiwanese company employing more than 1 million workers in mainland China; the Chinese workers only locked in 1.8 percent of the value added. This echoes a persistent myth about Chinese manufacturing: They are good at assembly, with the more profitable segments such as product design and marketing controlled by their western counterparts.

If it remains at the low end of the value chain, a company, regardless of its operation scale, simply cannot create much value and gain widespread respect in the marketplace. Recall "the Linsanity" during the 2011–2012 NBA season. Both iPhone and the NBA Player Jeremy Lin have been popular in China. As a famous joke goes, Jeremy Lin and Apple have three things in common: raw materials from Taiwan, an American brand, and the largest market share in China. Influential brands are in short supply in China and scarcity creates overblown fame. Chinese media once circulated a jaw-dropping formula, 1 = 800,000,000: As the world's largest textile exporter, China needs 800,000,000 shirts to get enough profits to purchase an Airbus 380 jet.

After accomplishing the breakthrough in firm size, corporate China is now facing a more arduous second "Long March." The theme of the second "Long March" is no longer more *Fortune* Global 500 companies. It is transforming the Chinese companies into great companies. Accompanying this new "Long March" will be the transition of China's economic growth model from investment- and export-led to consumption- and efficiency-driven. Those forces that had sustained the Chinese firms' rapid growth in size are on the wane.

A FRAMEWORK NEEDED

What is behind a great company's greatness? In their bestselling book *Built to Last: Successful Habits of Visionary Companies*, Jim Collins and Jerry Porras noted:[4]

> What is a visionary company? Visionary companies are premier institutions—the crown jewels—in their industries, widely admired by their peers and having a long track record of making a significant impact on the world around them.
>
> ...
>
> All individual leaders, no matter how charismatic and visionary, eventually die; and all visionary products and services—all "great ideas"—eventually become obsolete. Indeed, entire markets can become obsolete and disappear. Yet visionary companies prosper over long periods of time, through multiple product life cycles and multiple generations of active leaders.

Jim Collins and Jerry Porras went on to explore the genes of visionary companies, and the six criteria that great companies meet drew wide attention and resonance from the business world. These criteria include: a premier institution in its industry; widely admired by businesspeople;

made an indelible imprint on the world; had multiple generations of chief executives; had been through multiple product (or service) life cycles; and had a minimum age of 50 years. Collins and Porras singled out 18 visionary companies, including GE, IBM, American Express, Boeing, Citibank, Wal-Mart, and Disney.

In his later writing, Collins simplified the six criteria to two. First, a great company must create value and bring high returns to its shareholders. Second, it must be able to change people's lives through products and services in a unique manner; if a great company dies, the void it leaves cannot be filled by other companies.

Dissatisfied with the studies on successful companies that fail to control for the effect of luck or randomness,[5] two consultants from Deloitte Consulting, Michael Rayor and Mumtaz Ahmed, conducted a statistical analysis of 25,453 listed companies in the US market over 44 years and had their findings published in *Harvard Business Review*. In the article titled "*Three rules for making a company truly great*," they detailed how they found the most important rules for making a company great.

Michael Rayor and Mumtaz Ahmed first identified several hundred firms that have done well enough for a long enough period of time to qualify as truly exceptional. Analyzing these truly exceptional firms, they found that the many and diverse choices that made certain companies great were consistent with just three seemingly elementary rules: (1) Better before cheaper—in other words, compete on differentiators other than price; (2) Revenue before cost, that is, prioritize increasing revenue over reducing costs; and (3) There are no other rules—so change anything you must to follow Rules (1) and (2).

According to the first rule, great companies should compete mainly by offering superior non-price benefits such as a great brand, an exciting style, or excellent functionality, durability, or convenience; or they can meet some minimal acceptable standard along these dimensions and try to attract customers with lower prices. Only mediocre companies choose to compete on price. According to the second rule, companies must not only create value but also capture it in the form of profits. By an overwhelming margin, exceptional companies garner superior profits by achieving higher revenue than their rivals, through either higher prices or greater volume. Very rarely is cost leadership a driver of superior profitability.

Obviously, the three rules do not dictate specific behaviors that a to-be-great company should follow, but they are foundational concepts on which companies have truly built greatness over many years. As the two authors note, they show how great companies think.

Dick Foster and Sarah Kaplan, in their 2001 bestseller *Creative Destruction*, went all out to promote the Enron model, and touted Enron as an innovative and great company. In their narrative, Enron had creatively disrupted the traditional energy business by building up capacity for perpetual innovation. Enron craftily transformed its major business from natural gas pipeline to trading futures and other derivatives on natural gas. This "light-asset strategy" had allowed Enron to achieve a soaring rise in profit. However, almost at the same time as the publication of *Creative Destruction*, the scandal of financial frauds was disclosed. With this scandal, Enron finally "creatively destructed" itself.

Despite the misuse of the Enron example, many analytical results in Foster and Kaplan are valuable. Specifically, the book highlighted one prominent empirical fact based on the analysis of a large sample of companies—creative destruction is everywhere, and achieving long-lasting prosperity is difficult. *Forbes* has published its well-known *Forbes 100* list since 1917.[6] In 1987, 70 years after the publication of the first list, *Forbes* reprinted the names of the 100 companies that appeared on the 1917 list, and asked one question: Where are these companies now? In hindsight, out of the 100 companies, 61 disappeared; 21 companies failed to maintain their past performance and exited the list. Only 18 companies were still on the 1987 list, including GE, Kodak, P&G, Exxon, and Citibank. Among the 18 companies, only GE and Kodak had reported stock market performance better than overall market performance during the 70-year period.[7] Twenty years later, Kodak also got itself into trouble. The company is now still struggling to remake itself simply because the whole business of film photography has been eclipsed by the digital photography revolution.

In a series of academic papers, Robert Wiggins and Tim Ruefli (2002, 2005) studied 6772 listed firms in the USA, spanning 40 industries from 1974 to 1997. They divided these firms into three categories based on their relative performance in their industries: excellent, average, and poor. The authors tracked these firms' performance and found the following: (1) only 5 percent of companies managed to maintain an excellent performance for ten consecutive years or longer; (2) only 32 companies, that is, less than 0.5 percent, maintained an excellent performance for 20 consecutive years or longer; and (3) only 3 companies were able to deliver an excellent performance for 50 consecutive years. The findings by Wiggins and Ruefli confirmed that competitive advantage is short-lived and rare. Maintaining lasting prosperity is far more difficult than imagined. In his book *The Origin of Wealth*, Eric Beinhocker summarizes:[8]

> *Taken together and viewed over a longer time frame, the story that the "excellent company" books tell is not one of sustainable competitive advantage and enduring high performance. Rather it is a story of the ephemeral nature of competitive advantage, and the incredible dynamism of markets as companies rise and fall.*

Either by the standards listed in *Built to Last* or by the criteria suggested by the researchers mentioned above, very few Chinese companies can be viewed as visionary companies or great companies. It is true that China has witnessed the rise of good-performing companies such as Huawei, which has built up core competences in telecommunication infrastructure, smartphones, as well as enterprise products and services.[9] BAT, shorthand for Baidu.com, Alibaba, and Tencent, are candidates for China's great companies as well.[10] But these companies are still young and need more time to prove their adaptability to ever-changing business conditions. They also need time to test that they have built their capacity for perpetual and revolutionary innovations.

Can great companies be selected according to the conventional standards that survive the test of time? Anecdotes seem to suggest "No." In one of the business bestsellers in the 1980s, *In Search of Excellence*, Tom Peters and Bob Waterman chose 43 sample great companies and tried to map out best practice based on those companies. Ironically, many of them, including Westinghouse and K-Mart, failed as a result of not being able to effectively address changes in their respective industries, internal bureaucracy, and arrogance that had gradually built up among the management team.

This gives rise to an interesting question: Is it still useful to study what is in a great company? The concept of visionary companies by Collins and Porras has been widely accepted in the business world. Nevertheless, the criteria they use to select visionary companies are largely subjective. Ironically, many visionary companies chosen by them later reported serious problems, exhibited mediocre performance, and turned out to be not great at all. In 2001, Collins published another book, *Good to Great*, in which he studied 11 companies that had transformed themselves from good to great. Through case studies, Collins identified seven important features that had led to successful transformation. The features highlighted by Collins contain leadership ability, team spirit, corporate culture, cutting-edge technologies, and so on. However, among the 11 sample companies touted by Collins, Circuit City went bankrupt in 2009 and Fannie Mae nearly collapsed during the 2008–2009 global financial crisis. Although Altria had delivered a handsome return to shareholders, it produces cigarettes. Can a tobacco company be a great company? The 11 companies reported an average annual return of 7 percent between 1996 and 2011, barely on par with that of the overall market. Between 2001 and 2012, the 11 companies even underperformed the S&P 500 index.

Any writings on great companies, especially the studies on successful cases, may not be able to escape such an embarrassment. Research on great companies typically studies winners and adopts a backward-looking approach. However, all the factors that are alleged to have caused past success do not necessarily ensure future success. The future is non-linear and full of unexpected twists. Indeed, the business world is filled with all sorts of disruptions, mostly unexpected.

In the process of writing this book, I also encountered similar questioning. Among 6772 listed companies in the USA, according to Wiggins and Ruefli, only three companies achieved excellent performance for 50 consecutive years. If the odds hold in a more general context, then what is the point of studying great companies? Could the experiences built upon 0.04 percent of the listed companies in the USA be generalized and applied to an ordinary firm in another corner of the world? Could they be applied to a Chinese company, which operates in a completely different institutional setting? While I admit that an exact formula for making a great company may not be available, fundamental principles underneath a great company's mission, value proposition, strategy, and operation surely shed light on the Chinese companies which are going through the arduous transformation from big to great.

A large number of Chinese companies have achieved breakthroughs in size during China's reform era. For example, in the household appliance industry, the three largest makers in the world (by profits) are all Chinese firms (Gree Electric Appliances, Midea Group, and Qingdao Haier) with combined revenue of $60 billion and profits of $45 billion. PetroChina and State Grid each employ close to 1.5 million people, and the electronics giant Hon Hai Precision employs 1.2 million people. But "size" does not mean profitability, and it does not capture value creation either. Many business leaders in China have developed an obsession with size simply because they believe in the principle of "too big to fail." A large size helps a firm survive in fiercer market competition; in addition, if a big firm fails, the damage caused may be so high that the government has to step in to lend its supporting hand.

However, this rule in the jungle is now changing in China—a large size does not necessarily provide better chance for survival and growth; it calls for a higher demand for input such as capital and labor. However, the credit-fueled growth model cannot be sustained as a result of mounting corporate debt; rising wages are also eroding Chinese companies' profits and casting a shadow on their further development. "Too big to fail" may still work. But corporate dinosaurs lack nimble ways to cope with disruptive factors in the market. Their long-term prosperity can hardly be achieved.

How to successfully achieve corporate China's rise to greatness, which would be characterized by the surge of a large number of companies with differentiated products or services and sustainable capacity for perpetual innovation? To address this issue, I have to go back to the attributes shared by great companies. Then I return to the starting line where a business begins, and ponder over what kind of qualities and force drives a startup to continuously walk forward until its final success. I get an exceptionally simple answer—value creation. To succeed, a firm should, as stated by the famous German soldier Carl von Clausewitz, "Pursue one great decisive aim with force and determination." For corporate China, value creation should be such a great and decisive aim.

GREAT AND DECISIVE AIM

If a company sets value creation as its ultimate and decisive goal, from a corporate finance perspective, achieving a higher level of return on invested capital (ROIC) is critical. Empirical studies have soundly established a positive correlation between ROIC and firm value. As I will show, ROIC is the most relevant financial indicator that is positively associated with a Chinese firm's value as well. Intuitively, a firm with a higher level of ROIC invests more efficiently, and therefore calls for a relatively smaller amount of capital spending to sustain future growth. All else equal, this leaves the firm with more free cash flow, which corresponds to higher firm value. Although the relation between ROIC and firm value may not be causal, ROIC is a reliable indicator showing the strength of a firm's fundamentals. Pursuing ROIC rather than sales, total assets, or other variables demonstrates a firm's determination to create value. And value creation is at the core of a great company's greatness.

By this way of thinking, I even believe that any innovations in business models are associated with certain innovative ways to systematically and significantly improve firms' ROIC.

The relevance and importance of ROIC can be better shown by using data. As in Fig. 2.1, between 1963 and 2001, the average ROIC of the listed companies in the USA is 11.6 percent. This suggests that every dollar of capital (fixed assets or working capital) put into these listed companies' operations is able to generate an after-tax profit of 11.6 cents. In the past one hundred years, the average ROIC of the listed companies in the USA is about 10 percent. And the annualized stock market return is also about 10 percent, on par with that of the listed companies' ROIC. The two are highly correlated, confirming the claim of neo-classical economics. As I will show in Chap. 3, over the period from 1998 to 2012, one dollar of capital put into a Chinese listed firm's operation can only generate an after-tax profit of 3 cents. From 1998 to 2012, investing in the Chinese

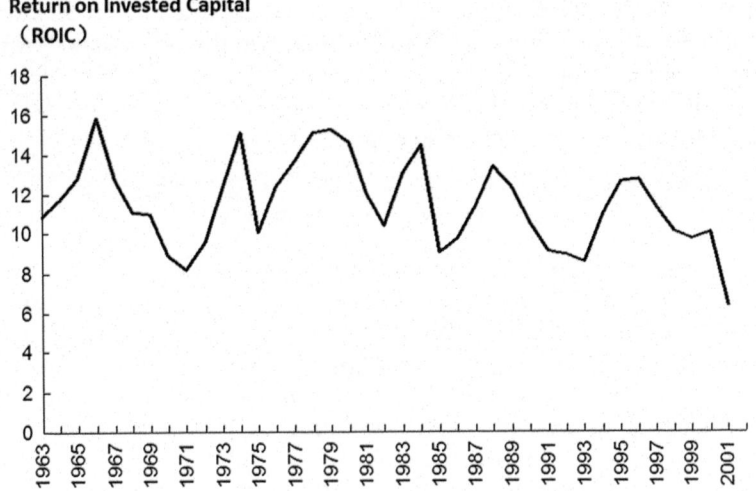

Fig. 2.1 Average ROIC of the listed companies in the USA: 1963–2001
Source: The data source is the Compustat database. The sample includes all listed companies in the New York Stock Exchange and NASDAQ. Following conventional practice, firms in financial services and utilities are excluded

stock market could only generate an average 3.5 percent of annual return. The Chinese listed companies' market performance was worse than that of their US counterparts, as a result of poor ROIC.

Another concept, WACC, is also important. WACC, shorthand for weighted average cost of capital, measures the cost of funding for a company. There are two main external financing sources for a firm: debt and equity, each of which may carry a different cost. WACC is the weighted average costs of debt and equity. It captures the opportunity cost of the capital that has been put into a company's operating activities. For example, if the debt-to-equity ratio of a company is 1, this suggests that half of the company's capital is financed through debt and the other half through equity. In this case, if the after-tax cost of debt is 6 percent and the cost of equity is 12 percent, then the company's WACC is 9 percent. This suggests that the company needs to deliver to its capital suppliers, shareholders and creditors inclusive, an annual rate of return of 9 percent. This in turn implies that the firm's ROIC has to be larger than 9 percent, otherwise what the firm earns cannot cover the cost of obtaining operating capital. The firm is not creating value at all.

Notably, economic value added (EVA), a concept coined in the 1980s, has been widely used to capture a firm's value creation. An easy way to calculate EVA is as follows: EVA = (ROIC − WACC) × Invested Capital. Clearly, at the core of EVA are ROIC and WACC. If and only if ROIC is bigger than WACC can a firm have a positive EVA.

ROIC ≥ WACC

When a company maintains ROIC higher than that of its peers and its WACC for a long enough time, the company can easily meet the criteria for a great company listed by Jim Collins and Jerry Porras in *Built to Last: Successful Habits of Visionary Companies*. The company with higher ROIC has excellent operating results and is more likely to be one of the best among its peers; since it generates value, the company can draw wide respect from people in the same line of business. Higher ROIC also makes the company financially able to produce great products or provide differentiated services over several life cycles, and ultimately exert inerasable influence on the world.

Michael Porter, a corporate strategy guru and a professor at Harvard Business School, stresses that a great company should be able to maintain competitive advantages over its competitors and potential entrants over a long period of time. In Porter's narrative, a company's long-term competitive advantages derive from its cost advantages, differentiated brand, cutting-edge technology, and, in particular, positioning in the marketplace relative to stakeholders such as clients, employees, rivals, potential entrants, and regulators.[11] Clearly, if a firm can consistently maintain an ROIC higher than that of its peers, the firm can very likely ensure its competitive advantages. Our corporate finance perspective on great companies is largely in line with the definitions of great companies raised in previous studies.

Take the listed companies in the NYSE and NASDAQ as examples. As shown in Fig. 2.1, from 1963 to 2001, the average ROIC of the listed companies was 11.6 percent. The main reason that the stock market in the USA had consistently delivered attractive returns to investors is closely related to the fact that the listed companies in the USA had managed to achieve higher levels of ROIC.

To better illustrate the relevance of ROIC to firm value, I use the rise and fall of Dell as one example. The changes in Dell's ROIC fully embodied key features of its business model. When Dell entered the PC market in 1984, the leaders in the industry such as IBM, HP, and Compaq used offline stores as the main platform to sell computers. Establishing and maintaining physical stores requires large amounts of capital spending, which surely lowers the level of ROIC. Dell introduced the integrated customer direct model by targeting technologically sophisticated customers. Rather than being used as a marketing gimmick, Dell's direct-sale model allowed customers to place their orders according to their preferences for speed, computing power, storage, and so on. After Dell received orders, it swiftly procured and assembled standardized and modularized accessories and parts into PCs, and mailed them to customers.

With "build to order" as one catchy line of its business model, Dell did not have much inventory, which significantly reduced the level of working capital, and translated into improved ROIC. With the dawn of the internet era, Dell pioneered the use of internet to develop ties to end consumers, who can order tailor-made products form Dell swiftly. Dell had thus achieved explosive growth and rapidly rose to one of the leaders in the PC business.

The troubles Dell encountered in recent years precisely reflect the bottlenecks facing the company. Dell's competitive advantages resulting from the "build to order" model had been on the wane when laptops gained popularity and took up the market share of the traditional PC business. Compared to desktops, assembling laptops based on individual consumers' idiosyncratic configuration is more difficult simply because there are fewer standardized accessories and parts for laptops. To meet consumers' specific requirements on certain features, Dell has to store numerous accessories and parts, and finished final goods, which inevitably increases its inventory and capital spending. In the laptop era, Dell's asset-light "build to order" model had become more like the traditional "build to stock" model. Not surprisingly, Dell's competitive advantages gradually waned, as reflected in its ROIC.

The rise and fall of Dell had been mirrored in the ups and downs of its ROIC. Certainly, Dell's fall was also related to tougher competition from cheaper and nimbler Asian companies such as Lenovo. But Dell's obsession with its "build to order" model and delay in adapting to changing business conditions were at the core of its failure.

ROIC AND IBM'S TRANSFORMATION

There are plenty of case examples highlighting the importance of a sustainable higher level of ROIC to a firm's greatness. IBM's transformation in the 1990s is one. Louis Gestner, former CEO of IBM, had detailed in his autobiography about how IBM achieved its transformation from a manufacturer to a service provider under his leadership. The book is titled *Who Says Elephants Can't Dance?* After this, people grew accustomed to using "a dancing elephant" to describe IBM's transformation in the 1990s.

IBM, established in 1911 and headquartered in Armonk, New York, is one of the world's largest multinational information technology companies. Employing 430,000 staff, IBM's businesses span more than 160 countries. The company started with commercial typewriters in its early stage. Its main businesses evolved and shifted to word processors, and then to computers. IBM is culture conscious. Under the leadership of Thomas J. Watson, IBM had developed a distinct culture which has been best reflected in its famous "THINK" slogan.

As a leading computer manufacturer, IBM gained its prominence in the 1980s. By then, IBM's leading product was the mainframe. IBM's mainframe business was so successful that the "mainframe thinking" took shape and became the core of IBM corporate culture. Although IBM successfully launched the world's first PC set as early as 1981, the PC was long viewed as inferior to mainframe computers. It was believed that the PC business was incompatible with IBM's "mainframe" culture, and hence received little attention within the firm. However, as PCs got more sophisticated in the early 1990s, the market share of IBM started to shrink and IBM was not well prepared for this disruptive change. The company's revenues and profits declined sharply. On January 19, 1993, IBM announced a loss of US$4.97 billion for the 1992 fiscal year, which set a record in the history of corporate America at the time. Between 1991 and 1993, IBM suffered a total loss of US$14.6 billion.

Figure 2.2 presents IBM's share prices from January 1990 to May 2013. As shown in this figure, IBM performed poorly in the early 1990s. On January 2, 1990, IBM's share price dropped to US$16.44. It continued to tumble and further dropped to US$8.35 on September 1, 1993. During the same period, Standard & Poor's 500 Index increased by almost 40 percent.

Against that backdrop, IBM kick-started a painful and arduous transformation under the leadership of new CEO Louis Gestner. Having a full-view description of IBM's transformation would be hard as it inevitably involves tears (a total of 40,000 employees were laid off by early 1993), laughter, failures, and joy. Here, I would like to analyze how IBM achieved

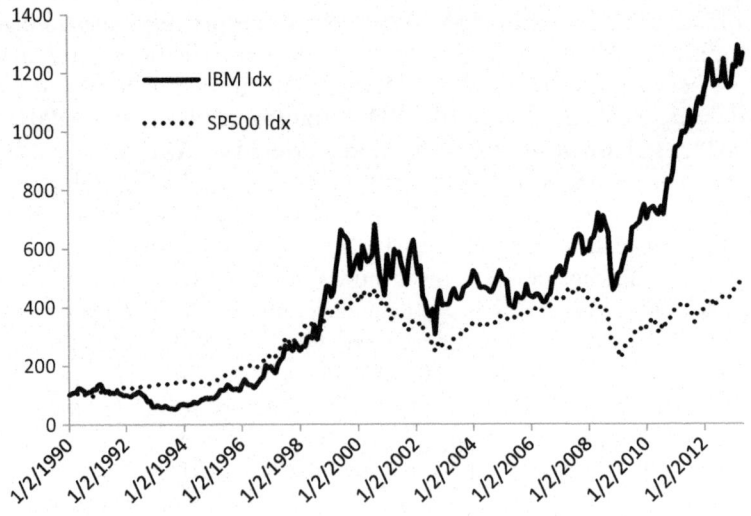

Fig. 2.2   IBM's share prices versus Standard & Poor's 500 Index
Notes: The share price and the index level on January 2, 1990, were set to be 100
Source: author's calculation based on data from CRSP (the Center for Research in Security Prices).

its successful transformation from the perspective of corporate finance. Especially, I focus on discussing how its ROIC evolved dynamically and how such dynamics were mirrored in the changes in IBM's business model.

Upon his arrival, Gerstner was reminded that he needed to stop the bleeding and restore IBM's cash flow as soon as possible. As the market demand for IBM's main products, computers, and peripheral hardware had become soft and the substitute products were fiercely eroding IBM's market share, downsizing seemed a natural choice. For example, IBM operated 125 independent data centers in 1993, and had 128 chief information officers at different levels, which had considerably lowered the company's profit margin. Louis Gestner orchestrated IBM's transformation. He stressed the "One IBM" policy, and made efforts to consolidate IBM's enormously complicated internal system, freeing up cash flow to meet immediate needs. While such measures helped stop the bleeding, over time it became clearer that IBM needed a more drastic approach to boost ROIC. IBM eventually chose to sell business units with low-profit margin. Manufacturing and hardware popped up as primary candidates—they were capital-intensive and yield was low. By stripping these businesses, IBM's ROIC increased significantly. As a result, IBM's cash flow situation greatly improved. In the meantime, IBM strengthened its investments in software and services, which boasted higher levels of profitability and required less capital spending. This, together with stripping capital-intensive manufacturing business, greatly increased IBM's ROIC.

To implement this transformation strategy, IBM conducted a series of mergers, business stripping, and reorganization. Figure 2.3 shows the changes in IBM's net assets and price-to-book ratio (P/B) in 1990–1999. In Fig. 2.3, the horizontal axis captures IBM's net assets, which measures size, and the vertical axis represents its P/B ratio (share price divided by book value per share), which measures its performance at the capital market. From 1990 to 1994, IBM stripped two major manufacturing units and this helped reduce the firm size. As a result, IBM's net assets declined from $42 billion in 1990 to $19 billion in 1993. By disposing of redundant assets and business units with a lower rate of return, IBM offloaded unnecessary burdens. At the same time, IBM chose to increase investments in software and services. It purchased Lotus with $3.5 billion in June 1995, which kicked off its transformation from hardware to software. Lotus mainly engaged in e-mail, social networking services, office software, mobile and wireless services, electronic forms, and content management. In 1996, IBM purchased Tivoli, a company focusing on services.

Market Performance: P/B Ratio

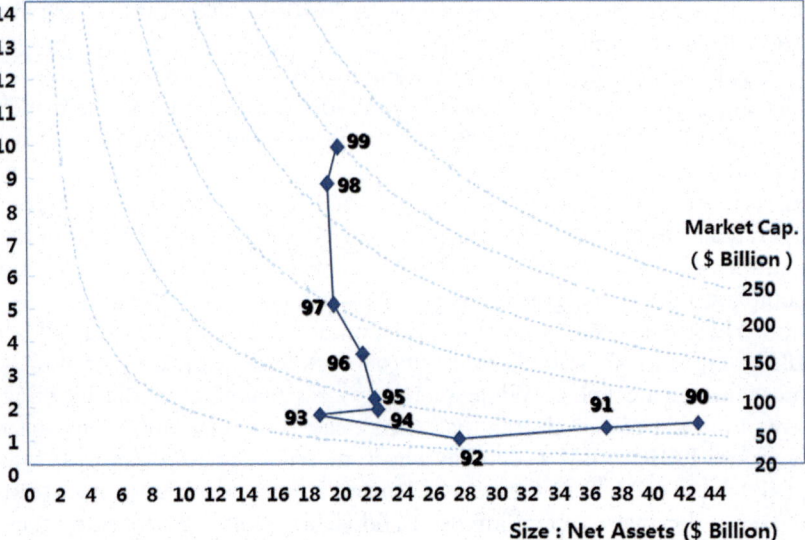

Fig. 2.3 IBM's size and market performance: 1990–1999
Source: Compustat; author's calculation

With investments and acquisitions, IBM marched into the area of information technology. When shifting business focus from hardware to software and services, IBM coined the term "e-commerce" in 1995, which summed up IBM's business vision. Continuing such a drive, IBM later purchased PricewaterhouseCoopers Consulting with $3.5 billion in July 2002, which greatly strengthened its service unit. In 2005, IBM sold its PC business to China's Lenovo, which was viewed by many as a continuation of IBM's transformation strategy.

Figure 2.3 vividly captures the dynamic changes in IBM's net assets (the horizontal axis) and market performance (the vertical axis; measured by P/B ratio) during its transition since 1990. Between 1990 and 1993, IBM focused on downsizing. Its net assets decreased significantly from close to $42 billion to $19 billion. Beginning in 1994, IBM started a series of mergers and acquisitions, which increased its net assets. However, its newly acquired businesses were mainly in service and software, which shared high profit margin but required less capital spending. IBM's net assets, which is a good proxy for the total amount of invested capital employed in operation, did not increase much. With much improved profit margin and lower invested capital, IBM's ROIC gradually recovered, which significantly boosted its stock market performance. From 1990 to 1999 IBM's net assets reduced by 55 percent, but its market value increased by more than 201 percent. More importantly, its P/B ratio increased by 600 percent. Once again, IBM became the darling of the stock market. A once cumbersome elephant finally walked brisk dancing steps.

IBM has once again proved that it is a great company. Its greatness lies in its decisiveness in making painful changes and its unrelenting efforts to seek new business models that can boost ROIC. Figure 2.4 presents IBM's ROIC for the period from 1971 to 2007. IBM's ROIC had been declining since the mid-1980s. It dropped to 4 percent in 1991, and further down to 0.5 percent in 1993. Between 1990 and 1993, IBM's rate of investment return could not even cover its cost of funding, which explains its deteriorating stock market performance. Thanks to IBM's light-asset transformation, its ROIC gradually picked up. In 1994, IBM's ROIC returned to 8 percent, and it further increased to 13 percent in 1999. IBM had since maintained a strong ROIC performance. In 2007, IBM's ROIC reached 25 percent.

The transformation of IBM from a manufacturer to a service company highlights the importance of pursuing value creation rather than size measured by assets. The connotation of a "great company" lies in whether

Fig. 2.4 IBM's ROIC from 1971 to 2007
Source: Author's calculation

a company has established a sound profit-driven business model, and whether it is able to deliver to investors high enough returns for a long enough time. And all of these crucially hinge on whether the firm can maintain a higher level of ROIC. If a company can dwarf its competitors in ROIC, the company is well positioned to maintain its competitive edge and is ready to leapfrog to a great company. From this perspective, what corporate China needs is to shift its mindset from pursuing size to pursuing value.

The transition of China's growth model from investment-led to efficiency-driven will surely speed up the pace of cleaning up the so-called zombie companies, which have built up enormous size through cheap loans from the state-owned banks but reported miserable bottom lines. If the Chinese firms can bravely embrace competitive business models characterized by higher ROIC and rapid growth, some of them will surely emerge from obscurity to become national or even world champions.

THE RISE AND FALL OF SUNTECH

This is a story about a failing Chinese company, Suntech, and its founder, Shi Zhengrong. Mr. Shi, a young and ambitious engineering student, went to Australia in 1988. With the support of a Chinese government scholarship, he enrolled in the Department of Physics at the University of New South Wales in Sydney, where he studied solar technology under the supervision of Professor Martin Green, a renowned scholar in the field. Shi obtained his PhD in 1992. He then started working as research director at Pacific Solar, a company founded by Martine Green. Over his eight-year tenure at Pacific Solar, Shi conducted extensive research on how to contain the cost of producing solar energy by reducing the amount of silicon used in the manufacturing process. Although Shi was very happy with his life in Sydney, he always felt a little bit like he was underachieving—when the Chinese economy had been growing rapidly, he was just a bystander. Finally, he decided to move back to his homeland to pursue a different life as an innovator and an entrepreneur.

Shi moved back to China in 2000. Solar energy was a new concept to most Chinese by then, and Shi had to spend more than a year trying to persuade the local governments to support his solar energy plan. Eventually, he convinced the Wuxi municipal government in Jiangsu Province. Wuxi government decided to invest $6 million of capital in Shi's venture, owning 75 percent of the shares, to get the project off the ground. With technology and an investment of $400,000, Shi owned 25 percent of the company. On January 21, 2001, Wuxi Suntech Co. was formally established.

Suntech's Surge and Sudden Fall

Suntech completed its first photovoltaic (PV) cell manufacturing line with a capacity of 10MW in August 2002. With its "leap-forward" approach, Suntech's business took off. As Suntech scaled up its operations, the quality of its products also improved. In 2004, Wuxi Suntech was rated by PHOTON International as one of the world's leading solar PV manufacturers. Suntech pursued a low-cost manufacturing model, and worked very hard to produce better than industry average PV conversion efficiency. At the end of 2005, Suntech rose to one of the world's top five PV companies, with a capacity of 150 MG.

With ownership restructuring, the Wuxi government exited in 2005. In the same year, Shi registered in the British Virgin Islands a company called Suntech Power Holdings Co. Ltd. (Suntech Power), which had 100 percent shares of Wuxi Suntech. Suntech Power went IPO on the NYSE in December 2005, making it the first Chinese private firm to do so. In 2006, the share price of Suntech Power climbed to over $40 per share, making Shi the richest person in China, with a wealth of $2.3 billion. By the end of 2007, Suntech had increased its capacity to 360 MG. Both sales and market capitalization of Suntech exceeded $10 billion in the same year, making it one of the world's top three PV cell producers. In 2008, with strong demand for PV cells in the USA and Europe, the global PV industry reached its peak. Suntech continued its strong investment with the support of bank loans. As of 2010, Suntech had become the world's largest PV cell manufacturer in terms of both capacity and realized output (see Fig. 2.5 for share prices of Suntech).

Right after Suntech reached its peak, its good fortune seemed to come to an end. As of the fourth quarter of 2008, the demand for PV components dropped significantly as a result of economic meltdown in the USA and Europe, Suntech's main export markets. However, the supply of PV cells was still kept at very high level because more and more Chinese competitors entered into the market, most of which had strong support from local governments. Overcapacity led to declining price and eroding profit margin. Despite the fact that Suntech managed to report a net profit of $262.3 million in the 2010 fiscal year, the majority of this profit was

Fig. 2.5 Share prices of Suntech Power: December 14, 2005–November 8, 2013
Source: Yahoo Finance

from investments rather than its core business—PV cells. Suntech's good fortune had seemingly come to an end.

In 2011, Suntech terminated a long-term contract with its main silicon provider, MEMC, and paid a large sum as fine for contract breach, which brought it a net loss. The share price of Suntech Power dropped to around $9 in 2011. The sharp drop continued in 2012 and the stock price lingered at $1 per share for most of 2012. Suntech's focus on low-cost manufacturing in China with global sales and marketing efforts was questioned by the market.

Suntech's aggressive expansion finally came to an end in September 2012, when its new CEO, Jin Wei, announced a reduction of capacity by one quarter and a cut of 1500 employees. On March 4, 2013, the Suntech board of directors dismissed Shi Zhengrong from his post as board chairman. On April 15, Wuxi Suntech, which contributed more than 90 percent of the output of the NYSE-listed Suntech Power, announced default on a convertible debt with the amount of $541 million. The share price of Suntech Power, Wuxi Suntech's parent company, tumbled by 24.91 percent to 44 cents in a single day.[12]

It took slightly more than twelve years for Suntech to rise to the top and then fall hard back to earth. The unbridled pursuit of operating scale rather than ROIC was behind Suntech's collapse. Suntech's predicament was related to a significant drop in the product price resulting from over-supply, the impact of the global financial crisis since 2008, as well as the anti-dumping campaigns staged by the USA and European Union. On top of these external factors, Suntech's predicament was inherently associated with its aggressive expansion strategy and a number of investment projects that had been poorly carried out.

From 2007 to 2010, the profit margin of Suntech Power dropped from 14.8 percent to 8.2 percent. In 2011, its main business suffered a huge loss, with a profit margin of negative 19.3 percent. Although Suntech maintained a strong sales growth from 2007 to 2010, due to declining profit margin, its earnings before interest and tax (EBIT) remained almost unchanged. However, the company's fixed assets increased significantly, leading to a declining ROIC.

Eroding profit margin was largely driven by overcapacity in China's PV industry. Dubbed "new and clean energy," the PV industry was once a darling to local governments. Companies like Suntech can easily get preferred tax treatment, land use rights, and access to external finance. As a result, capital swarmed into the industry. Many firms tried to replicate Suntech's miraculous journey. In early 2007, more than 100 municipal cities across China announced their plans to construct their own PV industrial parks. After years of leap-forward development, oversupply became a serious issue in the industry.

The declining profit margin had a lot to do with the development model of China's PV industry. Companies such as Suntech focused on low-cost manufacturing strategy, with technology, raw materials, and sales relying heavily on global markets. Most had not formed their core competence, and had to compete on price. After 2010, the global demand for PV cell products grew weaker as a result of anti-dumping tariffs imposed by the EU and the USA on Chinese solar PV companies, which further worsened their profitability.

Reflection on Suntech's Failure

Rather than rising to greatness after it became the world's largest PV supplier in 2010, Suntech fell hard. Suntech's sudden fall is enlightening for the Chinese companies as a whole. Suntech's failure had much to do with the local government, which had generously supported Suntech in the early stage of its development. The subsidies and tax breaks provided by the local government greatly spurred Suntech's growth. But the government also pressured Suntech to pursue even larger capacity through more investments. Because almost all local governments had adopted a similar approach to promote the solar PV industry under their jurisdiction, the capital spending spree caused serious overcapacity in the industry. Suntech, despite its leading position, was not immune to increasing competition and declining product prices. The political tournament based on economic performance, which largely characterizes the behavioral patterns of the Chinese local governments, not only brewed the birth and surge of China's solar PV industry, but also pre-determined its short-lived prosperity.

Of course, Suntech's failure is more associated with its immature business model and extremely aggressive strategy. As one of the world's leading solar PV manufacturers, Suntech had not proactively cultivated its competitive edge by building up a strong base of intellectual assets. Suntech committed only one percent of its sales to research and development (R&D). Its core technologies were imported and its largest competitive edge was cost. However, when facing fiercer competition and weaker demand, Suntech's cost advantage quickly evaporated. Suntech had managed to achieve a high ROIC for a short while, but it failed to maintain the momentum for a long enough time. In Fig. 2.6, I provide Suntech's ROIC from 2007 to 2012, the period Suntech experienced its rapid rise and dramatic fall. In the Technical Appendix of this book, I provide a detailed explanation on how I calculate Suntech's ROIC and how I decompose this into several branches in order to better understand the drivers behind Suntech's changing ROIC.

Suntech's pre-tax ROIC peaked at 20.8 percent in 2007. After this, it steadily declined, from 11.1 percent in 2008 and 12.4 percent in 2009, to 9.8 percent in 2010. Suntech reported a negative ROIC in 2011. According to my estimation (see Technical Appendix), Suntech's WACC ranged from 10 percent to 12 percent during 2007–2012, suggesting that its ROIC cannot cover its cost of funding since 2009. A firm with negative EVA does not create value, and shows no signs of becoming a great company.

The analysis of Suntech's ROIC, as shown in Fig. 2.6, clearly explains the rise and fall of Suntech. First, Suntech's profit margin dropped from 14.8 percent to negative 19.3 percent, reflecting the adverse impact of

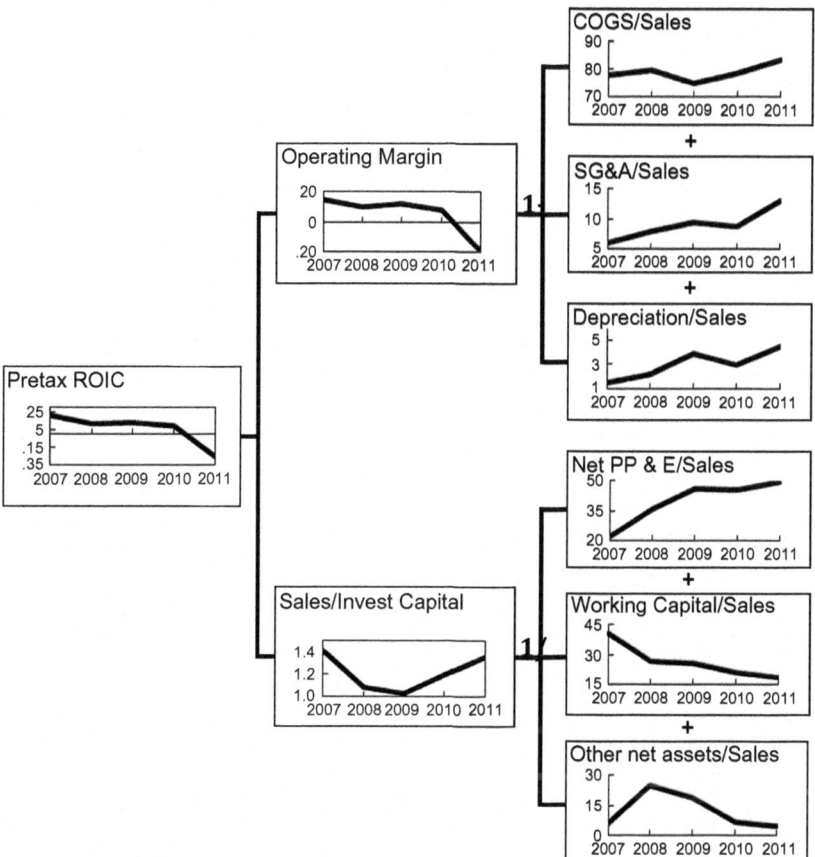

Fig. 2.6 Suntech's Pre-tax ROIC: 2007–2011
Source: Author's calculation. See technical appendix for details

oversupply. However, Suntech continued its investment spree despite eroding profit margin. The fixed assets-to-sales ratio more than doubled from 2007 to 2011. A significant rise in the level of its fixed assets had also led to a larger amount of depreciation, which further reduced the firm's profit margin.

Behind the capital spending spree was Suntech's tenacious pursuit of market share rather than profit or value creation. Shi Zhengrong was determined to make Suntech the largest solar PV manufacturer in the world. The Wuxi municipal government also expressed the same wish repeatedly. With such sentiments dominating the mind of the decision-makers, it is quite easy to understand why Suntech had been so eager to expand its capacity. In hindsight, Suntech had unfortunately chosen a pro-cyclical investment strategy: When market demand was strong, Suntech used credit-fueled investments to expand its capacity; it continued to do so until the demand got soft. Investments were largely irreversible. When the demand went under, a large portion of Suntech's capacity was left unused. A bloated balance sheet, coupled with a decline in profit margin, explains Suntech's deteriorating ROIC since 2010.

Pro-cyclicality in investment is not the best strategy for an industry like solar PV manufacturing. In this case, to mitigate upstream risks surrounding supply and the pricing of silicon, Suntech initiated a number of equity investments in several silicon suppliers. Suntech aimed to secure adequate and high-quality silicon. Meanwhile, it signed a number of long-term contracts with silicon suppliers, in hope of mitigating its risk exposure to silicon supply shortage. For example, in 2006, when the demand for solar PV products was at its peak, Suntech signed a ten-year contract with MEMC, which was valued at $6 billion, to support its aggressive expansion plan. In October 2007, Suntech signed a contract with Asia Silicon Co., Ltd. to purchase up to $1.5 billion of high-purity silicon over a seven-year period.

These investments, largely driven by the motive to enlarge production capacity, failed to generate the desired outcome in the aftermath of the global financial crisis. Numbers help here: When signing the silicon supply contract with MEMC, the price of silicon was at $500 per kilogram; the price dropped to $50 per kilogram by 2009. After a short rebound in 2011, the price of polycrystalline silicon further dropped to $2.4 per kilogram. By locking in silicon supply with fixed price through long-term contracts, Suntech suffered a huge loss when the economy turned weak.

To finance investments, Suntech relied on debt financing. By the end of 2011, Suntech had total debt amounting to $2.3 billion, of which $1.57 billion would be due within two years, and $580 million was con-vertible. High leverage ratio was one of the direct reasons for Suntech's fall: Suntech filed for bankruptcy in April 2013 because it was not able to honor the convertible debt.

Controversial corporate governance practice has also been held account-able for Suntech's predicament. When Wuxi Suntech filed for bankruptcy, Shi Zhengrong's ownership in Suntech was almost worthless. However, Shi and his family had set up a number of tightly controlled companies through cross-holding structure. These affiliates had engaged in all sorts of transactions with Suntech Power, the listed company. For example, Asia Silicon Co., Ltd and Glory Silicon Co., Ltd., both of which were controlled by Shi and his family, signed several long-term contracts with Suntech to supply fixed-priced silicon. Both locked in handsome profit despite the fact that the market price of silicon fell to below 10 percent of the contracted price. It is not clear whether this was due to misjudgments or whether it was intricately designed to hedge the risk faced by Shi and his family. In either case, Shi and his family were winners. The dynamics of ROIC, as shown in Fig. 2.6, vividly unravel the reasons behind Suntech's quick rise and sudden fall. Investment-led growth strategy is surely powerful in promoting large companies. But size is not tantamount to value creation. If a firm lacks a convincing business model that is associated with a high and sustainable level of ROIC, the firm cannot be a great company.

Stan Shih, founder of Acer Group in Taiwan, once put forward a "Smiling Curve" theory. Back in 1992, Mr. Shih used this framework to diagnose the company he ran and frame Acer's future strategies (see Fig. 2.7). The "Smiling Curve" theory argues that out of the three segments associated with manufacturing—R&D, assembly and production, and brand and marketing—R&D and marketing and branding have a much higher profit margin than does assembly and production. Shih continued to suggest that most Asian firms began with assembling, and had them positioned at the low end of the value chain. To get into high ends

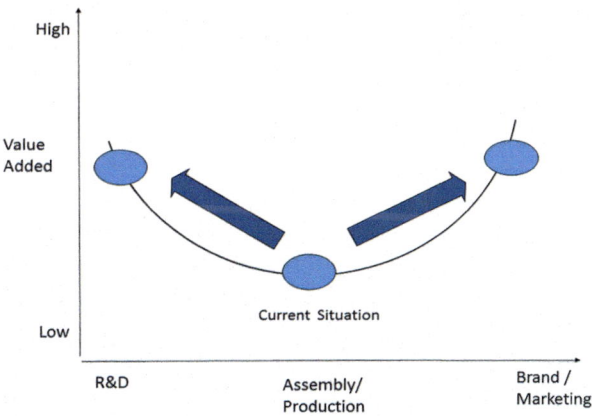

Fig. 2.7 Smiling curve

of the value chain and secure high profit margin, Asian companies need to build their own brands and proactively pursue R&D. Without R&D, a firm only acts as an original equipment manufacturer (OEM); without marketing and brands, even the best products would be useless once their life cycles are over.

Applying the "Smiling Curve" theory to Suntech, one can easily draw a conclusion that the fall of Suntech might have been inevitable. Suntech's main businesses concentrated in the low-profit margin assembly and production. Without a solid footing in either R&D or marketing, Suntech was still an OEM in a high-tech industry. While Suntech could enjoy a high ROIC for a while, thanks to government subsidies and favorable market conditions, maintaining high ROIC for a long enough time was rather difficult. Suntech should have tapped into R&D and brand-building much earlier and should have been extremely careful with its pro-cyclical investment strategy. In any case, the solar PV industry is an emerging industry with many uncharted risk areas.

BORN IN RECESSION

One plausible way to search for the rules that make companies great is to study the great companies. Investigating the commonalities of well-perceived great companies, one may find some cues. GE, Microsoft, and Federal Express are all widely viewed as great companies. What do they have in common? One thing most may not have realized is that they were all born in recession. According to a research by the Kauffman Foundation in 2011, more than 50 percent of Standard & Poor's 500 companies were founded during the recession periods, while the recession periods only accounted for 15 percent of the time in the past one hundred years. What special features do firms born in recession have? Can these features explain these great companies' greatness?

I address these issues together with my collaborator Xiaoquan Wang. In a recent academic paper,[13] we investigate more than 9000 listed companies in the USA including the universe of companies that have gone IPO since 1975. After carefully cleaning the data, we identify 1281 firms that were born in recession (they are dubbed recession firms hereafter). Comparing the 1281 recession firms with other firms, we find robust empirical evidence that the recession firms boast much better stock market performance and ROIC.

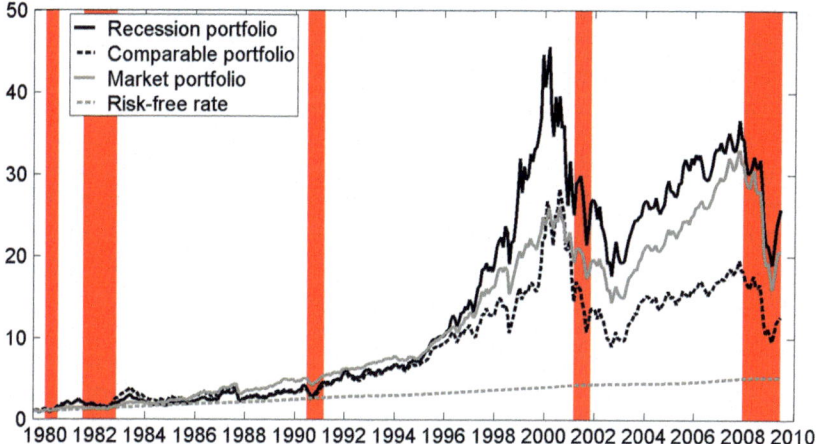

Fig. 2.8 Market performance of firms born in recession: 1980–2010
Source: Liu and Wang (2015)

In Fig. 2.8, a reproduction of Fig. 2.1 in Qiao Liu and Xiaoquan Wang's paper (Liu and Wang 2015), we compare the market performance of four portfolios: the portfolio consisting of the stocks of recession firms, the portfolio consisting of the stocks of other firms (non-recession firms), risk-free assets, and the market portfolio. Obviously, the portfolio consisting of the stocks of the recession firms outperforms the other three portfolios by a large margin. Particularly, one dollar invested in the stocks of the recession firms in 1980 would grow to $26 by end 2010; as a comparison, one dollar invested in the stocks of other firms (non-recession firms) would only grow to $13 by end 2010, just half of that of the recession firms. Moreover, one dollar invested in the market portfolio in 1980 would only grow to $21 by 2010. Although the market portfolio outperformed the portfolio consisting of stocks of non-recession firms, the stocks of recession firms outperformed the market during 1980–2010. Note that in Fig. 2.8 the red bars indicate the recession years.

Why do the recession firms outperform other firms? We find that firms born in recession are more persistent in their corporate decisions. Their investment, financing, dividend payout, and R&D decisions are less affected by the macroeconomic conditions. Unlike other firms, which tend to make pro-cyclical corporate decisions, firms born in recession are less likely to make excessive investments when the economy booms; they are more likely to stick to their value-oriented investment plans even during recessions. That is, they are cautious when others are greedy and behave normally when others are over-cautious. The persistence in their decision-making style, to a great extent, accounts for their better performance.

What shaped recession firms' unique decision-making style remains an empirical puzzle. The persistence in the recession firms' various corporate decisions could result from corporate culture or genes shaped in the early years of a recession firm's development. In the latter case, when a firm is born, its external business conditions may leave a deep imprint, which tends to remain with the firm over a long time. Such an imprint affects the firm's decisions, practice, and, finally, operation outcome. Firms born in recession are usually more disciplined, and have a better awareness of potential risk exposure. *"Those born in the winter know how to weather the storm,"* as the old saying suggests; firms born in recession know how to better manage. Interestingly, compared with other firms, those born in recession usually have more patents, and tend to adopt a low-risk approach. As a result, they are able to maintain a relatively higher level of ROIC.

The empirical findings on the recession firms are particularly enlightening for Chinese firms. Entering into the 2010s, the Chinese economy started wrestling with slow growth, an aging population, excessive debts, and widespread overcapacity. Intractable anxiety is building up among the Chinese firms. However, adverse external conditions may hone a firm's adeptness in dealing with uncertainties. For the Chinese firms, especially those state-owned "zombie companies," taking a long-term view and shifting the focus from the size to value creation is their best preparation for the upcoming disruptive forces. In any case, the greatness of a firm lies in its strong capability of upholding high ROIC for a long enough time. Slowing down economy is, without a doubt, a challenge; it however could provide a window opportunity.

NOTES

1. There are 106 *Fortune* Global 500 companies in China (including companies in Hong Kong and Taiwan) in 2015, among which 98 are mainland Chinese companies.
2. See Xiaolin Yang, "Homegrown auto brands upgrading paradox," The Economic Observer, July 14, 2013.

3. See Kraemer, Kenneth, Greg Linden, and Jason Dedrick, Capturing value in global networks: Apple's iPad and iPhone. UC Irvine, UC Berkeley and Syracuse Working Paper 2011.
4. See p. 1 of *Built to Last: Successful Habits of Visionary Companies.*
5. As Rayor and Ahmed wrote in their Harvard Business Review article, "Randomness can crown an average company king for a year, two years, even a decade, before performance reverts to the mean. If we can't be sure that the performance of companies mentioned in success studies was caused by more than just luck, we can't know whether to imitate their behaviors." For more detail, see "Three rules for making a company truly great," *Harvard Business Review*, April Issue.
6. See Foster and Kaplan (2001).
7. Kodak filed for bankruptcy in 2012.
8. See p. 331 of Beinhocker (2006).
9. I will discuss Huawei Technologies, Alibaba Group, Xiaomi, and SF Express in Chap. 8. These four companies have a good chance of becoming truly exceptional companies.
10. I will analyze these companies in detail in Chap. 8.
11. See Porter (1980, 1985).
12. Wuxi Suntech accounted for more than 90 percent of Suntech Power's production capacity.
13. See "Those born in the winter know how to weather the storm: an empirical investigation of firms born in recession" (Liu and Wang 2015), PKU Guanghua working paper.

CHAPTER 3

Does ROIC Apply to Corporate China?

The greatness of a company lies in its ability to maintain a return on invested capital (ROIC) higher than its main competitors and the industry average for long enough time. More importantly, a great company's ROIC should be kept at a level higher than its weighted average cost of capital (WACC). In my narrative of IBM and Suntech in the previous chapter, I view high ROIC as the most relevant variable indicating a firm's greatness. Can the conclusion derived from those anecdotes be generalized to a broad context? Can this criterion be applied in China, where firms in the modern sense did not even exist before 1978? Should Chinese entrepreneurs and corporate executives care about ROIC?

The Chinese firms have a penchant for fancy and glamorous projects. When I speak of ROIC to Chinese businesspeople, most of whom I have held very high respect, the usual reaction is that this concept makes a lot of sense, but it just does not apply in China. "Firm size is more important." Chinese entrepreneurs tend to explain, "Operating scale measured by total asset or the number of employees is what we can count on when applying for bank loans, government subsidies, land use right, and business licenses." "With a bigger firm size, I am more assured of my company's survival." Some entrepreneurs would even put it this way: "To grow a business in China, you need government support. Larger firms contribute more to local employment and tax revenue; they are more likely to gain attentions from the government. Only with such kind of attention can a business get support and grow."

© The Editor(s) (if applicable) and The Author(s) 2016
Q. Liu, *Corporate China 2.0*, DOI 10.1057/978-1-137-55089-7_3

I once interviewed a highly respected entrepreneur, who is known for being gifted at fostering government relations. After several rounds of drinks and some warm-up questions, he told me that when facing fierce product market competition and severe external financing constraints, the best way for a company to survive is to quickly expand its operating scale through credit-fueled investments.

"Does the increasing debt level concern you?" I asked cautiously, trying not to be too offensive.

"Too big to fail!" he laughed—he was much more frank than I had expected and obviously in a buoyant mood.

Such an ethos is not unusual. Growing outsized and breaking into the *Fortune* Global 500 list has been one primary goal, and, once achieved, a milestone for many Chinese companies. Obsession with firm size, or, more specifically, obsession with the *Fortune* Global 500 list, has driven many Chinese firms to invest ceaselessly. However, in addition to survival, the Chinese firms have to aim higher, especially when the Chinese economy is entering the so-called new normal, under which the importance of ROIC clearly dominates investment rate, as I have shown in Chap. 1. It is about time to call an end to the size-driven corporate strategy. There is an old Chinese saying, "A broader vision will temper a higher quality." What vision should a Chinese firm take? What goal should a Chinese firm work hard to achieve?

There is a famous case in the American corporate history, *Dodge v. Ford Motor Company*. By 1916, the Ford Company had accumulated a capital surplus of over $60 million. The company's president and major shareholder, Henry Ford, sought to end special dividends for shareholders in favor of massive investments in new plants. He believed that such a strategy might be in the long-term benefit of the company. However, the minority shareholders objected to this strategy. The Dodge brothers, who together owned 10 percent of the company, sued Ford. The Michigan Supreme Court was called upon to decide on the case. In 1916, the Michigan Supreme Court gave its verdict against Henry Ford[1]:

> A business corporation is organized and carried on primarily for the profit of the stockholders. The powers of the directors are to be employed for that end. The discretion of directors is to be exercised in the choice of means to attain that end, and does not extends to a change in the end itself, to the reduction of profits, or to the non-distribution of profits among stock holders in order to devote them to other purposes.

This ruling has often been cited as having embodied the fundamental principle of Anglo-Saxon capitalism—it is a company's most important fiduciary duty to maximize shareholder value. This principle has been widely accepted and is also reflected in Collins and Porras' definition of great companies. In *Built to Last*, they wrote the following[2]:

> Profitability is a necessary condition for existence and a means to more important ends, but it is not the end in itself for many of the visionary companies. Profit is like oxygen, food, water, and blood for the body; they are the point of life, but without them, there is no life.

Defining a company's ultimate goal as profit maximization or shareholder value maximization is surely controversial. Do shareholders represent the company as a whole? In addition to shareholders, there are creditors, customers, employees, suppliers, and other kinds of stakeholders. They may have interests that completely conflict with those of shareholders. Should the company also care about their rights and interests? Not long ago, several high-profile companies touting shareholder value maximization blew themselves up: Enron, WorldCom, and Arthur Andersen, among others. In 2008, the collapse of Bear Stearns and Lehman Brothers triggered a global financial crisis. A consensus has yet to be reached regarding whose value a company should serve and whose interests should come first. Despite the hot debate, there is not much dispute that firms should take value creation, definitely not firm size, as their purpose. The real issue can hence be rephrased as how we correctly define and measure value. Among numerous noisy and flawed indicators that are related to firm value, I would like to take an unambiguous stand that ROIC is by far the most relevant one and could be effectively used to guide a value-oriented firm's operation.

When I began my research on corporate China and tried to answer the obvious puzzle of why Chinese firms succeeded impressively in growing their size but failed to grow their value, one piece of sage advice I received was "Try to compare the Chinese firms with their western counterparts; you may find answer in those great international firms." In hindsight, this is how ROIC surges onto the scene. In Chap. 2, I have documented that the greatness behind firms such as IBM is their strong capability to maintain a high level of ROIC for a long enough time. If the Chinese firms want to transform themselves from big to great, achieving a higher ROIC might be the right thing to do.

Over the past three and a half decades, with the deepening of China's reform and opening up initiatives, it has gradually become a consensus that Chinese companies, state owned or privately run, should first of all create value. Certainly, value is a broad concept. In addition to economic value, it may also include social value and value for certain entrenched political groups. Although many Chinese companies, especially those large SOEs, also have to shoulder many social and political responsibilities, maximizing value does not necessarily conflict with these responsibilities if we interpret value as a combination of economic, political, and social value. A company has to create value to justify its existence.

In their book *Creative Destruction*, Dick Foster and Sarah Kaplan examine a large sample of companies and provide convincing evidence that those survivors of fierce market competition usually performed worse in the stock market. They argue that surviving market competition alone does not make a great company. For a company to be great, it must creatively adapt itself to ever-changing market conditions, and must be bold enough to disrupt itself by turning its established business models upside down. In doing so, the company must be able to maintain a high ROIC for a long enough time. This corporate finance perspective of a great company, which I have detailed in Chap. 2, not only applies to companies in the USA and other developed economies, it also applies to corporate China, although they compete against each other and against the international firms in a very different institutional setting.

Having advocated the importance of value creation and ROIC, I next use data on China's listed companies to illustrate the relevance and importance of ROIC. I provide evidence from different perspectives that ROIC is closely related to a firm's operating performance, lasting prosperity, as well as great performance in China's young stock market, which has been denounced by many as chaotic, disorderly, and even inferior to gambling houses.[3] I show that companies who manage to achieve a high level of ROIC for a long enough time can consistently deliver good returns to their investors. As in other parts of the world, ROIC is the most relevant indicator that showcases a firm's value-creating capability in China.

STRONG ECONOMY, WEAK STOCK MARKET

Academics and professionals interested in China and the Chinese economy are often puzzled by one paradoxical fact about the Chinese economy and the Chinese stock market: While China has maintained a GDP growth rate

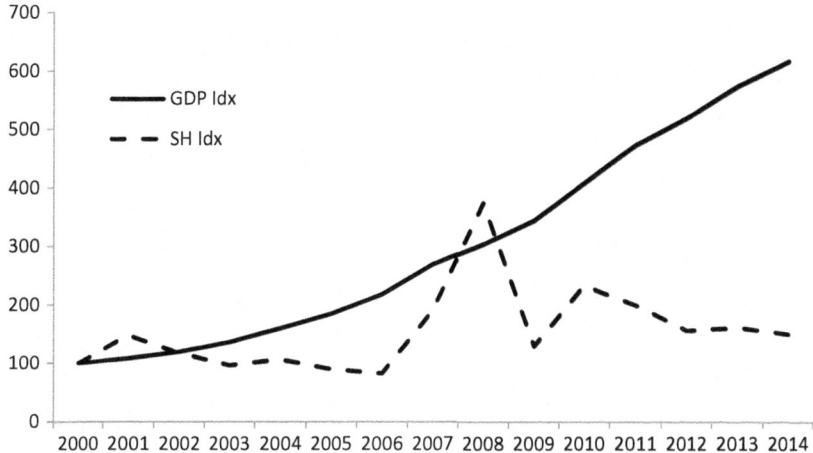

Fig. 3.1   China's GDP and the Shanghai Composite Stock Index, 2000–2014
Note: Both the level of the Shanghai Composite Stock Index at the beginning of
2000 and China's GDP in 2000 have been reset to be 100.
Source: Author's calculation

of close to 10 percent in the past three and a half decades, its stock market remains one of the worst performing markets in the world for quite a long time. It seems that there is a hard-to-understand disconnect between China's stock market and its real economy.

Figure 3.1 depicts how China's GDP and the Shanghai Composite Stock Index, which has been widely used to measure the overall performance of China's A-share market (RMB-denominated market), evolved dynamically from 2000 to 2014. From 2000 to 2014, China's GDP grew by almost seven times, from around RMB 9 trillion to over RMB 62 trillion. In a striking contrast, after going through several ups and downs, the Shanghai Composite Stock Index only rose from 1406 at the beginning of 2000 to slightly over 3000 at the end of 2014. Against the conventional wisdom, China's stock market is not the barometer of its real economy at all.

In finance terminology, the difference between the return on a portfolio or a stock and the expected return or the benchmark return is labeled α. The bigger the α, the more profitable the investment portfolio. The expected return is usually proxied by return on the market portfolio or calculated based on various asset pricing models. The most standard method is known as the capital asset pricing model, or CAPM, which comes with all the usual assumptions about perfectly rational investors, efficient markets, and equilibrium. While CAPM had failed to fanfare in empirical tests, Nobel Economics Laureate Eugene Fama and his long-time coauthor Kenneth French introduced a model that uses three factors to capture the expected returns. These three factors are constructed to capture the effects of market returns, size, and book-to-market ratio, respectively. The model has been dubbed the Fama-French three-factor model and has been widely adopted in empirical research as well as in practice.

Looking back, investing in China's stock market does not generate much α. One can even claim that the Chinese stock market does not have any invest-ability at all, given its poor record in the past. China's stock market is not the only market reporting such a woeful performance in recent years. In fact, almost all emerging markets exhibited weak performance between 2011 and 2014. Take 2010 and 2011 as one example. Emerging markets as a whole reported a GDP growth of 12 percent in these two years, far better than the growth of 4 percent achieved by developed countries. But they demonstrated completely different performance in the stock markets. According to the MSCI (Morgan Stanley Capital International) global stock indices, developed countries witnessed an accumulated increase of 7 percent in their composite stock index in 2010 and 2011, while emerging markets, with much better real economic performance, experienced a drop of two percent in their composite stock index.

For savvy investors, disconnect between China's stock market and the real economy is not new. The Chinese stock market has long been derided as a gambling house. The stock market is small relative to the economy, with a tradable value of slightly more than a third of GDP, compared with more than 100 percent in developed countries. China's stock market has never been viewed as a barometer of the real economy. The ups and downs of the stock market more closely follow macroeconomic policies but not economic fundamentals. In fact, the property market in China matters far more for China's economy than stock market does. Housing and land account for the vast majority of collateral in the financial system and play a much bigger role in spurring growth. The stock market does not—it is a side show.

Despite the fact that the stock market and the real economy have little in common, individual investors still care much more about where to find a positive alpha (α) for their investments. Unlike the markets in the USA and Europe where institutional investors dominate, retail investors account for the majority of trades. As of 2011, there had been a total of

160 million investment accounts opened in China, and probably half of these accounts are still actively engaging in stock trades. How to ensure that these small individual investors also benefit from China's booming economy poses a daunting challenge to China's regulators and policy-makers. Without being appropriately rewarded, people may question the value of establishing a stock market in the first place.

Examining the Chinese stock market's performance over the past two decades, we find that this market did have good times occasionally, and also generated quite decent returns to shareholders in a longer time frame. However, such booms in the stock market typically took place when the real economy performed extremely well. In contrast, when the real economy endured certain uncertainties and was experiencing downturns, the stock market tended to fall at a magnitude that could be justified by the changing fundamentals.

Comparing the Chinese stock market to those of the developed economies indicates that they all perform quite well when real economies are performing, but the Chinese market tends to fall deeper when investors raise doubts about the real economy. Lacking a reasonable performance in economic downturns is one important reason that the overall performance of the Chinese stock market lags behind. The Chinese stock market lacks the recession-resistant capability. But how do we explain such a lack?

The disconnect between China's lackluster stock market performance and its strong real sector growth remains one of the most intriguing puzzles concerning the Chinese economy. According to the argument of the neo-classical school of economics, at equilibrium, stock market performance should be determined by the performance of the real economy. Controlling for firm-level leverage, at equilibrium, a firm's stock return should be equal to its ROIC. Obviously, to understand the Chinese stock market, one needs to go back to the listed firms' fundamentals—firm-level information is more insightful than the macroeconomic-level information.

Low ROIC Is the Culprit

The mediocre stock market performance in China has long been attributed to poor corporate governance including a lack of transparency, limited disclosure of financial information, unchecked insider trading, and rampant related-party transactions between the listed firms and their affiliates. Corporate governance by all means is one important factor driving China's capital market performance. I will also discuss in detail its implications in Chap. 5 of this book. What I would like to focus on now is a more essential cause of poor stock market performance: There is a lack of quality listed firms in the Chinese stock market. When I say quality firms, I refer to those with a sustainable high level of ROIC.

Stock market performance is eventually determined by economic fundamentals. The single most important factor that best captures firm fundamentals is ROIC. Studying the level and distribution of ROIC of the Chinese listed companies helps one understand their market performance. According to the reasoning of the neo-classical school, after controlling for leverage ratio, a company's ROIC in the long run should be equal to its expected stock return. Otherwise, the mispricing may lead to arbitrage opportunities. When a stock market is filled with sound and quality listed firms with high levels of ROIC, this market is more robust and is able to better cope with adverse shocks and negative sentiments hitting the market. This market may also demonstrate much resilience in resisting the negative impact of economic downturns. On the contrary, when a market lacks quality firms, any negative shocks and sentiments hitting the market tend to spread across the whole market, generating a downward spiral and causing investors to flee the market, which may eventually lead to financial tumult.

Research has shown that the US stock market over the past 100 years has brought to its investors an average rate of return of 10 percent annually. Consistent with such a stock market performance, over the same time period, the listed companies in the USA on average reported an ROIC of 10 percent. Over the period from 1963 to 2001, the average ROIC of the listed firms in the USA was 11.6 percent. Strong firm-level fundamentals have laid down a solid micro-foundation for a relatively robust stock market in the USA, despite occasional fluctuations.

How about China? Ultimately, the strength of my argument depends on what the data in China suggests. Surprisingly, given its very importance, few attempts have been made to systematically understand the values and the distribution of ROIC among China's more than 2700 listed companies. Bai et al. (2006) had estimated the return on capital for the aggregate Chinese economy and found that the rate of return had been consistently high in the early stage of China's reform era (around 20 percent). However, they relied on the statistical data released by the National Bureau of Statistics rather than corporate data.[4] Although their conclusion about high return on capital in China was largely consistent with strong macroeconomic growth, it runs against a few studies based on corporate data. For example, a McKinsey report published in 2011 suggests that China's listed companies on average have an ROIC 6 percentage points lower than that of the listed firms in the USA over 2006–2010.[5]

I endeavor to calculate ROIC of the Chinese listed companies from 1998 to 2012. Knowing the level and distribution of ROIC of the listed companies is essential to understand the firm fundamentals. In my calculation, I exclude listed firms in financial services and utilities, both of which are heavily regulated. Following the conventional practice in the academic research, I truncate the calculated ROICs at the one percent level at both ends to control for the impact of outliers. I then average the Chinese listed firms' ROIC in each year from 1998 to 2012 and report the results in Fig. 3.2. Note that in Fig. 3.2, I use the equal-weighted method to compute average ROIC, that is, every firm in my sample is treated equally.

From 1998 to 2012, the average ROIC of China's listed companies ranges from 0.5 percent in 2005 to 7.3 percent in 2011. The 15-year average stands at a meager level of 3 percent only. That is, for every 1 yuan of capital put into the listed companies' operating activities, only 3 cents of after-tax profit will be generated. The operating performance of the Chinese listed companies is much worse than that of the US firms, which

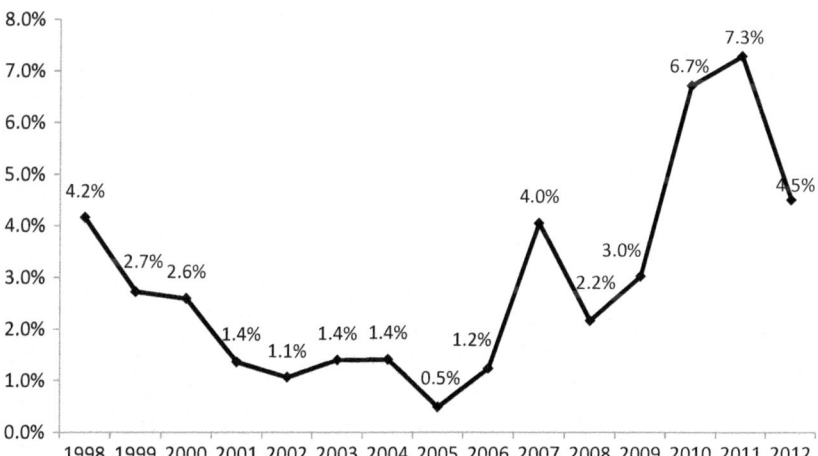

Fig. 3.2 Average ROIC of China's listed companies (equal weight): 1998–2012
Source: The Wind database; author's calculation

boast an average ROIC of more than 10 percent over the past one hundred years. This confirms the fact that there is indeed a disconnect between the aggregate Chinese economy and its micro-units—the Chinese companies.

Figure 3.2 also shows that the Chinese listed companies' average ROIC fluctuates quite significantly from year to year over 1998–2012 when China had reported an impressive economic growth in real terms. The fluctuation in ROIC over time unravels the underpinnings of the lack of quality firms in the Chinese stock market—the competitive advantages developed by the Chinese listed companies are largely short-lived; and the Chinese listed companies have yet to develop more mature business models.

In addition to calculating the equally weighted average ROIC, I also compute value-weighted average ROIC of the Chinese listed companies for the same time period, where a firm's total asset is used as the weight. Figure 3.3 presents the results. The weighted average controls for the influence of large firms, which in the Chinese context mainly concentrate in protected industries providing resources and energy and are widely believed to be more profitable. As shown in Fig. 3.3, the weighted average ROIC of China's listed companies ranges from 1.3 percent to 11.5

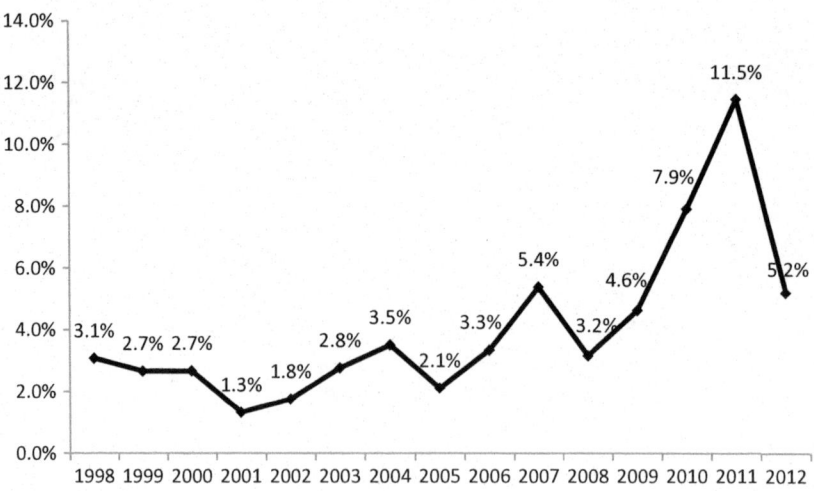

Fig. 3.3 Weighted average ROIC of China's listed companies (by total asset), 1998–2012
Source: The Wind database; author's calculation

percent over 1998–2012. The 15 years' average is 4.1 percent, slightly higher than the equally weighted average ROIC.

Analyzing ROIC of China's listed companies clearly suggests that lacking quality listed companies is the essential explanation for the lackluster performance of China's stock market. The strong aggregate economic performance contrasts significantly with the weak performance of the micro-units of the Chinese economy. Poor stock market performance is not a myth.

In a way, my thesis is quite straightforward. Return on invested capital (ROIC) captures my attention not just because it is an important concept in corporate finance and I am obsessed with a finance concept, but also because its values and distributions indeed reflect the fundamentals of the Chinese listed companies. However, it is not the main theme of this chapter to offer a full-length explanation for why the Chinese listed firms in general fail to deliver a higher level of ROIC. This involves multifaceted pitfalls in China's institutional infrastructure, poor design of the listing and delisting mechanisms, rampant inside trading, as well as market speculators' frantic rent-seeking and arbitraging activities intended to profit from those institutional loopholes. I will tackle these issues in a later part of this book.

When the institutional foundation of a market is tenuous, as one can observe in the Chinese stock market, the adverse selection problem widely discussed in the economics literature surfaces. Ill-behaved companies tend to drive out well-behaved companies, causing a low efficiency level in the marketplace. In this kind of market, fewer firms are willing to plot out a long-term strategic plan aiming at sustainable growth and lasting profitability. To break this vicious cycle, what China needs most is a large number of quality companies that put ROIC and value creation ahead of other ends.

High ROIC Pays Off

In the narrative of this book, great companies are defined as those that can long maintain a high enough ROIC. The meaning of 'enough' here is twofold: First, a great company's ROIC should be much higher than that of its comparables; and second, the ROIC should exceed WACC. This simple message should be taken seriously by Chinese companies. To strengthen the power of this argument, I provide evidence below that ROIC is a variable of primacy in China. Achieving higher ROIC pays. To do so, I examine the universe of China's listed companies from 1998 to 2012. I did not include earlier years simply because China's young stock market was not that sizable until the late 1990s. For this part of the analysis, I raise and try to address a simple research question: Will higher ROIC bring higher returns to shareholders?

I compute the listed companies' ROIC in each year based on the method discussed in the technical appendix, which I have detailed in Chap. 2. Simply put, I first calculate ROIC for all firms in the sample beginning in 1998. I then follow the conventional practice in academic finance research to annualize a listed company's stock return. Specifically, I compute the annual stock returns by cumulating each listed company's monthly stock returns. To ensure that a firm's operating results measured by ROIC is public information when investors form investment portfolios, I cumulate monthly stock returns from May of year t to April of year t + 1 to obtain a firm's annual stock return in year t.

I examine the correlation between stock returns and ROIC. I find that there is a significantly positive correlation between these two variables, suggesting that higher ROIC is related to higher stock returns. Specifically, for every two-digit industry,[6] I sort firms in the industry into deciles by their ROIC. I then group the firms in the same deciles and across different two-digit industries to form ten different portfolios. For example, I pool

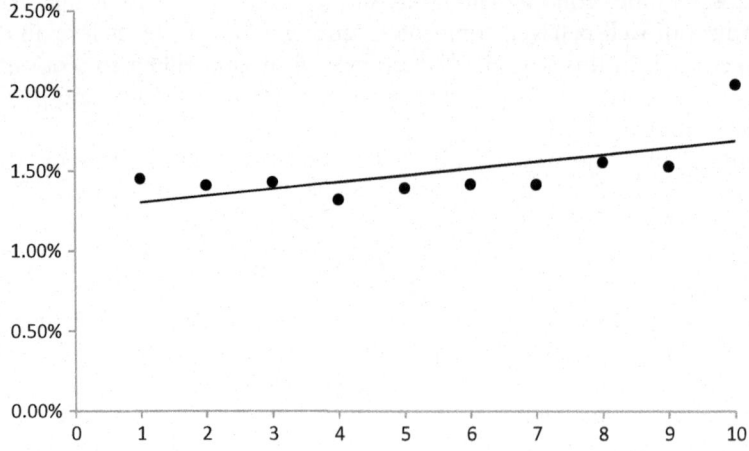

Fig. 3.4 Equal-weighted monthly portfolio returns versus ROIC
Source: Author's analysis

the firms with the lowest 10 percent of ROIC in their respective industries to form the bottom decile, and firms with the highest 10 percent of ROIC in their respective industries to form the top decile, and so on. After I form the ten portfolios, I calculate their returns on a monthly basis by using both equal-weighted and value-weighted approaches.

Figure 3.4 presents the relation between ROIC and portfolio returns in the case of using the equally weighted method to compute portfolio returns. Here, the horizontal axis captures ROIC; and the vertical axis captures the average monthly portfolio returns of the ten deciles over the period from May 1998 to December 2012.[7] We observe a significant and positive correlation between the two variables, suggesting that firms with a higher level of ROIC yield higher returns to their shareholders. For example, when a firm leapfrogs from the first portfolio (the lowest ROIC portfolio) to the tenth portfolio (the highest ROIC portfolio), its average monthly return increases from 1.45 percent to 2.04 percent, which by all means is significant. High ROIC does pay off.

Notably, in the regression in which monthly portfolio return is used as the dependent variable and the standardized ROIC with values ranging from 1 to 10 is used as the sole explanatory variable, the R squared of the regression is as high as 41 percent. This suggests that a single variable—the standardized ROIC—is able to account for up to 41 percent of the cross-sectional variation in portfolio returns. ROIC matters tremendously in explaining a firm's or a portfolio's market performance.

I repeat the analysis by using the value-weighted method to calculate monthly portfolio returns. Here, for each stock, its market capitalization in the previous year is used as the weight when computing weighted average portfolio returns. I investigate the relation between monthly portfolio returns and the standardized ROIC, and report the results in Fig. 3.5. The main finding derived from Fig. 3.5 is the same as that in Fig. 3.4—there is a positive correlation between portfolio returns and ROIC.

Note that in Fig. 3.5, the slope of the regression fitting line is 0.2, suggesting that when a firm's ROIC increases by one unit, its average monthly return increases by 0.2 percentage point, which can translate into an annualized return of 2.4 percentage points. The economic magnitude of the ROIC effect on stock return is sizable: If a firm is able to move from the first decile to the tenth decile, its stock will yield an extra annual return as large as 24 percentage points. Enhancing ROIC is directly correlated with higher returns to shareholders. R squared from the regression in which monthly portfolio return is used as the dependent variable and

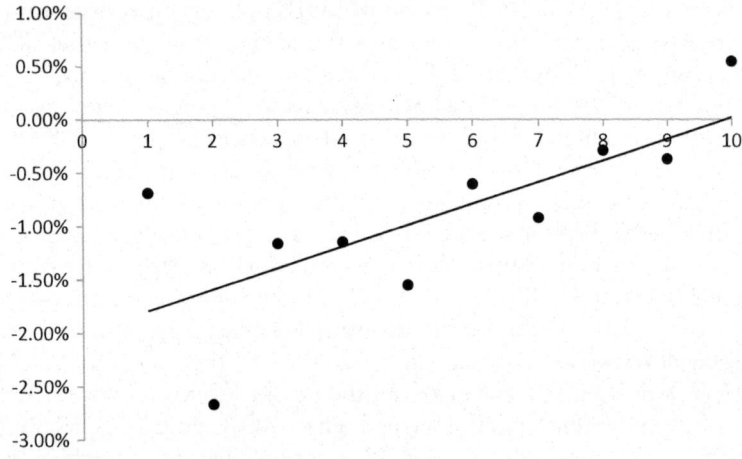

Fig. 3.5 Value-weighted monthly portfolio return versus ROIC
Source: Author's analysis

the standardized ROIC is used as the independent variable is 51 percent. In plain language, this means that standardized ROIC, as the sole explanatory variable, is able to explain 51 percent of cross-sectional variation in portfolio returns.

Given that ROIC is an important indicator correlating closely with a firm's capital market performance, enhancing ROIC helps boost its stock market performance. This explains the disconnect between the real economy and the stock market in China. At the aggregate level, the Chinese economy has maintained strong growth momentum in recent years as a result of credit-fueled fixed-asset investment; but at the firm level, the listed companies' ROIC has been unimpressive. The differences in the performance at the macro level versus the firm level explain the deviation of the stock market performance from the real economic growth. The root cause, as I have argued throughout this chapter, is the lack of quality listed companies.

In a robust analysis, I provide evidence from another perspective to further demonstrate the importance of ROIC. I divide all of the listed firms in the Chinese stock market into five groups based on their respective ROICs. The five groups are respectively labeled P1, P2, P3, P4, and P5. P1 is composed of the listed firms with the lowest 20 percent of ROIC in their own industries; and P5 is composed of the listed firms with the highest 20 percent of ROIC in their own industries. The other three groups are formed accordingly.

For groups P1 to P5, I calculate their monthly portfolio returns using both equal-weighted and value-weighted methods. As firms' performance changes from year to year, I need to rebalance the portfolio. Portfolio rebalancing is carried out every year in May when firms' financial statements are disclosed to the public and ROIC can be computed. Take 1999, the first year in my analysis, as the example. Based on ROIC in 1998, I assign each firm in the sample to one of the five portfolios. After the five portfolios are formed, I compute portfolio returns for each from May 1999 to April 2000. As a conventional practice, I choose May as the beginning month.[8]

Figure 3.6 presents the cumulative returns of four portfolios from May 1999 to December 2012: P5 (high-ROIC portfolio), P1 (low-ROIC portfolio), the A-share market portfolio, and risk-free asset. In this analysis, I use the weighted average method to calculate portfolio returns and the market capitalization of the listed firms in the previous year is used as the weight. Figure 3.6 reveals several findings consistent with the earlier results. First, portfolio P5, consisting of firms with the highest 20 percent

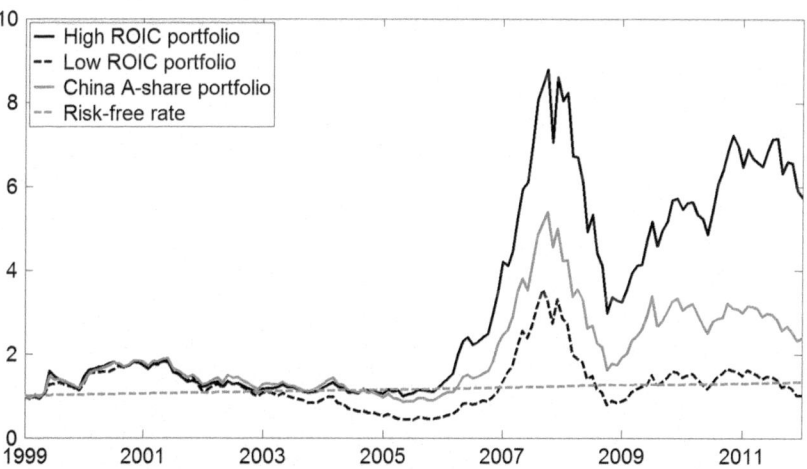

Fig. 3.6 Cumulative returns of various portfolios from May 1999 to April 2012
Source: Author's calculation

of ROIC in their own industries, registers a strong market performance. For example, investing one dollar in this portfolio at the beginning of the sample period, May 1999, one could harvest 5.7 dollars by December 2012. The average annualized rate of return from an investment in portfolio P5 is 13.2 percent, which is largely on par with China's nominal GDP growth rate over the same time period. From this perspective, the performance difference in the real economy and the stock market can be reconciled if China's stock market is composed of firms in P5 only. Having high-ROIC listed companies is the key to improving the stock market performance. For ordinary investors, investing in high-ROIC firms can generate a very decent rate of return.

Second, as a comparison, I compute the returns of portfolio P1, which consists of the stocks of the firms with the lowest 20 percent of ROIC in their respective industries. I find that one dollar of investment in this portfolio in May 1999 will shrink to 70 cents by December 2012, representing an annualized rate of return of negative 2.5 percent—a huge loss in wealth.

Third, I study the performance of the market portfolio. Over the same sample period, one dollar of investment in the market portfolio in May 1999 would grow to 2.2 dollars by end 2012, representing an annualized rate of return of 5.8 percent only, which is much lower than the annualized rate of return generated by investing in portfolio P5.

Finally, investing in the high-ROIC portfolio yields a return that is much higher than that of investing in the risk-free government bonds. In the latter case, one dollar of investment in the risk-free government bonds could grow to 1.5 dollars more than 12 years later, representing quite a disappointing performance.

To sum up, the findings in Fig. 3.6 offer further support for the relevance and importance of ROIC in determining a firm's stock market performance. Economist Burton Malkiel, in his bestseller *A Random Walk Down Wall Street*, notes that on average and over time, mutual funds and professional investors cannot beat broad market indices such as S&P 500 on a statistically significant, risk-adjusted basis.[9] My analysis, however, shows that an ordinary investor in China, if forming his investment strategy based on ROIC, can consistently beat the market. For most people investing in the Chinese stock market, this probably sounds a bit surprising. One of China's best known economists, Wu Jinglian, once said: "*China's stock market is even worse than a casino. At least at a casino, there are rules.*" Mr. Wu might be right. But seeing through the chaotic and oftentimes volatile movements of stock prices, one can still identify a simple rule at work—firm fundamentals matter in China and ROIC is the most reliable measure of such fundamentals.

WHERE DOES α HIDE?

I have presented evidence that high ROIC is associated with high stock returns in China. However, one may still question that such a correlation may be driven by a high level of risk associated with firms with high ROIC. Without clearly controlling for risk factors, high returns are very likely just compensation for additional risks investors have to bear. To address this concern, I need to take care of the risk premium associated with high-ROIC firms. Fortunately, the empirical finance literature pioneered by Eugene Fama has offered plenty of well-accepted methods. In the next part of the chapter, I will calculate risk-adjusted abnormal returns associated with ROIC after controlling for various risk factors. In other words, I will try to prove that there is an α in the Chinese stock market, and it is closely related to ROIC.

In the empirical finance literature, α is defined as follows:

$\alpha = portfolio\ returns - expected\ portfolio\ returns\ (benchmark\ returns)$

Expected portfolio returns are also benchmark returns, which could be calculated based on various asset pricing models. The most widely used model is the CAPM. The extra part of returns, which cannot be explained by factors driving expected returns, is dubbed α. The sources of α are diverse and indefinite. It could be related to investors' stock picking skills; it could be related to hidden risks which have not been clearly spelled out by conventional asset pricing models; and it could be behavioral—investors may have underestimated the value of a certain stock. In this case, α captures a positive surprise.

In our context, if I can provide evidence that α exists and is related to ROIC, then I can simply argue that higher ROIC brings higher realized returns to investors, which corresponds to better stock market performance. Thinking in this way, I do not need to be particularly concerned about whether the identified α is risk-based or behavioral—it is still an unresolved issue in academic research.

According to the conventional practice, typical asset pricing models employed to calculate benchmark returns include the market model, the CAPM, the Fama-French three-factor model, and the Carhart four-factor model. In my analysis below, I use all of them except the market model to compute α.

I first form five ROIC-based portfolios. Specifically, I follow the same procedures as in Fig. 3.6, and use portfolio P1 to represent a low-ROIC portfolio and portfolio P5 to represent a high-ROIC portfolio. Additionally, I construct a zero-cost hedge portfolio which long stocks in portfolio P5 and short stocks in portfolio P1. This portfolio is intended to capture the economic magnitude of the trading strategy based on ROIC.

Table 3.1 presents the results. In this table, I use the value-weighted method to compute the returns to different portfolios, in which market capitalization in previous month is used as the weight. To demonstrate

Table 3.1 Value-weighted annualized abnormal returns (α) based on different asset pricing models, May 1999–December 2012

	Low-ROIC portfolio (1)	High-ROIC portfolio (2)	High-low (3)
	Capital asset pricing model (CAPM)		
α(%)	–5.78*	7.52**	13.30***
	(–1.73)	(2.05)	(3.07)
MKT	1.04 ***	0.95 ***	–0.09
	(19.34)	(16.78)	(–0.98)
R^2 (%)	84.67	79.52	2.10
	Fama-French three-factor model		
α(%)	–7.77***	11.97***	19.74***
	(–2.65)	(3.67)	(5.72)
MKT	1.04***	0.99***	–0.05
	(22.26)	(20.54)	(–0.61)
SMB	0.39***	–0.20***	–0.59***
	(4.76)	(–2.66)	(–6.61)
HML	–0.16	–0.68***	–0.51***
	(–1.42)	(–7.91)	(–3.97)
R^2 (%)	89.97	84.39	29.66
	Carhart four-factor model		
α (%)	–8.78***	8.11***	16.89***
	(–3.05)	(3.01)	(5.54)
MKT	1.04***	1.02***	–0.03
	(21.40)	(23.65)	(–0.33)
SMB	0.42***	–0.10	–0.52***
	(4.85)	(–1.65)	(–6.48)
HML	–0.16	–0.66***	–0.50***
	(–1.36)	(–7.30)	(–3.83)
UMD	0.14	0.51***	0.38***
	(1.65)	(6.55)	(4.68)
R^2 (%)	88.54	89.76	38.33

*, **, and *** denote statistically significance at the 10, 5, and 1 percent respectively.

the effect of ROIC, I focus my discussions on the results based on the Fama-French three-factor model, which I discussed earlier in this chapter. The Fama-French three-factor model has been widely applied in empirical finance research. Eugene Fama and Kenneth French study what drives the cross-sectional stock returns in the USA market.[10] They find that three constructed variables, namely SMB, HML, and MKT, can effectively explain the cross-sectional variation of stock returns. The three variables are related to firm size, the firm's growing prospects, and the stock market return, respectively. Fama and French suggest that what has been left out of the explanatory power of the three factors could be attributed to the mysterious α.

When I use the Fama-French three- factor model to calculate expected portfolio returns (i.e., the benchmark returns), I find that portfolio P1 yields an average annualized abnormal return of –7.77 percent, confirming my earlier finding that a low level of ROIC is associated with poor stock market performance. In a stark contrast, portfolio P5, which consists of the stocks of the firm with the highest 20 percent of ROIC in their own industries, yields an α of 11.97 percent. α is both statistically and economically significant. Investing in high-ROIC stocks brings extra payoff. If short sale is allowed (technically, Chinese investors can now implement short sale strategy through options on the stock market indices), the zero-cost hedge strategy, P5—P1, could generate an abnormal return of 19.74 percent per year, which suggests that ROIC-based strategy can effectively bring handsome rewards to investors.

To offer a robust check on the main findings in Table 3.1, I use the equal-weighted method to calculate portfolio returns. Using the equal-weighted method can control for the bias due to over-representation by large stocks. I report the results in Table 3.2, which is structured in the same way as Table 3.1. I also use CAPM, the Fama-French three-factor model, and the Carhart four-factor model to calculate the benchmark returns.

To illustrate how ROIC is associated with extraordinary stock market performance, I use the results based on the Carhart four-factor model as the example. On the basis of the Fama-French three-factor model, the Carhart four-factor model includes one additional factor, UMD, to capture expected returns. UMD, intended to capture the momentum effect, mainly controls for the effects on returns of the stock's previous performance.

Table 3.2 Equal-weighted annualized abnormal returns (α) based on different asset pricing models, May 1999–December 2012

	Low-ROIC portfolio (1)	High-ROIC portfolio (2)	High-low (3)
	Capital asset pricing model (CAPM)		
α(%)	5.75	10.10***	4.35
	(1.05)	(2.80)	(1.10)
MKT	1.08***	1.02***	−0.06
	(13.20)	(19.84)	(−0.98)
R^2 (%)	70.95	84.45	0.66
	Fama-French three-factor model		
α(%)	−2.84	7.44***	10.27***
	(−1.17)	(2.86)	(3.13)
MKT	1.04***	1.01***	−0.03
	(29.47)	(29.53)	(−0.56)
SMB	1.19***	0.52***	−0.67***
	(19.81)	(6.39)	(−9.49)
HML	0.07	−0.22***	−0.28***
	(1.01)	(−2.79)	(−2.92)
R^2 (%)	93.89	91.31	42.18
	Carhart four-factor model		
α (%)	−3.06	5.02**	8.08**
	(−1.30)	(2.06)	(2.60)
MKT	1.04***	1.03***	−0.01
	(28.65)	(34.19)	(−0.20)
SMB	1.19***	0.58***	−0.61***
	(18.75)	(7.97)	(−9.74)
HML	0.07	−0.20***	−0.27***
	(1.02)	(−2.65)	(−3.10)
UMD	0.03	0.32***	0.29***
	(0.38)	(4.89)	(3.77)
R^2 (%)	93.86	93.24	49.00

*, **, and *** denote statistically significance at the 10, 5, and 1 percent respectively.

As shown in Table 3.2, portfolio P1, which consists of stocks of the firms with the lowest 20 percent of ROIC in their own industries, yields an α of −3.06 percent, which is not statistically significant. This suggests that after controlling for factors affecting benchmark returns, low-ROIC firms do not deliver returns significantly lower than the expected returns. Still, we can conclude that firms with low ROIC cannot beat the benchmark to generate a positive α. I then investigate portfolio P5, which is composed of the stocks of the firms with high ROIC. Consistent with earlier findings, this portfolio yields an α of 5.02 percent, which is statistically significant. The zero-cost hedge portfolio, which shorts portfolio P1 and longs portfolio P5, generates a statistically and economically significant α of 8.08 percent. Although the economic magnitude is much smaller than that of using the value-weighted approach to compute portfolio return (16.89 percent, as shown in Table 3.1), 8.08 percent of abnormal return is still sizable.

Who says there is no investment opportunity in the Chinese stock market? The extra payoff, α, hides where a high level of ROIC is.

It is striking to note that a simple concept such as ROIC is so closely tied to a firm's value-creating capability and its stock market performance. It is equally striking that such an important concept has failed to draw resonance from the Chinese entrepreneurs and executives. When corporate decisions are made by size- or scale-occupied minds, a concept as simple and powerful as ROIC fails to get much deserved respect.

What this has deeply implied is that any Chinese firms aiming at creating value and transforming into great companies should shift their focus from size to ROIC. Overly focusing on size sows the seeds of lower ROIC. ROIC, the concept I have repeatedly stressed in this book, should be placed ahead of other ends a firm pursues.

Cross-Industry and Within-Industry ROIC Distribution

China lacks quality listed companies, as illustrated by the low average ROIC of the listed companies. To better understand the performance of the Chinese listed companies' ROIC and what could be the underlying drivers, I present evidence of the cross-sectional distribution of ROIC across industries.

Based on the industrial classifications designated by the China Securities Regulatory Commission (CSRC), I assign the listed companies to one of the 20 two-digit industries based on their core businesses. I calculate every listed firm's ROIC in each year from 1998 to 2012. I then compute the cross-industry and within-industry distribution of ROIC. Figure 3.7 shows the results.

Note that in Fig. 3.7, I report the ROIC statistics for the 20 industries classified by CSRC, with each row standing for one particular industry. Following the conventional practice, I do not include firms in utilities and financial services. The horizontal axis lists different ROIC levels. For each

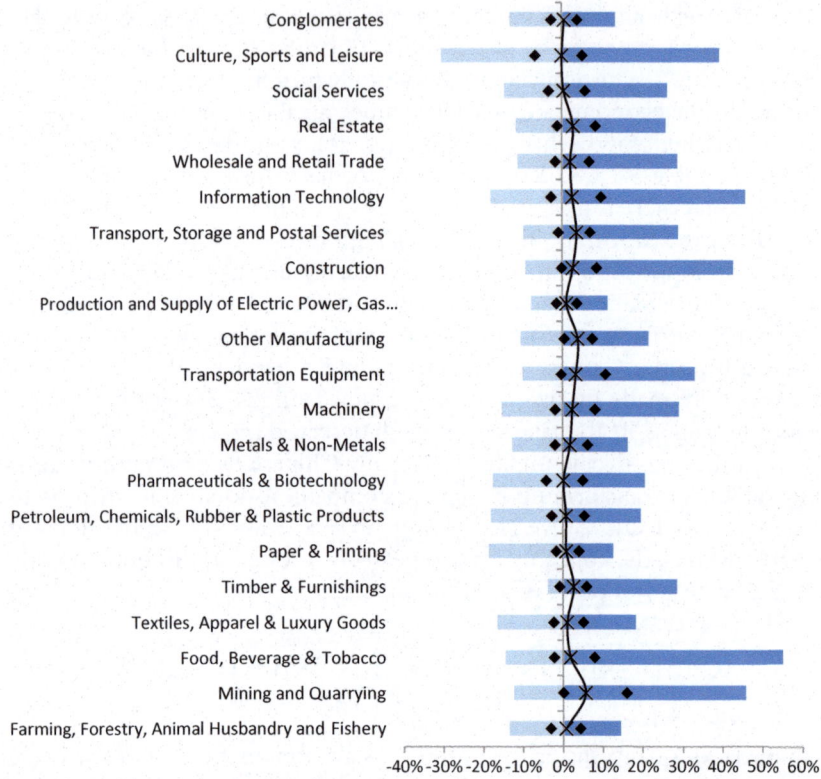

Fig. 3.7 Cross-industry and within-industry ROIC in China: 1998–2012
Source: Author's calculation

industry, I reported five ROIC numbers, corresponding respectively (from left to right) to the 95th percentile, the 75th percentile, median, the 25th percentile and, finally, the 5th percentile. For each industry, the two small rhombuses "◆" respectively represent the 75th and 25th percentiles; the distance between the two rhombuses is a measure of the within-industry variation of ROIC. Also note that "✕" in each row represents the median ROIC in that industry.

A careful read of Fig. 3.7 immediately yields several findings about the distribution of ROIC of the Chinese listed companies. First, when the industries were ranked based on their average ROIC, transportation, storage, and postal services has the highest ROIC among China's listed companies, with its median ROIC standing at 4.58 percent, which is higher than the market-wide average, 3 percent. Second to transportation, storage, and postal services is the industry dubbed "other manufacturing"—its average ROIC stands at 3.91 percent. The transportation and communication equipment industry is ranked as the third with an average ROIC of 3.39 percent, followed by mining (2.93 percent), real estate (2.86 percent), and electrical information technology (2.7 percent).

During the 1998–2012 period, the industry with the lowest average ROIC is culture, sports, and entertainment. Its average ROIC stands at 0.03 percent. The biology and medicine industry is slightly better than culture, sports, and entertainment with an average ROIC of 0.22 percent. It is followed by social services (0.41 percent) and diversified businesses (0.65 percent).

I calculate the within-industry variation of ROIC by subtracting the 75th percentile from the 25th percentile. That is, I use the ROIC distance between the two small rhombuses " ♦ " to measure within-industry variation. The industry dubbed "mining" presents the largest within-industry difference—12.61 percent; electrical information technology reports the second largest within-industry difference, 12.42 percent. These two industries are followed by transportation and communication equipment, which reports a within-industry ROIC difference of 11.19 percent. Power, gas, and water production and supply reports the smallest within-industry ROIC difference, 5.08 percent only, followed by paper, printing, and stationary (5.68 percent) and diversified businesses (6.54 percent).

Figure 3.7 reveals several interesting facts about China's listed companies, which shed light on their corporate strategy and future development. While I defer a more detailed and elaborate discussion about corporate China's corporate strategy to Chap. 6, here I summarize the key results that are about ROIC or related to ROIC. First, as shown in Fig. 3.7, diversified businesses, which refer to firms with more than one core businesses, has on average the third lowest ROIC among the 20 industries during 1998–2012. Although diversification has been an alluring strategy for the Chinese listed companies, diversification does not necessarily generate firm value. This could be a wake-up call for many Chinese businesspeople who have their minds occupied by size rather than value.

Second, as shown in Fig. 3.7, the median industry ROIC of the 20 industries ranges from 0.03 percent to 4.58 percent during 1998–2012. However, the within-industry ROIC difference ranges between 5.08 percent and 12.61 percent. Obviously, the within-industry ROIC difference is much bigger than the between-industry ROIC difference. This fact, if taken seriously, will have far-reaching influence on corporate China's strategic thinking going forward. As I mention earlier in the book, one of the malaises the investment-led Chinese economy has suffered in recent years is widespread overcapacity, which has eroded Chinese firms' profit margin and caused a pile-up of corporate debt. To deal with this problem, many Chinese firms pay attention to new industries or industries with relatively higher profit margin, which have been labeled "blue sea." While diversification has been a common choice for many Chinese firms, real estate and financial services stand out as the two most popular choices. My research, however, shows that getting into a new industry, no matter how profitable it seems, does not necessarily lead to an improved ROIC. Despite the arresting aspect of moving into industries that boast of higher profit margin, the Chinese data tell us that the within-industry ROIC difference is much larger than the between-industry ROIC difference. By specializing in its core business and striving to be a top-notch player in its own way, a firm has a better chance of achieving a higher ROIC and eventually becoming a great company.

NOTES

1. For details on this case, refer to "The Company: A short history of an evolutionary idea" by John Micklethwait and Adrian Wooldridge, which was published as A Modern Library Chronicles Book in (2003). It is worth noting that now most states regard the balancing of stakeholder interests as within a director's business judgment. Dodge has not been explicitly overruled, but ceased to represent the law in most states.
2. See p55 of Collins and Porras (1994).
3. One of China's best known economists, Wu Jinglian, once said, "China's stock market is worse than casinos—there are at least rules at casinos."
4. See Bai, C.E., T. Hsieh, and Y. Qian "The return to capital in China," 2006. Available at: http://www.nber.org/papers/w12755.
5. See "Can Chinese companies live up to investor expectations" (by David Cogman and Emma Wang), McKinsey on Finance, Spring, 2011.
6. The industry classifications are based on the codes designated by the China Securities Regulatory Commission (CSRC).
7. Thus, the ROIC information is publicly available when investors form their portfolios.
8. Most Chinese listed companies' annual reports come out in March and the latest April.
9. See Malkiel (2000), pp. 161–172.
10. See Fama and French (1992).

CHAPTER 4

The "Great" Hope Struggles

China is in the midst of a challenging transition. After more than three decades of rapid growth, the economic growth is slowing down. Structural challenges are emerging: population is aging; labor force will soon start to shrink; debt, especially corporate debt, has been rising rapidly to fuel investment in infrastructure and property, but return on invested capital (ROIC) is declining. China can no longer rely on the traditional investment-led growth model to sustain GDP growth. The future growth will have to come from improvement in productivity. The implications of China's economic transition for Chinese firms are profound. After corporate China has successfully achieved its first Long March and surged in the global markets, the challenge facing it now is that it needs to significantly improve its ROIC. As such, the micro-foundations of the Chinese economy have to be greatly strengthened and China does not need to count on additions to the labor force and fixed-asset investment to grow its economy. The daunting task for the Chinese companies is: China needs to breed a large number of great companies.

A great company is able to maintain a high level of ROIC for a long enough time. Why are there many big companies but few great Chinese companies? Why is it particularly difficult for the Chinese companies to achieve high enough ROIC for a long enough time? What are the constraints that are holding the Chinese firms back? Through which mechanisms are those factors affecting Chinese companies' behavioral patterns?

© The Editor(s) (if applicable) and The Author(s) 2016
Q. Liu, *Corporate China 2.0*, DOI 10.1057/978-1-137-55089-7_4

Why is it a conventional practice that the majority of the Chinese firms put operation scale ahead of ROIC and value creation?

To address these questions, one has to first identify the structural factors driving the rapid growth of the Chinese economy in the past three and a half decades, and then investigate how these factors have shaped corporate China's decisions and made it what it is. Outside firms, two structural factors are decisive: investment-led growth model and weak institutional infrastructure. In this chapter, I argue that these two factors largely account for the abundance of large companies but the paucity of great companies in China.

INVESTMENT-LED GROWTH MODEL

For more than three decades, China averaged a double-digit growth rate. China's economic growth has mainly been driven by investment, export, and consumption—the so-called trioka in the conventional wisdom. Among the "troika," consumption has long played a feeble role in driving China's economic growth. With the worsening external economic environment faced by China in recent years—weaker demand for Chinese products and services in European and North American countries—the significance of export to China's economic growth is also declining. Only fixed-asset investment has continued to power China's economic growth. As evidenced by the most recent global financial crisis, when China's exports experienced a significant drop as a result of weak external demand in the developed economies, investments became the single most important pillar that China has to count on to sustain its economic growth.

Two distinct features characterize fixed-asset investment during China's reform era. First, the rate of fixed-asset investment has always hovered at a high level, partly due to high domestic savings ratio and partly due to China's success in attracting foreign direct investment. Over the period from 1970 to 2010, fixed-asset investment on average accounted for close to 40 percent of China's GDP. It has increased to close to 50 percent since 2010, which from time to time raises the concern that the Chinese economy has been overheating due to over-investment. Second, the state sector, consisting of SOEs and the governments at various levels, has tightly controlled the scale of fixed-asset investments and how they are allocated.[1]

Political Tournament and the Investment Frenzy

During its transition from a planned economy to a market-oriented economy, China can be described as a *de facto* federalism, with local governments having significant autonomy in economic matters.[2] China's economic reform strategy so far can be described as a combination of political centralization and economic decentralization. From the political perspective, through its organization departments at different levels, the Chinese Communist Party (CCP hereafter) has applied a "one-level down" appointment system.[3] The evaluation of local officials lies in the hands of party officials at a higher level. CCP frequently rotates the party officials to address potential entrenched interests and fight corruption. While the central government tightly controls the promotion of local officials, it relegates the economic decision power to local governments. In the earlier stage of China's economic reform, economic decentralization was important—in the absence of market competition, competition among local governments provided the local officials with incentives compatible with economic growth.

Economic decentralization has been accompanied by a series of tax reforms. Under the new tax system, the central government and the local governments share fiscal revenues. The more fiscal revenue a local government solicits, the more will be retained at the local level. In addition, the extra income exceeding the fiscal budget goes solely to the local governments.

To advance his political career, a local official needs to demonstrate his competence and political loyalty.[4] Regional decentralization gives local officials power over economic development, public services, and law enforcement in their jurisdictions. Local officials retain a great deal of flexibility in enforcing laws, levying taxes, providing subsidies, and regulating competition. They also control SOEs in their regions. They can select SOE managers, and significantly influence SOEs' business decisions. Local officials who can achieve better outcomes of their autonomous power relative to their peers are likely to be rewarded with promotions. By promoting yardstick competition among officials, the CCP's cadre management system operates quite well in stimulating economic performance. It was exactly this political competition among local government officials for promotion that substituted for the lack of product market competition in the early stage of China's reform era.

In short, to transform a grabbing hand into a helping hand, the central government employs political tournaments based on economic growth to motivate local political leaders who have discretion and capacity to promote local economic growth. Given such an institutional arrangement, when local leaders compete for performance-based political promotion, GDP growth becomes a key performance indicator. In an academic article published in 2005, economists Hongbin Li and Li-an Zhou find empirical evidence that local GDP growth has been the most relevant variable in explaining local politicians' promotion.[5]

Since local governments hold control over key inputs for business success, dealing with local governments is the key for doing business in China. As players in political tournaments, local political leaders have strong career concerns. They care a great deal about what contributes to local economic performance. Big and visible projects that contribute significantly to local GDP and tax revenues are strongly preferred by local politicians. For both state-owned and privately owned companies, maintaining strong investment momentum can appease local governments' desire to promote GDP growth through investment. This incentive is even stronger for SOEs as they are plagued by the soft budget constraint problem. The debt they borrow from state-owned banks is default-free as the government implicitly guarantees the repayment. As a result, many investments fueled by bank loans are inefficient and mostly excessive. Credit-fueled investments boost firm size, increase market share, gain corporate executives attention in the political media, and improve the levels of local GDP, fiscal revenue, and employment. Excessive investments hence enhance the chance of SOE executives being promoted to a higher government position. While SOEs and local governments have a strong investment impulse, they tend to focus on size and do not particularly pay attention to ROIC.

Private firms in China also demonstrate strong incentives to invest. Growing in size through investments helps improve their visibility and recognition by local governments. Such politically motivated investments made by private firms are more involved, oftentimes concerning projects that can appease local governments' headaches and boost local glamor. For example, investments in the form of acquiring unprofitable local plants may benefit local governments by offloading unpleasant burden due to widespread bankruptcies, for example, layoffs, and likely, a subsequent increase in crime rate.

The case of Mr. Yin Mingshan illustrates how excessive investments help entrepreneurs advance in their political status. Mr. Yin, one of China's wealthiest private entrepreneurs, became president of the Chongqing Federation of Industry and Commerce in April 2002. He was promoted to be vice chairman of the Chongqing Chinese People's Political Consultative Committee (CPPCC) in January 2003. Before being politically recognized, Yin Mingshan had invested tremendous amounts of money in soccer and basketball clubs in Chongqing, and renovated several local stadiums. None of those investments were related to the main businesses of the Lifan Group, the company founded by Yin Mingshan and listed in the Shanghai Stock Exchange. In hindsight, none can be counted as a success—Lifan withdrew from sports several years later. Of course, Yin Mingshan was rewarded by the local government—he was elected as vice chairman of the Chongqing CPPCC not only because he was influential and successful, but also because he helped boost local glamor, for which local officials had openly expressed their appreciation.

Another case example concerns Mr. Xu Ming, the founder of Dalian Shide Group and a key figure in the scandal involving former member of the CCP Politburo Bo Xilai. Mr. Bo, the mayor of Dalian at that time, stated that soccer had a long tradition in Dalian and expressed a strong desire that it should become a calling card of the city. In December 1999, Xu Ming spent RMB 120 million purchasing Dalian Wanda Soccer Club and renamed it Dalian Shide Club. Since then, Mr. Xu has invested huge amounts of money and time in the Shide Club, which won almost all national championships from 2000 to 2003. Xu was rewarded by being "elected" to the CPPCC at the provincial level in 2003.

Politically motivated investments, although they cause efficiency loss, may bring private benefits in different forms to corporate founders. Gauging the costs and benefits involved, Chinese corporate founders and executives may find it appealing to make excessive investments. The irony about these investments is that although they definitely help boost local GDP and enable companies undertaking these investments to rapidly build up operation scale, they are not profit-driven and in most cases fail to generate high enough ROIC.

The Rise and Fall of COSCO

An investment spree can lead to a quick surge of a company. However, if the investment fails to generate high enough ROIC, it may also leave the company with a massive amount of debt and cause its unexpected fall. A notable case in point is the rise and fall of China Ocean Shipping

Company (COSCO hereafter). Established in 1961, COSCO has since developed into one of the largest central government-controlled SOEs in China. China COSCO Holdings Co., Ltd., with dual listings in both Shanghai and Hong Kong (stock codes: 601919.SH and 01919.HK, respectively), is the listed vehicle of COSCO, accounting for more than 90 percent of COSCO's revenue. I hence do not distinguish the parent company and the listed company in the rest of discussion.

COSCO operates a wide range of businesses including cargo transport as well as peripheral services supporting shipping business (e.g., ports, ship maintenance, construction). COSCO is one of the world's leading shipping service providers, operating the world's largest dry bulk shipping fleet and the world's fifth largest container fleet, thanks to the company's rapid expansion as a result of its spending binge since 2007.

Since its listing in the Shanghai Stock Exchange, the share price of COSCO has experienced drastic fluctuations (see Fig. 4.1), which largely reflect the company's volatile operating results. For example, the company reported a net profit of RMB 19.09 billion in 2007 and a profit of RMB 10.83 billion in 2008. As a result, its share price once

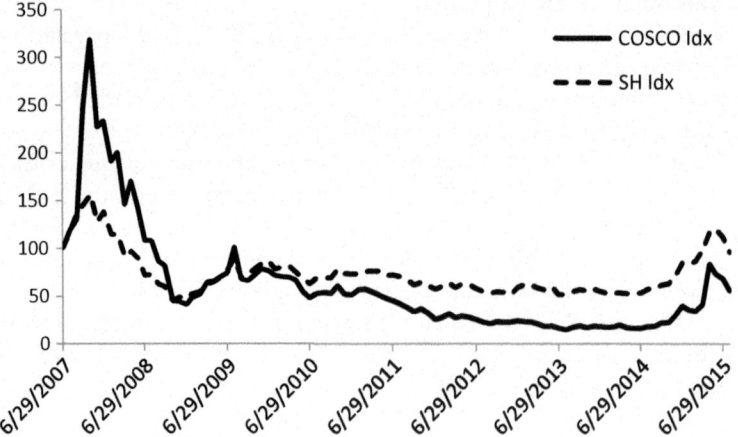

Fig. 4.1 COSCO share price versus the Shanghai composite index: June 29, 2007–June 28, 2013
Note: Both the index value and the share price of COSCO on June 29, 2007, are set to be 100.
Source: Author's calculation

rose to RMB 68.40 per share between 2007 and 2008. However, as one of the world's largest bulk carriers, which carries things such as iron ore, coal, and other commodities, COSCO had been hit hard by massive overcapacity and sluggish demand due to a slowing down economy. The company reported a net loss of RMB 7.54 billion in 2009, in the wake of the global financial crisis. After a temporary rebound in performance, COSCO suffered heavy loss again in both 2011 and 2012. The net loss in these two years was reported at RMB 10.449 billion and RMB 9.56 billion respectively. As a result, the stock code of COSCO was changed to "ST COSCO" by the Shanghai Stock Exchange on March 29, 2013, meaning that the company had been exposed to some financial abnormalities and become riskier, calling for investors' special attentions. ST is shorthand for special treatment. Once a company is dubbed ST, it will have one year to turn profitable, otherwise, the company's stock trading will be suspended—a precursor of being delisted. COSCO is the first central government-controlled SOE that has ever been dubbed ST.

If the share price of COSCO on June 29, 2007 was set to be 100 (its actual value was RMB 18.26), it dropped to 16.5 six years later (the share price on June 28, 2013 was RMB 3.01). More than 80 percent of the market value of COSCO had been wiped out in six years. Although China's stock market did not perform well during the same time period, the benchmark index—the Shanghai Composite Index—only dropped from 100 to 51, still significantly outperforming the COSCO stock.

While COSCO invested to build its capacity, its share price went in the opposite direction. Something must have gone terribly wrong with COSCO. Without doubt, COSCO has been operating in a cyclical industry. While it seems that COSCO's problems are due to factors beyond its control, facing the same market turbulences, COSCO's main international competitors, Maersk and Mediterranean Shipping Company (MSC), have managed to stay profitable. Of course, both Maersk and MSC have benefited from being based in Europe: demand to transport goods across the Atlantic has remained strong, even in the wake of the global financial crisis. Still, they operate on a global scale, and face weak demand, hiking fuel prices, and the adverse impact of other market-wide factors as much as COSCO does. Clearly, something else must have been behind COSCO's sudden fall.

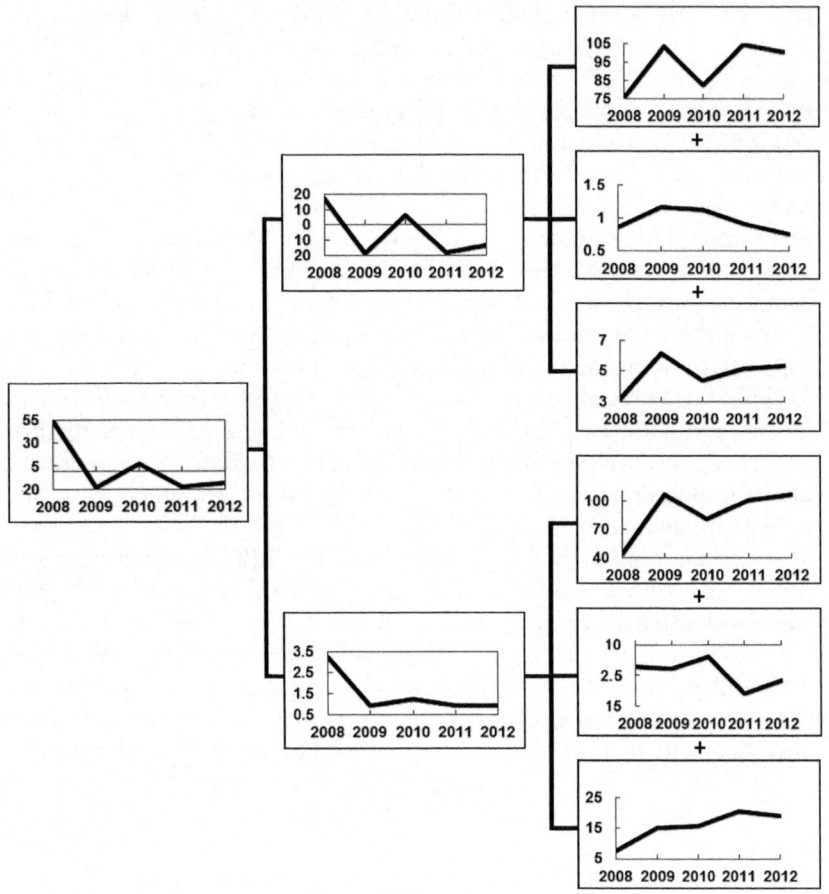

Fig. 4.2   COSCO's pre-tax ROIC: 2008–2012
Source: Author's calculation

Diagnosing COSCO's ROIC and its dynamic changes over time helps isolate the relevant factors determining its performance. Figure 4.2 presents the analysis of COSCO's pre-tax ROIC from 2008 to 2012. I analyze pre-tax ROIC to avoid the influence of varying marginal tax rate. A careful read of COSCO's ROIC over time leads to several insightful findings. First, declining ROIC may well explain what had happened to COSCO's stock market performance—deteriorated market performance was largely driven by declining ROIC. Second, declining ROIC was mainly driven by reduced profit margin and significant increase in fixed-asset investments. From 2008 to 2012, COSCO's operating profit margin dropped from 16.9 percent to negative 13.8 percent, reflecting the influence of the worsening external environment—the demand for commodity shipping dropped dramatically in the wake of the 2008–2009 global financial crisis. Notably, COSCO's depreciation skyrocketed from 3.2 percent of sales in 2008 to 5.3 percent in 2012, resulting from its aggressive investments catering to its expansion strategy. As shown in Fig. 4.2, the fixed assets-to-sales ratio increased from 44.2 percent to over 100 percent during 2008–2012. The rapid expansion in fixed assets surely pushed down COCO's ROIC.

COSCO had embarked on an investment boom in 2007 and 2008. It almost doubled its shipping capacity, making its CEO and a former captain, Mr. Jiafu Wei, a national celebrity. Mr. Wei was named as one of ten most influential business leaders in China in 2005 and was selected as one of the ten most influential business leaders of the decade in 2009, by the China Central TV Station (CCTV), China's most influential TV station. The public value size and capacity. The government regards it as vital to have a national merchant fleet. The management of COSCO had every reason to cater to the government's desire and deliver what the public want. Mr. Wei was the main force behind COSCO's expansion strategy. He chose to rationally follow the fad and was rewarded. While he was personally rewarded for making COSCO a bloated corporate behemoth, the company he once ran is now struggling to deal with piling debt, excessive capacity, and eroding margin. The company tentatively turned profitable in 2014, thanks to the generous state aid and proceeds from divesting unprofitable assets.

Now, the falling volume of seaborne trade and declining freight rates are forcing the whole shipping industry to consolidate. COSCO and China Shipping Group, two of China's biggest lines, are in the process of merging. The end game of the shipping industry might be fewer, bigger lines sailing ever-larger ships to fewer, bigger ports. Regardless of how COSCO will position itself, the tremendous amounts of investments made in 2007 and 2008 had gone to waste. Becoming a great company, the goal that COSCO once set, is now a distant memory.

Out of Investment Feast

With an investment spree, companies, especially SOEs, have strong motives to put operation scale ahead of shareholder returns or value creation. This sentiment has been reflected in almost every aspect of the

Chinese economy. In July 2013, the Broad Group, a real estate developer in Hunan Province, launched a project dubbed "Sky City" in Changsha, the capital city of Hunan. According to the plan, the Broad Group would build the world's tallest skyscraper with a height of 838 meters, 8 meters taller than Burj Khalifa in Dubai (approximately 2722 feet). While people were amazed by the planned height and excited about the fact that China might harvest another world record, few seriously discussed what value such a skyscraper would add and whether the project made any economic sense at all. The project, once touted with great fanfare, has been completely abandoned due to the developer's financial problems. Today, almost three years later, the excavated foundations lie submerged in a fish-farming pond.

Despite the fact that the "Sky City" never got off the ground, the world's second tallest skyscraper, Shanghai Tower, at Lujiazui, Pudong, Shanghai, opened to the public in 2015. It measures 2073 feet (632 meters) with 128 stories in the financial district of Shanghai. Built for about $3 billion by the Shanghai Tower Construction and Development Co., an SOE, the building now sees 20,000 to 30,000 people pass through each day.

The solar PV industry mentioned in Chap. 2 also vividly shows the investment spree seen everywhere in China. When the industry peaked between 2008 and 2011, almost every province in China had prioritized solar PV as the strategically preferred industry that the local government would like to strongly support. Developing solar PV is consistent with the strategic themes the government has been busy promoting: high-tech and green. Arrangements in the form of beneficial tax policies, government-backed investment funds, and easier access to bank loans had been orchestrated to spur the rapid growth of the industry. More than 300 municipal cities developed their own solar PV plants, and over 100 cities established industry parks where a large number of plants clustered. The investment projects driven by local governments contributed to the rapid formation of capacity in the solar PV industry. However, similar to the case of Suntech discussed in Chap. 2, the ROIC of these projects was unimpressive. Without cutting-edge technologies and well planned development strategy, most plants were competing at the low end of the value chain. Most had suffered huge losses, and were forced out of business in 2013 and 2014.

As a result of China's investment-led growth model, China's large companies mainly concentrate in industries providing production factors that are closely related to fixed-asset investment: finance, energy, and commodities including coal, copper, steel and aluminum. Investment stoked China's appetite for these production factors, making it a sponge for raw materials all over the world. As China has maintained a fixed-asset investment-to-GDP ratio close to 50 percent in recent years, many corporate giants surged in sectors providing those factors. Since the Chinese government tightly controls the factor markets and does not give private companies many opportunities, the giants are largely bloated and inefficient SOEs.

It seems that China is kick-starting a new round of economic reform, aiming at shifting its growth emphasis from fixed-asset investment to consumption. It takes time to see real effects, if any. Corporate China is used to extrapolating economic success into future success, and, to a great extent, has them trapped by the mindset that size always comes first. However, as I have shown in earlier parts of the book, pursuing size facilitates the emergence of large companies, but not great companies.

WEAK INSTITUTIONS

Institutions play important roles in spurring economic growth. Empirically, it is difficult to establish a robust causal relationship between institutions and economic growth simply because the causality can be easily reversed— it is economic growth that provides foundations for better institutions, not the other way around. In an influential empirical study published in 2001, the trio of economists Daron Acemoglu, James Robinson, and Simon Johnson employ a novel natural experiment aiming to address the potential reverse causality between institutional and economic growth. They cleverly use European colonization as the setting, arguing that some societies that are otherwise similar were affected by historical processes (e.g., different colonization policies) leading to divergent institutions. Using colonization policy several hundred years ago as a source of exogenous variation that affects institutions, they find convincing empirical results that nations with better institutions tend to have a higher level of per capita income nowadays.

Acemoglu and Robinson expanded their findings into a bestseller titled *Why Nations Fail: The Origins of Power, Prosperity, and Poverty*. In this book, they argue that the lack of absolute "inclusive" political institutions such as democracy has been the root cause of poverty and stagnation around the world. They use the Egyptian Jasmine Revolution as the primary example and argue that "Egypt is poor precisely because it has been ruled by a narrow elite that have organized society for their own benefits at the expense of the vast mass of people."[6] The theory put forward by Acemoglu and Robinson has since triggered a heated debate. The critics raise many counterexamples. For example, the Acemoglu and Robinson theory is highly inadequate to explain China's economic miracle since 1978 under an authoritarian political regime, as well as Singapore's post-independence economic miracle. The debate eventually boils down to one single point: How can one clearly define "inclusive institutions" and "extractive institutions?" While the former support economic development, the latter constrain economic development.

Many academics have used China as one important counterexample to dispute the importance of institutions. In the absence of sound institutional infrastructure including well-defined and well-protected property rights, rule of law, and efficient financial system, China has achieved rapid growth for over 35 years.[7] Does this suggest that institutions were irrelevant for economic development, at least in China? I take a slightly different approach to address this question. On the one hand, I firmly believe in the importance of institutions; on the other hand, I would like to argue that the importance of institutional elements varies across different socio-economic contexts. Take China as the example. Even under the authoritative political regime, alternative institutional arrangements such as family ties, reputation concerns, and arm's length relationships still matter. Bearing this in mind, the appropriate questions to ask therefore are: What institutions are inclusive institutions and what are extractive institutions in China?

I believe that the state-dominated financial system and administrative approaches used by the government to intervene in economic matters are the most relevant "extractive" institutions at work in China. They induce certain types of corporate and government behavior, and pre-determine the Chinese companies' preference for operation scale rather than firm value. They are important institutional reasons explaining why there are big but not great companies in China.

State-Dominated Financial System

During China's reform era, the Chinese government adopted a moderate degree of financial repression, ensuring that the scarce financial resources could be prioritized and allocated to the state's preferred areas. Financial repression in China takes two forms. First, the key interest rates are tightly controlled by the government, which ensures a stable interest spread for financial institutions such as commercial banks. Second, the government monopolizes financial intermediation through a merciless control over the licenses to provide financial services.

Financial repression unavoidably results in undesirable economic consequences. First, scarce funds are allocated to the firms and sectors favored by the government. However, it is believed that the state sectors do not have good enough investment efficiency because of the soft budget constraint problem facing them.[8] With soft budget constraint, a firm does not have to honor its debt. The firm manager therefore may perceive a very low level of cost of capital, which may greatly enhance his incentives to invest more. This over-investment tendency is typically associated with lower efficiency.

Second, when interest rates are regulated, the cost of capital facing firms is not determined by the market supply and demand. By keeping rates well below where they would have settled in a free market, the government transferred wealth from savers to banks and then to borrowers. Banks benefit because regulators create a large and stable interest spread, about three percentage points, between saving rates and lending rates, guaranteeing them easy profits when turning deposits to loans. This has made them rich but lazy. Borrowers are happy too because lending rates are held artificially low, providing them with cheap credit to fuel China's investment boom. In the meantime, savers, who put their hard-earned salary in the bank accounts, earn poor returns.

Distorted cost of capital causes misallocation of capital and loss of efficiency. When cost of capital is biased downward, firms with access to finance may find it tempting to use "cheap" credits to fund unnecessary investments. A rational entrepreneur will only invest if and only if the project has an ROIC higher than WACC. However, when the interest rate is regulated by the government, the lending rates do not really reflect the demand and supply of funds in the market. The state-controlled financial system may lend an SOE funds with an interest rate considerably lower than the market rate, which provides this SOE with a strong incentive to invest. For example, given an SOE's credit rating, its market-based cost of capital should be 12 percent, suggesting that the firm will decide to invest if and only if its ROIC is higher than 12 percent. However, if the state-dominated financial system lowers the lending rate to 7 percent, the threshold of investment becomes much lower. In addition, the conventional wisdom and practice has long been that the SOEs will never be allowed to go bankrupt no matter how much their financial situations have deteriorated. As long as the SOEs feel that they are default-free, borrowing as much as they can to invest is a dominating strategy to use. As such, projects which otherwise would never be undertaken may be launched. Those projects may greatly increase the size of the firm, but do not necessarily help enhance the firm's ROIC and value.

If local governments are the decision-makers, the situation can be even worse. As a result of the political tournament based on economic growth, local governments have strong incentives to invest. Due to the soft budget constraint, local bureaucrats' perceived cost of capital could be very low. In extreme cases, cost of capital perceived by local government officials could even be zero as they do not need to repay the amounts they borrow given that the banks are also controlled by the state. As such, ill-conceived projects may be undertaken, which of course help boost local GDP growth, but contribute little to economic value.

Here, both local governments and SOEs are rational. They also follow the principle of value-oriented investment: ROIC ≥ WACC. However, their seemingly rational decisions fail to generate desired outcome because WACC has been distorted and hence has been perceived at a level lower than market rate, as a result of the distorted financial intermediation.

Financial repression has profound effects on the private sector as well. When the financial intermediation process is biased toward the state sector, private companies and SMEs have difficulties in accessing finance. Many resort to informal financial systems such as underground money lenders, pawn shops, trust companies, and, now, P2P (peer to peer) platforms for funds. They unavoidably bear very high cost of capital. This, to a certain degree, explains the boom of China's shadow banking system in recent years—it provides the private firms and SMEs some sort of financing support, which helps relax the financing constraints facing these firms.

Still, the private firms and SMEs cannot scale up their operation as easily as do SOEs. For example, a typical private company may have to bear a cost of capital as high as 24 percent through the shadow banking system. Given this fact, a rational private entrepreneur should only undertake investment projects that could generate a rate of return over 24 percent. How many such projects are available after an economy has rapidly expanded for more than three and a half decades? Private companies in China may have to pass up many good investment opportunities because of the inefficient financial intermediation. As a result, there are few large private companies in China.

Market Competition Matters

Another fundamental problem associated with China's institutional infrastructure is the lack of an open and integrated domestic market. During China's reform era, China became sufficiently open to the outside world. But the domestic market is still segmented, largely due to local protectionism. As mentioned earlier in this book, China's economic reforms began with the delegation of economic decision-making power from the central government to the local governments. By promoting competition among local governments, China successfully overcame the constraints resulting from the lack of market competition. While the political tournament based on economic performance spurs economic growth, it has obvious side effects. It promotes local protectionism, which greatly increases transaction costs in the domestic market.

As many industries in China such as steel, coal, aluminum, glass, cement, and so on are suffering from overcapacity, cross-region mergers and acquisitions may be an effective way to consolidate these industries and absorb excessive capacity. However, local governments have a strong tendency to meddle with firms in their jurisdictions. Administrative hurdles set by local governments make such transactions difficult to implement.

One empirical anomaly in the international trade literature vividly demonstrates the severity of local protectionism and how it impacts Chinese firms' behavioral patterns. In his 2003 *Econometrica* paper, Marc Melitz, a Harvard economics professor, investigates the impact of international trade on intra-industry reallocation and aggregate industry productivity. One important empirical implication from Melitz's model is that only the more productive firms will enter the export market and the less productive firms will continue to produce only for the domestic market. That is, exporting firms tend to have a higher level of productivity than non-exporting firms. What are the reasons? According to Melitz, only the more productive firms are able to overcome the cross-country trade barriers and successfully compete in foreign markets.

Empirical evidence since then has been largely consistent with Melitz's prediction, with only one exception—China. It has been found that in China, exporting firms usually have a lower level of productivity than non-exporting firms. How can one account for such an empirical paradox?[9] A deep-rooted cause for this empirical puzzle lies in the lack of an open and integrated domestic market in China. In this case, competing in domestic markets is even more costly than in foreign markets. The local

94   Q. LIU

governments have strong incentives to use administrative approaches to intervene in market competition. Those less productive firms, most of which do not receive preferential treatment form the government, choose to enter the export markets. We hence observe an empirical pattern that is exactly the opposite of that in other nations.

Market competition breeds better and more productive firms regardless of the companies' ownership. SOEs could be productive if they operated in regions or industries where market competition prevails. For example, Gree Electric, a state-owned appliances producer, under the leadership of Ms. Dong Mingzhu, has transformed into a highly competitive firm.

One Economy, Divergent Paths

Institutions decide corporate conducts; corporate conducts decide firm performance. The S-C-P framework, first put forward by Edward Mason in the 1930s, was rejuvenated by Michael Porter in the 1980s through his famous series on competitive strategies. S-C-P is shorthand for structure, conduct, and performance. In Michael Porter's narrative, every industry has to cope with different conditions of supply and demand, from which emerges industry structure. Structure in turn shapes the conduct of the players and the choices they make and can make, which in turn determine their performance measured by profitability, efficiency, and innovativeness. As such, the important task is to uncover what structural factors created opportunities in an industry that a company could exploit to its competitive advantage. The S-C-P framework is very insightful in understanding the behavior and performance of corporate China. It illustrates what structural factors, under the current institutional and market institutions, have shaped Chinese firms' behavior and determined their performance.

As a result of historical factors and the characteristics of a transitional economy, there are mainly three types of companies competing in the Chinese economy: the central government-controlled SOEs, concentrating in finance, telecommunication, energy, and other state-controlled industries; local government-controlled SOEs, distributed in state-controlled industries (e.g., tobacco and construction), and competitive industries; and a large number of private firms, SMEs, and joint ventures distributed in competitive industries. Such a structure to a great extent decides the specific behavioral patterns of different types of companies.

We analyze these one by one and begin with the central government-controlled SOEs. They are the legacy of central planning and dominate sectors such as oil and gas, financial services, and raw materials. Because of their size and the protectionism approach adopted by the Chinese government during the reform era, private capital can hardly enter into these industries and compete effectively with those large SOEs. With the support of the state-controlled financing system, they can easily become outsized and harvest handsome profits when the economy is booming. Low-hanging fruits, however, could distort their behavior and cultivate a size-oriented mindset. Given that these companies are an important and reliable source of fiscal revenue (e.g., PetroChina pays more than RMB 100 billion of income tax every year, in addition to value-added and other types of taxes), the central government, while extending to these companies a wide range of protection and support, meddles with them in their strategies, important decisions, and even routine operations. When the central government has not completely kept its hands off these companies' activities, how can we expect them to operate by the market standards and take value creation rather than their political assignments as the top priority? How can we expect them to make sufficient returns to cover their cost of capital?

Since the central government-controlled SOEs mainly concentrate in the sectors providing production factors, and the prices of production factors are still regulated, the central government-controlled SOEs exhibit a strong pro-cyclical pattern in their profitability. When the economy is booming and the fixed-asset investments hover at a higher level, these SOEs could be very profitable. When the economy goes under, few can escape the trap of stagnation. Thanks to the low-hanging fruits in the Chinese economy, the central SOEs do not exhibit strong incentives to hone their business models and invest in R&D. According to the State-owned Assets Supervision and Administration Commission (SASAC), the watchdog of slightly more than 100 central SOEs (excluding financial institutions), these central SOEs on average spend less than one percent of their sales on R&D. As a comparison, the privately owned Huawei Technology spends more than 10 percent of sales on R&D every year, as I will discuss in detail in Chap. 8.

SOEs in competitive industries, most of which are local government-controlled, face a similar problem. Compared to the central government-controlled SOEs, most of them are smaller and their managers' incentives are misaligned. But they are important sources of local fiscal revenue. They also play an important role in maintaining local employment. Their performance, if better than those in other regions, helps local politicians win in the political tournament based on economic performance. The local governments tend to grant them preferential access to external financing, low financing costs, government contracts and bailouts, tax benefits, government subsidies, and favorable policies. Too big to fail. These politically connected firms are largely size-oriented and care little about ROIC.

SOEs, with their political backing, have easier access to finance and monopolize a series of sectors ranging from banking and energy to transport. However, these privileges carry with them political duties, including an obligation to help maintain social stability by refraining from laying off workers. Investment efficiency and operation efficiency is not the only goal pursued by SOEs, large or small. This, to a certain extent, explains why SOEs are not ROIC-driven.

Private companies are more likely to be profit-driven. But they are competing in highly competitive industries. The majority of them lack the support of the formal financial system. They operate in the low-end segments of the value chain and are not armed with the ability to move up along the value chain or infiltrate the value chain. Few of them are able to develop into large and great companies.

Institutional loopholes and biased policy designs have provided the Chinese firms, state owned or privately owned, with various types of "rent-seeking" opportunities. When the government still meddles in many areas from cost of capital to the price of electricity and water, there are many profitable arbitrage opportunities for firms with political connections. When seeking arbitrage opportunities with haste becomes a conventional way of thinking, innovation will not be rewarded.

Indeed, with the investment-led growth model and weak institutional infrastructure, it would be difficult for the Chinese companies to put bottom line (e.g., profitability and ROIC) ahead of top line (e.g., sales); it would also be difficult for more innovative and profitable private companies to compete with SOEs on equal terms to grow their size. To transform the Chinese companies from big to brilliant calls for an overhaul of China's growth approach and beefing up the institutions. The struggles of the Chinese companies in the process of rising to greatness can be best epitomized in Anne Sexton's *The Fury of Sunsets*:

> *All day I've built*
> *a lifetime and now*
> *the sun sinks to*
> *undo it.*

HERE COMES THE EMPIRICAL EVIDENCE

The unprecedented economic growth over the past three-five years in China has been based largely on weak institutions and inefficient financial intermediation. While China has maintained a fixed-asset investments-to-GDP ratio as high as 40–50 percent over the past decade, the credit-fueled investments largely concentrate in the state sectors. If we measure the success of a company by size, many Chinese companies have emerged triumphant. However, as I suggested in Chap. 2, what distinguishes a great company from its peers is a high enough ROIC for a long enough time.

Despite numerous anecdotes that investments made by the state sectors are not as efficient as those made by the private firms, it remains empirically challenging to map out the dynamic relation between corporate investment efficiency levels and institutional factors such as ownership. The asymmetric concentration of China's investment in certain industries (e.g., real estate, raw materials), certain ownership types (e.g., SOEs), and certain regions (e.g., coastal areas), however, has drawn widespread concerns among policy-makers. Investment inefficiency has been held accountable for ever-increasing non-perforating loans (NPLs) in China, which may potentially undermine further development of the Chinese economy. However, how to quantify the investment inefficiency poses a daunting empirical challenge, partly due to data limitation and partly due to a lack of appropriate empirical approach. There are only slightly more than 2700 publicly listed companies in China which have accounting information available. Even for these companies, the credibility of their disclosed information remains questionable.

The National Bureau of Statistics of China (NBS hereafter) surveys the industrial firms with annual revenue and total assets over RMB 5 million every year.[10] The surveyed results are mainly used to construct China's industry value-added and GDP data in each year. The number of industrial firms surveyed ranges from 200,000 to 400,000 from year to year. The survey covers six ownership categories including private firms, SOEs, collective firms, Hong Kong/Taiwan invested firms, foreign firms, and mixed firms (i.e., partially privatized firms). Relatively speaking, the NBS dataset is a reliable source of information to understand the behavior and performance of corporate China.

While ROIC is a credible indicator reflecting these firms' investment efficiency and value creation, it is not readily available. The NBS survey does not provide all information needed for the calculation of ROIC, especially the components of invested capital. Some scholars instead use return on equity (ROE) to capture a company's return on capital. ROE unavoidably suffers from two problems. First, a company's net profit (the bottom line of income statement) contains non-operating profit such as earnings from stock market investment and other non-operating activities, and thus may distort the company's actual operating performance. For example, a company may sell nothing but still report a large amount of profit. Second, the level of ROE closely depends on the debt-equity ratio of the company and high debt-equity ratio may inflate ROE. Therefore, ROE is not an accurate indicator measuring a company's fundamentals.

In an academic paper by Alan Siu from University of Hong Kong and myself, we design a novel empirical approach to overcome obstacles facing researchers. We employ an important economic intuition: at equilibrium, a company's marginal cost of investment should equal its marginal return. If this equilibrium condition holds, we can, based on a company's actual capital spending (investment), back out the discount rate the company has used to guide its investment decision. This discount rate, inferred from the firm's actual capital spending, captures the ROIC the firm perceives. It is therefore a good proxy for a company's ROIC. Another way to explain the logic goes like this: A company has incentive to invest if and only if its ROIC is equal to the discount rate that the company uses to discount future payoffs.

Using the actual corporate investment data obtained from the NBS, we estimate the discount rates "perceived" by firm managers based on the aforementioned assumption that firm managers choose the amount of investment to make the cost of capital equal to the marginal return of investment. Specifically, we employ an investment Euler equation framework to examine the extent to which institutions affect Chinese firms' investment behavior. Applying generalized method of moments (GMM) estimators to large samples of Chinese industrial firms, we estimate the rates these firms use to discount future investment payoffs.

This investment-implied return on capital reveals firm managers' true propensity for investment and can be interpreted in an intuitive way. In addition, this empirical approach is not restricted to publicly listed firms and hence imposes minimal requirements on capital market information. In the analysis, our sample contains more than 200,000 industrial companies. The estimated results based on the sample are more reliable than those obtained from the samples consisting of listed companies only.

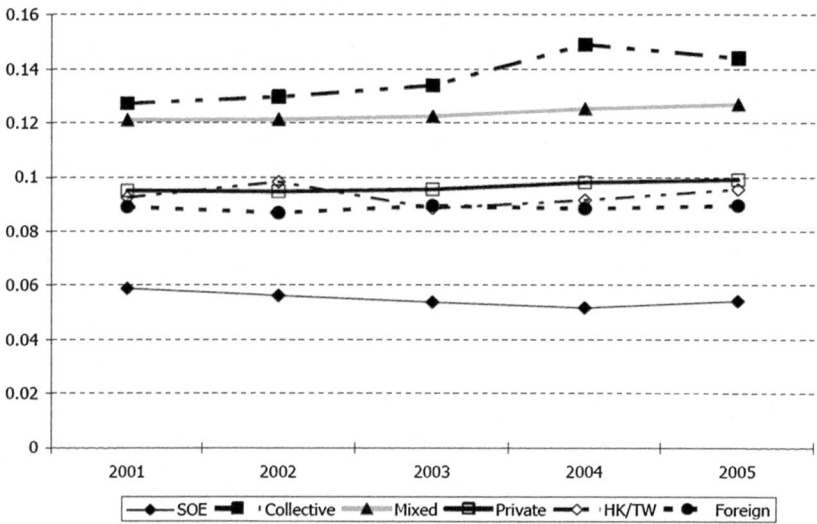

Fig. 4.3   ROIC by ownership
Source: Liu and Siu (2011)

With the investment-implied return on capital or discount rate perceived by firm managers in hand, we examine how institutional elements affect their distributions. We document robust evidence that ownership is the primary institutional factor affecting firm-level ROIC in China. Based on the estimated parameter values, we compute the discount rate (ROIC) for all of the firms in the sample. We then average these firm-level ROIC across different ownerships. Figure 4.3 presents the results. As shown in Fig. 4.3, the average ROIC of China's SOEs is much lower than that of non-state firms including collectives firms, foreign firms, Hong Kong/Taiwan invested firms, private firms, and mixed firms. Based on our estimation, between 2001 and 2005, the average ROIC of the SOEs ranged from 5.3 to 5.8 percent, implying that one dollar of capital used in firm operation, after controlling for regional and industrial differences, generates less than six cents of after-tax profit. Non-state firms in China on average generate an ROIC 4 to 6 percentage points higher than that of SOEs.

SOE managers tend to perceive lower cost of capital simply because they can easily borrow money from state-run banks or state-administrated stock markets, while private firms or foreign firms are more likely to perceive higher cost of capital. Clearly, the pattern of cost of capital across regions, industries, and especially ownership can help policy-makers understand a wide range of issues, which may generate relevant policy implications.

One relevant policy implication is the allocation of capital in China. Despite the fact that SOEs have relatively lower levels of ROIC, the state-dominated financial system still allocates more than 70 percent of bank loans to them. With easy and cheap credit fueled by state-owned banks, SOEs exhibit a strong impulse to invest. With such a capital spending spree, it is easy for SOEs to achieve a breakthrough in operation scale. But it remains extremely challenging for them to achieve an impressive ROIC. In fact, one of the consequences of China's investment-led growth model in the past three and a half decades is that corporate debts are piling up in the economy, amounting to more than 125 percent of China's GDP as of mid-2014. The majority of corporate debt concentrates in the state sector, which breeds many corporate zombies. These corporate zombies have to rely on new loans to roll over their existing debts. Assume that the average cost of debt is 8 percent in China. Then every year, corporate China's total interest expenses could amount to 10 percent of China's GDP.

Even worse, when the state is still the dominant power in the Chinese economy and the majority of financial resources are allocated to the less efficient state sector, we see a crowding-out effect in the Chinese economy. Indeed, although both the number and the output of China's SOEs are declining, their political clout looms large. By using up a disproportionate share of resources, especially credit, they crowd out the private sector—more efficient parts of the economy are underfunded and may not be able to undertake profitable projects simply because of the lack of strong financial support, making it difficult for them to capitalize opportunities for further development and become larger and greater.

As China launches its economic transformation from an investment-led to an efficiency-driven economy, ROIC will largely determine whether such a transformation can eventually be accomplished. For the transformation to happen, the government must push ahead with difficult reforms to curb the power of the state. It must expose SOEs to the discipline of genuine market competition and the scrutiny of independent antitrust regulation. Financial intermediation should be improved so that credit goes to the most dynamic firms. It is also highly desirable to enforce the rule of law so that all firms, private or state owned, are treated equally, and to encourage competition across the economy to make it more efficient and more innovative. At the micro- and firm level, taking value creation rather than size enlargement as the ultimate goal of firm operation should be deeply implanted in corporate China. The biggest reason for optimism about China's future growth is the emergence of fresh waves of entrepreneurism and innovation that are propelling China forward. While the "great" hope still struggles, we have finally found what may eventually take us there. I will discuss this less traveled road at length in Chap. 7.

NOTES

1. See Qiao Liu and Alan Siu, "Institutions and corporate investment: evidence from an investment-implied return on capital in China," (*Journal of Financial and Quantitative Analysis*, 2011), for a detailed discussion about the institutional factors driving China's high fixed-asset investment.
2. For detailed discussions about the roles played by the Chinese government in economic matters during China's reform era, read "The fundamental institutions of China's reforms and development," by Chenggang Xu. *Journal of Economic Literature* (2011), 49 (4): 1076–1151.
3. See Yasheng Huang, "Inflation and Investment Controls in China: The Political Economy of Central-Local Relations during the Reform Era," (Cambridge, New York and Melbourne: Cambridge University Press, 1996).
4. See A. Nathan and B. Gilley, "China's New Rulers: The Secret Files," (New York: New York Review of Books, 2002).
5. See Hongbin Li and Li-an Zhou, "Political Turnover and Economic Performance: The Incentive Role of Personnel Control in China," (*Journal of Public Economics*, 2005).
6. Acemoglu and Robinson (2012), p. 3.
7. See Allen et al. (2005).
8. For research on the state-dominated financial system and its impact, refer to Brandt and Li (2003); Cull and Xu (2003); and Boyreau-Debray and Wei (2005).
9. See Dan Lu, "Exceptional exporter performance? evidence from Chinese manufacturing firms," University of Rochester working paper, 2015.
10. The threshold had increased to RMB 20 million of sales and total assets since 2010.

CHAPTER 5

It Is Also About Corporate Governance

On the afternoon of May 10, 2013, in the Finance District of Beijing, a spokesman for the China Securities Regulatory Commission (CSRC), China's capital market watchdog, announced the punitive measures taken by CSRC against suspects involved in the Wanfu Biotechnology scandal. During the period from 2008 to 2010, the company had over-reported its sales and profits by RMB 740 million and RMB 180 million respectively. As a result, the company's IPO application was approved by CSRC and it successfully went public in the Shenzhen Stock Exchange on September 27, 2011. The financial fraud committed by Wanfu Biotechnology was eventually uncovered by CSRC in September 2012—one year after its public floatation. Despite the severe damage the Wanfu Biotechnology scandal had caused, CSRC's punitive announcement shocked everyone— the final punishment for Wanfu Biotechnology was extremely light—a fine of RMB 300,000. Out of the concern that suspending the trading of the company's stock might cause further turmoil in the capital market, CSRC even allowed the stock of Wanfu Biotechnology to continue trading, explaining, "It has not violated conditions for trading suspension."

The Wanfu Biotechnology episode sparked a heated debate on the Chinese listed companies' corporate governance practices. "With corporate governance practices like *Wanfu Biotechnology*, how should we expect the Chinese listed companies to deliver fair returns to their shareholders?" inquires one Chinese newspaper. "It bears almost no cost committing financial frauds in China!"[1]

© The Editor(s) (if applicable) and The Author(s) 2016
Q. Liu, *Corporate China 2.0*, DOI 10.1057/978-1-137-55089-7_5

Let us have a look at another interesting puzzle about Chinese listed companies. In 1998, CSRC introduced a special delisting mechanism in China to govern the listed companies' governance practices. Under the guidelines set forth by CSRC, China's two stock exchanges began to classify firms as special treatment firms (ST firms) if they have experienced two consecutive annual losses.[2] The ST firms face the possibility of being delisted if they fail to turn profitable within a certain time frame. In one of my academic papers that came out in 2004,[3] my co-authors and I study the ST firms' stock market performance before and after they had been designated "ST" firms. We find that the 66 ST firms in our sample on average outperformed the market by 32 percent points during the period from 3 months before their ST designations to 24 months after.[4]

How could such an obviously bad piece of news generate such overwhelmingly favorable market reactions in China? Our explanation for the puzzle is that the abnormal returns accrued to the ST firms reflect the price paid by their controlling shareholders (incumbent or entrant) in resources commitment in order to retain or gain control over these firms. As the controlling shareholders commit their own resources to prop up the performance of the ST firms, the stock prices of the ST firms naturally go up. The abnormal returns around the ST designations hence reflect the private benefits the controlling shareholders are able to extract from the listed companies. In a market where necessary corporate governance mechanisms are ill-functioning and private benefits abound, how could one expect these listed companies to take value creation rather than private benefits as their ultimate goal?

Corporate episodes like Wanfu Biotechnology and the ST firms are everywhere. It is not hard to understand why the Chinese listed firms have reported such a low level of ROIC in recent years.[5] Poor corporate governance practiced by Wanfu Biotechnology and other companies is one important reason that there is a lack of great companies in China.

A BURGEONING MARKET

China did not reopen its stock market until 1990, when the Shanghai Stock Exchange and the Shenzhen Stock Exchange were established. Since then, the Chinese stock market has developed into an important financing channel for corporate China. China has the second largest stock market both by trading volume and market capitalization. The number of listed companies has risen from 53 in 1992 to 2827 in 2015. While the main boards of the Shanghai and Shenzhen Stock Exchanges list larger and more mature stocks, like the NYSE in the USA, the Shenzhen Stock Exchange also includes two other boards, the Small and Medium Enterprise Board and the ChiNext Board, also known as the Growth Enterprise Board, which provide capital for smaller or high-technology stocks, just like the NASDAQ in the USA.

To understand the Chinese stock market, one has to bear in mind that China has just gone through a transition from a planned economy to a market-oriented economy; and that China started its reforms in an environment where most important elements characterizing a sound institutional infrastructure, including the constitutional protection of property rights, rule of law, democratic accountability, well-functioning financial system, and so on, were missing. These institutional constraints pre-shape the behavior of the listed companies and scope out a number of distinctive features regarding the Chinese stock market. They have also determined the regulatory framework adopted in China.

Over the years, China's stock market has developed a number of distinctive features. First, the link between firm fundamentals and stock prices is tenuous. The stock price fluctuations are driven by macroeconomic policies and market sentiment. The Chinese stock market is largely dominated by retail investors, who account for more than 80 percent of trading. With such a market microstructure, the efficiency of the market is questionable. For example, in 2015, when the Shanghai Composite Index increased from around 3000 to 5100, and then dropped to around 3000 by the end of the year, the total trading volume amounted to RMB 254 trillion, implying that a tradable share on average changed hands five times in a single year. Different opinions make horses run: How much trading was actually driven by investors' differentiated opinions?

Second, from the very beginning, the Chinese stock market was organized by the government as a vehicle for SOEs to raise capital and to help instill some elements of market discipline in SOE executives. The CSRC manages the tradeoff between growth and control.[6] As a result, the stock market is tightly controlled by the regulators. Since the primary reason for developing equity markets in China is to help SOEs relax external financing constraints and enhance performance, regulations typically favor SOEs or firms with close ties to the government.

One of the consequences of such a stock market growth strategy is that the best companies in the economy, in the absence of close ties to regulators and other key stakeholders, may not be able to go public. Meanwhile, the poorly performing companies, once they have gone public, may not be easily delisted. As a result, the overall quality of the listed companies in China is not very high. As I have documented in Chap. 3, over the period from 1998 to 2012, the average ROIC of the listed companies in China, excluding financial services and utilities firms, is only 3 percent.

Third, because of the various institutional constraints and the regulatory framework adopted by Chinese regulators, several notable features about different aspects of the market surface onto the scene. Take ownership structure as the example. The ownership of the Chinese listed firms is heavily concentrated, mostly in the hands of the state. As of 2010, the state still controlled over 60 percent of the listed companies, and more than 95 percent of the Chinese listed firms have one ultimate controlling shareholder.[7]

In the IPO system, China implemented a quota system when it reopened its stock market in 1990–1991. With the IPO quota system implemented by CSRC, listed companies typically allocated their productive assets to the listed vehicles according to the number of shares they were allowed to issue to the public. This practice had led to suboptimal ownership structure. More than 70 percent of the Chinese listed companies are subsidiaries of certain business groups, that is, they have parent companies.

Although the Chinese government has announced its plan to change the IPO system to the registration system, like the one used in the USA, sometime in 2016 or 2017, most market participants still believe that the government can easily resort to tactical maneuvers to control the IPO pace and screen the IPO candidates. Without doubt, with the implementation of the registration system, government control over who can be listed will be greatly loosened up. But the profound impact of the administrative governance approach will last for many years to come.

This immediately gives rise to the question as to whose interest these listed firms should serve, their own shareholders or their parent companies (the largest, and likely the controlling, shareholders). A well-functioning capital market not only helps companies raise capital more cheaply and conveniently, it also facilities better allocation and more efficient use of scarce capital among competing uses. By these two standards, the Chinese stock market has fallen terribly short. Most believe that poor corporate governance practices by the Chinese listed companies should be held accountable for this.

Lots to Do with Corporate Governance

What is corporate governance? The seminal work by Berle and Means (1932) suggests that, in practice, managers of a firm pursue their own interests rather than the interests of shareholders. This had been labeled "agency problem" and a theory was built around how to cope with the agency problems in the academic literature. Economists Michael Jensen and William Meckling revived what was known as agency theory about four decades later.[8] Starting from the premise that the purpose of a company was to maximize value for its shareholders, they argued that managers, particularly those without large ownership stake in the corporation, often had motives and interests different from those of shareholders. Such managers needed the discipline imposed by an active market for corporate control, including the threat of takeover. Jensen and Meckling not only pinpointed the nature of the agency problems, but also suggested a potential mechanism to cope with them—takeovers, especially hostile ones.

The agency problems inevitably bring different types of agency costs, making it difficult for a company to focus on value maximization. In recent years, another set of conflicts of interest has arisen as controlling shareholders take actions to benefit themselves at the expense of minority shareholders. La Porta, Lopez de Silanes, Shleifer, and Vishny (aka LLSV in academic circles) (1998) even assert that the central agency problem in large corporations is to restrict expropriation of minority shareholders by controlling shareholders.[9] This seriously challenges the conglomerate or business group model widely adopted in East Asia and increasingly in China.

Taking into consideration different sets of conflicts of interest due to the separation between ownership and management, Denis and McConnell (2003) define corporate governance as a set of mechanisms, both institutional and market-based, which induce the self-interested controller of a company (including both managers and controlling shareholders) to make decisions that maximize the value of the company to its owners. Practitioners share the same view. For example, the US pension fund, TIAA-CREF (Teachers Insurance and Annuity Association—College Retirement Equities Fund), defines corporate governance as a set of mechanisms that maintains an appropriate balance between the rights of shareholders and the needs of the board and management to direct and manage the corporation's affairs. Becht et al. (2003) provide a more general conceptual framework. They define corporate governance as a set of mechanisms that are necessary for two reasons: "first, to overcome the collective action problem resulting from the dispersion among shareholders, and second, to ensure that the interests of all relevant constituencies besides shareholders face the same basic collective action problem."[10]

As good corporate governance aims to resolve the various types of agency problems and maximize firm value, I propose an even simpler definition in this book: Corporate governance comprises a set of mechanisms, institutional or market-based, to ensure a firm's ROIC can squarely cover its WACC.

What sorts of mechanisms could ensure ROIC ≥ WACC? Becht et al. (2003) define five ways to mitigate the agency problems: (1) election of a board of directors representing shareholders' interests; (2) a takeover or proxy fight can be launched when necessary; (3) active and continuous monitoring by a large block-holder; (4) alignment of managerial interests with investors through executive compensation contracts; and (5) clearly defined fiduciary duties for CEOs and the threat of class-action suits that either block corporate decisions that go against investors' interests, or seek compensation for past actions that have harmed their interests.[11]

A more generic framework suggests two types of mechanisms that can resolve the conflicts among different corporate claim-holders, especially, the conflicts between owners and managers, and those between controlling shareholders and minority shareholders. The first type consists of various internal mechanisms including, for example, the ownership structure, executive compensation, the board of directors, and financial disclosure. The second are external mechanisms including, for example, the effective takeover market, legal system, and investor base.

What mechanisms can collectively best address the agency problems? In the USA and UK, where capital markets are well developed, the corresponding corporate governance mechanisms are basically designed around the available market mechanisms. As a result, the so-called market model of corporate governance has taken shape. The market model has several unique features: (1) ownership is dispersed; (2) financial disclosures are relatively more frequent and generally more accurate; (3) the boards are dominated by independent board members, which ensures their objectivity; (4) there is an active takeover and PE/VC (private equity/venture capital) market, imposing external monitoring on corporate executives; (5) the investors are largely institutional investors, who can better monitor executives and defend shareholder rights; and finally (6) the law protecting shareholders, especially minority shareholders, is well enforced.

In emerging markets including China, the capital markets are less developed, and not all of the corporate governance mechanisms associated with the market model are well in place. A control approach, which stresses "control" and "regulation," has been extensively adopted. In China, the government has adopted an administrative governance approach to develop the stock market. The control over the stock market by the government has been reflected in many aspects of the market. Take the IPO system, which I have discussed earlier, as the example. Using a quota system and a similar IPO system to govern the IPOs causes many undesirable outcomes, including concentrated ownership and rampant rent-seeking activities, to name just a few.

As a result of the administrative approach used by the Chinese government, a control model ensues. The control model used in China has several prominent features including: (1) ownership is concentrated and almost every listed company has one ultimate owner; (2) financial disclosures are limited and selective; (3) although every board has to elect several independent directors according to the corporate governance regulation, these independent board members are in most cases inactive; (4) the M&As and PE/VC investments are not active until the most recent years; (5) as discussed earlier, the Chinese stock market is dominated by retail investors, who account for more than 80 percent of trading, which largely reflects the underdevelopment of China's wealth management business; and (6) the protection of minority shareholders is weak, and the enforcement of law is not effective.

Obviously, a corporate governance model is largely characterized by a combination of the aforementioned mechanisms used to resolve potential agency problems. From this perspective, the market model and the control model are two extremes. There are many potential alternatives lying in between. The debates about the virtues and vices of these two extreme models have never come to a conclusion. They co-existed before the 1997–1998 Asian financial crisis. None had been perceived to be superior. However, in the aftermath of the 1997–1998 Asian financial crisis, many Asian companies linked the breakout of the crisis to their own corporate governance practices, which were very much like a control model. Since then, Asian countries have successively worked out a series of measures to improve their corporate governance practices, and the market model was used by many as the benchmark.

History has always been naughty. In the second half of 2007, exactly ten years after the Asian financial crisis, when the whole world was celebrating the triumph of the Washington Consensus and the free market system, a larger and more devastating financial crisis erupted. This time, the culprits were large financial institutions in the USA and UK, where the market model of corporate governance has been practiced. Since then, the debate resumed on which model is better. As the rise of Chinese companies as competitors shook up the comfortable world of traditional corporate empires, people started to look to China for cues. Some even advocated that the China model and the Beijing Consensus, distinguishing it from the Washington Consensus, would be the answer to the mess all around the world. The creators of the term "the Beijing Consensus," however, failed to provide precise explanations about this concept. At the corporate governance level, does it mean the control model widely adopted by the Chinese listed firms?

Why do I go to great lengths to chronicle the debates on corporate governance? I want to stress a misperception most people have about corporate governance: They tend to place much emphasis on the debates over the "model," but ignore the fact that the goal of corporate governance is to mitigate the agency problems. No matter which model eventually prevails, it has to first be able to address the agency problems. In this regard, the prevailing agency problems are more important determinants of the corporate governance practices. For Chinese companies, the most devastating agency problem, for the time being, is that the Chinese firms are much obsessed with size, but eschew the ultimate goal of firm operation—creating value. Can the control model wielded by the Chinese firms address this problem? If the answer is no, then the prevailing governance model should be reformed.

WHEN THE MODEL MEETS THE REALITY

Good governance helps address the agency problems and improve firm value. The control model falls short on this aspect. A few years ago, I teamed up with several researchers to examine how various governance mechanisms affect the value of Chinese listed companies. In one of the papers, we investigated how the commonly used governance mechanisms, which characterize the control model, affect Chinese listed firms' market valuation.[12] There are several interesting findings in this study. First, we find that the effect of the largest shareholder's ownership on firm value is non-linear. There seems to be a U-shaped relationship between a firm's market valuation and the proportion of shares held by the largest shareholder. Concentrated ownership, which is a common feature of the control model, does not necessarily generate value.

We also find that the degree of concentration of shares held by other large shareholders, excluding the largest one, positively affects firms' market valuation. When shares are also concentrated in the hands of other large shareholders, they are more likely to check balance the largest shareholder and prevent him from tunneling firm resources. In a related paper,[13] we document evidence that the degree of concentration of shares by other large shareholders is a good proxy for the likelihood of triggering a corporate control market. As such, it captures the effects on firm performance of an active takeover market, which is lacking in the control model.

We find that issuing shares to foreign investors helps improve firms' valuation, partly due to the monitoring effect of the relatively more sophisticated foreign investors, and partly due to more transparent financial disclosure required for cross-border listings. Among other governance mechanisms, we find that CEOs being the chairmen of boards negatively affects firm valuation, indicating that increasing board independence helps enhance firm performance. We also find that when the largest shareholder is the state, firms tend to have lower market valuation. The empirical results thus strongly suggest that the control-based corporate governance model does go along with value maximization.

The control-based corporate governance model also has a direct impact on the market transparency and informativeness of the stock prices. Under the control model, if the managers or the largest shareholders intend to expropriate the minority shareholders and tunnel firm resources, they have incentives to camouflage the true performance of the firms they are running. Not surprisingly, the concentrated ownership structure and the absence of effective external monitoring mechanisms, which are still the key features of China's control-based corporate governance model, have made earnings management or even falsifying financial reports easier and less costly by listed companies. Such incentives are further strengthened, since CSRC has been using an administrative approach and has simply relied on accounting numbers such as return on equity (ROE) to govern the listed companies. To comply with the requirements of the regulators, Chinese listed firms may demonstrate greater incentives to manage their earnings above the threshold levels of certain accounting indicators, especially ROE.

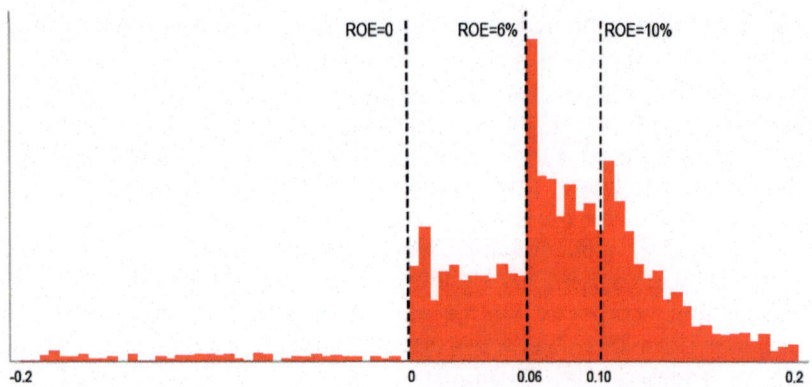

Fig. 5.1   ROE histogram of China's listed companies: 1999 to 2005
Source: Liu and Lu (2007)

Figure 5.1 presents a histogram of ROE for China's listed companies from 1999 to 2005, during which CSRC clearly specified that a listed company's ROE performance directly decides whether it would be allowed to refinance through rights issuing; and whether it would be delisted.[14] In normal situations, when the sample size is large enough, the distribution of listed companies' ROE should follow a normal distribution. In plain language, the ROE histogram should look like a bell. However, the ROE distribution of China's listed companies is very "abnormal." It is not smooth, and it is apparent that a disproportionately high number of companies reported ROEs just slightly over 0, 6, and 10 percent—there were three rather than just one spike in the Chinese listed companies' ROE distribution.

The three spikes demonstrate two important incentives for the Chinese listed companies to manage ROE: avoiding losses; and making ROEs above 10 percent or at least 6 percent. In the former case, CSRC regulates that a firm will be labeled "ST," a precursor of being delisted, if it has experienced two consecutive losses. This provides the listed companies with strong incentives to manage earnings to avoid a net loss. In the latter case, CSRC had for quite a while regulated that a listed firm had to maintain a minimum of 6 percent of reported ROE and a three-year average of 10 percent in order to obtain the rights to offer new shares. Thus, ROE being above 6 percent and 10 is quite critical for fund-raising. The listed companies' best response to the regulation is therefore to provide whatever the regulator needs. This reflects the primary purpose of going public—raising capital.

With an ROE distribution like the one in Fig. 5.1, one cannot help questioning the quality and credibility of financial statements released by listed companies in China. Motivated by Fig. 5.1, I collaborated with Joe Lu to study the relationship between governance mechanisms and earnings management[15]. Using data covering Chinese listed firms over 1999–2005, we found that the severity of earnings management, measured by several accruals-based variables, was positively related to the proportion of shares held by the largest shareholder, the shares held by the top management, and the dummy variable indicating CEO as the chairman of the board, but negatively correlated to the dummy variable indicating whether a firm issues stocks to foreign investors. These results suggest that the control-based corporate governance model, which has been pervasively practiced by the Chinese listed companies, is associated with poor earnings quality.

Figure 5.1 depicts an extremely depressing picture. When the majority of listed companies can "massage" their earnings on a discretionary basis, how can one trust that these companies are pursuing value rather than private benefits of the controlling shareholders? How can one trust what these companies take into consideration is higher ROIC but not firm size when making investment decisions? If value maximization and higher ROIC is not what these companies target, how can they transform themselves to become great companies?

INSTITUTIONAL DETERMINANTS

Laura Cha, a vice chairman of CRSC from March 2001 to September 2004, orchestrated CSRC's early attempts to discipline the listed companies. She once stated, "The concept of corporate governance has not been well developed or understood in our country. This may be partly due to our transitional stage from a planned economy to a market economy, and partly due to the entanglement of ownership rights with management responsibilities."[16] Indeed, the features mentioned in Laura Cha's comment largely explain why the control-based governance model has prevailed in China.

Several specific features, which are unique to the Chinese economy, shaped the emergence and development of China's stock market. First, China is a transition economy, where most components of the institutional infrastructure are lacking or inefficiently enforced, as I have discussed in Chap. 4. Second, in order to improve SOE efficiency, the Chinese government has adopted the corporatization policy in the past three decades. The main purpose of "corporatization" is to reform the business processes of SOEs by subjecting them to the rules of the "modern enterprise system." Developing a stock market and allowing the SOEs to raise capital through equity issuance is one part of the consideration.[17] Third, financial markets are still poorly developed in China. Attractive investment vehicles are in short supply in China. The stock market, soon after it was established, became a tempting investment vehicle for the general public. The general public had shown tremendous enthusiasm for the opportunities provided by China's infant stock market. As a result of their heavy involvement, the security regulators are constrained in their policy spectrum. Any turmoil in the stock market may potentially spread out and endanger social stability. Maintaining social stability has always been one of the most important goals for the regulators.

Reforming the SOEs

The Chinese stock market was organized by the government as a vehicle for its SOEs to raise capital and improve operating performance. Since the reopening of the Chinese stock market, the regulations have been evolving to address problems typically found in emerging markets. In particular, CSRC has been managing the tradeoff between growth and control. Since the primary objective of developing equity markets in China is to help SOEs relax external financing constraints, regulations introduced have been asymmetrically in favor of SOEs or the companies with close ties to the government.

As pointed out in Clarke (2003), a fundamental dilemma of the above approach stems from the state policy of maintaining a full or controlling ownership interest in enterprises. The state wants the enterprises it owns to be run efficiently, but not solely for the purpose of wealth maximization. Other more immediate purposes include maintenance of urban employment, direct control of sensitive industries, and politically motivated job placement. The state therefore wants to continue its involvement in the buildup of the Chinese stock market. However, such state involvement creates a conflict of interest between the state as controlling shareholder and other shareholders. Even worse, the state is playing two roles at the same time—controlling shareholder and regulator.

This dilemma generates many implications, which directly or indirectly explain Chinese firms' corporate governance practices. First, the ownership of Chinese listed companies is heavily concentrated in the hands of the state, simply because the state wants to keep enough equity interest to control the listed firms. Furthermore, the largest shareholder controls close to 40 percent of the listed companies' shares, a level much higher than that of the developed market companies. Ownership structure directly influences the growth strategies and operating style of the listed companies. A listed company with the state being the controlling shareholder is more likely to aggressively pursue growth, especially growth of operation scale.

Second, since the state or state-affiliated legal persons are normally the largest shareholders of the listed companies, the state representative generally dominates the board of directors. The independence of boards is thus greatly compromised. Third, developing the stock market in China serves multiple purposes such as allowing SOEs to leverage the market to get more capital, improving SOE efficiency, and maintaining employment. Shareholder value maximization is not the only and not even the primary objective. Providing investors with timely and accurate information is not the priority. Corporate transparency in China is low despite the fact that the laws and regulations introduced have consistently required more disclosure.

Weak Legal Environment and Administrative Governance

The growing law and finance literature has established the importance of the legal environment, and more specifically the extent of investor protection, in fostering good corporate governance practice.[18] China underperforms in both legal infrastructure and actual law enforcement. Both the private enforcement of investor rights and the public enforcement of contractual disputes have been extremely weak in China. A weak legal system, on the one hand, limits the spectrum of corporate governance practices a firm can select from; on the other hand, it predetermines the set of regulatory frameworks that the Chinese government can adopt.

Katharina Pistor and Chenggang Xu argue that effective law enforcement is lacking in China, and therefore the country has to rely primarily on an administrative governance structure built around the quota system to regulate the stock market.[19] Under the quota system, CSRC assigns the listing quota to the planning commissions of various provinces, then to

IPO candidates. The quota system serves two important functions with respect to the development of the stock market. It helps mitigate the asymmetric information problems investors and regulators face and also provides the local bureaucrats with an incentive to choose viable companies to go IPO. Partly due to the quota system, China has achieved partial success in its stock market development. The quota system, however, has an inherent weakness. Like any other quota system employed in the transition economies, the adoption of quota provides the local bureaucrats with "rent-seeking" opportunities.[20] The local bureaucrats thus have incentives to select the firms (IPO candidates) from which they can grab the largest rents. Similarly, they also choose the ownership structure by which their benefits can be maximized. The utility function of the local bureaucrats is definitely different from those of minority shareholders. As a consequence, although the privatization route adopted in China is less rapid and less massive than those in Russia and other eastern European transition economies, self-dealing conducted by local bureaucrats and controlling shareholders is still pervasive.

In addition, because of the implementation of the quota system, the corporatization of SOEs in China is not complete. A firm obtains a certain amount of quota and will corporatize itself according to the amount of shares it can issue. Suboptimal ownerships are thus selected to maximize the state's control and the local bureaucrats' utilities. This can explain why ownership has been so concentrated in the hands of the state in China through direct control or the control of legal persons.

The current control-based governance model practiced by the Chinese listed firms is rooted in China's institutional setting. Improving corporate governance is hence not just a firm-level campaign. Its success cannot be achieved within the stock market. Switching attentions to the macro-level institutional factors and making efforts to fix institutional loopholes is a must, and will surely pay off.

Beginning in 2001, the Chinese government has taken corporate governance improvement as one of the top priorities in developing its young stock market. Over time, key mechanisms including independent boards, more frequent and timely disclosures, cultivating institutional investors, promoting M&As and PE/VC investments, cracking down on insider trading, and enacting laws and regulations to protect minority shareholders have been introduced and implemented. These efforts are changing the behavioral patterns of Chinese listed companies and shaking up the foundations of the Chinese stock market. Despite all this progress, however, ownership structure, a corporate governance mechanism deeply rooted in institutions, remains a tenuous link.

FINALLY, OWNERSHIP STRUCTURE

Among all the corporate governance mechanisms, ownership structure remains the most decisive one. To a certain extent, the functioning of internal mechanisms such as boards and financial disclosure largely hinges on a firm's ownership structure. If a firm has a controlling shareholder, the controller very likely will have the final say on the board members and board procedures, which will surely affect board independence. Similarly, the controlling shareholder may exert his influence on the firm's disclosure policy and practices, which may also affect the information quality of earnings.

What ownership structure may be conducive to value creation? Economists Harold Demsetz and Kenneth Lehn have found that ownership structure is not exogenously given—firm-level characteristics and product market-based factors may decide a firm's ownership.[21] If one also includes institutions as determinants of ownership structure, then the Demsetz and Lehn proposition may apply to China's listed companies as well. Given the China-specific institutional setting, over time, several features of the Chinese listed companies' ownership structure have emerged, which are profoundly affecting Chinese firms.

Since 2001, although the Chinese listed companies have made great progress in almost all corporate governance aspects, ownership structure remains the least changed corporate governance mechanism. Understanding the features of the ownership structure and knowing the factors shaping it helps understand the behavioral patterns of corporate China, and map out its future dynamics.

What do we talk about when we talk about ownership structure? Three ownership structure aspects are of particular importance. First, is a firm's ownership concentrated in a few shareholders or widely dispersed? Second, is the firm's shareholding structure transparent? Is who owns how much of the firm public information? Third, does the firm follow one share—one vote policy? Are there equal rights among the firm's shareholders? In the next part of this chapter, I will discuss the Chinese listed companies' ownership structure around these three aspects, probe into their evolution, and analyze how ownership structure may influence corporate China.

Concentrated Ownership

The market model of corporate governance, also known as the Anglo-Saxon model, hails the virtues of dispersed ownership structure. However, it remains a hotly debated issue whether dispersed ownership structure is conducive to enhancing firm value. Even in the developed world, a rising number of new companies have dominant owners, and in most cases they are corporate founders. Founders like Mark Zuckerberg at Facebook and Jack Ma at Alibaba, because of their entrenched interest, are willing to sacrifice short-term results in order to pursue long-term benefits. In China, it has also been found that the relation between firm performance measured by Tobin's Q or ROE and the share in the listed company by the largest shareholder is U-shaped.[22] Concentrated ownership does not necessarily cause poorer firm performance.

In an academic paper published in 2012,[23] my co-authors and myself found that as of 2008, more than 95 percent of the Chinese listed companies had ultimate controlling shareholders, who owned at least 10 percent of the firms they control. On average, the largest shareholders owned 36.9 percent of the listed firms. Corporate China's ownership structure tended to concentrate in the hands of the largest shareholders. In the same research, we found that about 60 percent of the listed companies in China were controlled by the state. That is, they were either central government-controlled SOEs or local government-controlled SOEs. About 35 percent of Chinese listed companies were owned by families. Less than 5 percent of the listed companies had dispersed ownership structure and did not have an ultimate controlling shareholder.

In the early 1990s when China reopened its stock market, all of the listed companies were state owned, and their ownership was also concentrated. For example, in the case of PetroChina, one of the largest SOEs with dual listings in Shanghai and overseas markets, the controlling shareholder, the state, still owns more than 86 percent of the listed company. With the development of the Chinese stock market and the surge of private companies, more and more private firms found ways to float their shares. As our study shows, as of 2008, private companies already accounted for 35 percent of the universe of Chinese listed companies. The proportion of privately owned listed companies will continue to increase as almost all IPO-able SOEs have been corporatized and gone public and the new additions are more likely to come from the private sector.

This bifurcation of ownership structure, that is, the controlling shareholders almost equally distributed between the state and families, is quite unique in China. The other example is Russia—in 2002, 53 percent of Russian listed companies were state owned and 34 percent of them were privately owned. Most stock markets in the emerging markets and the developed markets are dominated by private firms. For example, in Brazil, 54 percent of listed companies are owned by families; the state only controls 15 percent of listed firms; about 27 percent of listed companies have a widely dispersed ownership structure. The proportion of the state to the proportion of families is 13–67 percent in Malaysia. In Mexico, the ratio is 0–100 percent. It is 0–83 percent in Chile; 8–62 percent in Thailand; and 18–50 percent in Turkey.[24]

When a listed company's shares concentrate in the hands of its controlling shareholder, its various decisions more likely reflect the interests of the ultimate owner. If the ultimate owner is obsessed with operation scale and ever-increasing business lines, the company's operation will very likely be size-driven. It may aggressively pursue growth through bank loans. Given the highly concentrated ownership among the listed companies in China, shifting the ultimate controllers' focus from size to value creation is the key to transforming the Chinese companies from big to great.

The Chinese Pyramids

In addition to highly concentrated ownership, Chinese listed companies have also extensively used pyramidal structure. Pyramidal structure generally refers to corporate ownership structure in which the ultimate controlling shareholders establish their control over firms (mostly listed firms) through several layers of intermediate firms. In contrast to a purely horizontal structure, in which the ultimate controller directly owns equity stakes in all the group firms, a pyramidal structure allows the ultimate owner to obtain control rights exceeding ownership rights.

In Fig. 5.2, I provide an example of pyramidal structure, in which the ultimate owner controls the listed companies through three intermediate firms. As shown in the figure, the ultimate controller, regardless of being the state or a family, instead of investing in the listed company directly, owns and controls 50 percent of firm A.[25] Firm A owns 50 percent of Firm B and then controls Firm B; Firm B then controls Firm C, and eventually Firm C controls the listed company.

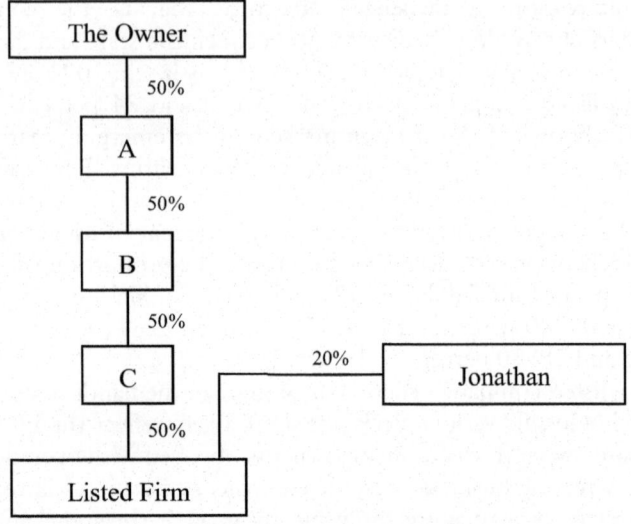

Fig. 5.2   An illustrative pyramidal structure

As the control over a firm is transitive, with the ownership structure specified in Fig. 5.2, the ultimate owner tightly controls the listed company. That is, the ultimate owner controls at least 50 percent of the listed company's votes. "The control right" (also known as voting right) owned by the controlling shareholder is thus 50 percent. However, the actual investment in the listed company made by the ultimate owner is only 6.25 percent. To illustrate this, suppose that the listed company pays $100 of dividend; only $6.25 will go to the ultimate owner. The ownership right (also known as cash flow right) of the ultimate owner is only 6.25 percent.

Under the ownership structure in Fig. 5.2, the ultimate owner uses 6.25 percent of investment to ensure absolute control over the listed company, which obviously violates the equitability and fairness principle on ownership. For example, another shareholder, Jonathan, directly invests 20 percent of capital in the listed company. He only has 20 percent of votes. Although he has invested much more capital than the ultimate owner, the ultimate owner, not Jonathan, controls the listed company. With pyramidal structure, the controlling shareholder at the top of the pyramid can use a small amount of capital to secure his control over a firm, making it easier for him to achieve a breakthrough in operation scale.

Since pyramidal structures grant ultimate owners *de facto* control in excess of their ownership, the literature predominantly associates pyramidal structures with various agency problems. Many academic studies,[26] for instance, find that an extensive use of pyramidal structures leads to a separation of control rights from cash flow rights, which encourages the expropriation of minority shareholders by a controlling shareholder and results in reduction in firm value.

Pyramidal structure is becoming more and more popular in corporate China. To quantify the extent of the use of pyramids by Chinese listed firms, I follow the conventional practice and use three measures: the number of layers (Layer), the ratio of the firm's ownership rights to control rights (OC), and the wedge between the firm's control rights and ownership rights (Wedge), which is defined as the firm's control rights minus ownership rights. Let me first introduce the terminology. Let O denote an ultimate owner's ownership rights, and C denote its control rights. The ratio of O to C (abbreviated as OC) tends to be small and Layer and Wedge tend to be big when the ultimate owner controls a firm through a longer control chain. When computing Layer, I count the number of players along the control chain between the ultimate owner and the listed firm, with the two ends included. For example, in Fig. 5.2, Layer equals 5. Since the ownership right is 6.25 percent and the control right is 50 percent, OC in this case is 12.5 percent and Wedge equals 43.75 percent. Among the three measures, OC is more intuitive. When OC has the value of 12.5 percent, it implies that the ultimate owner has maneuvered to use 12.5 percent of capital to completely control the listed company.

Empirical evidence so far predominantly associates corporate pyramids with the agency problems and political rent-seeking.[27] Why do Chinese firms still have incentives to extensively use pyramidal structure? The answer lies in the institutional context in which corporate China operates. In the case of private firms, they are disadvantaged in obtaining important resources such as permits and licenses, land use rights, and bank lending. In addition, external financing constraints faced by private firms give rise to a strong demand for well-functioning internal capital markets. Private firms thus have strong incentives to adopt more novel ownership structures to get around regulatory hurdles and to control more assets with as little capital as possible. Pyramidal business groups therefore emerge. In a sense, they are substitutes for weak legal and market institutions in China.

The same motives do not necessarily apply to SOEs. State-controlled firms are less subject to external financing constraints and unfavorable treatments typically found in private firms. However, SOEs are confronted with another set of agency problems—vaguely defined state ownership rights and the delegation of management to bureaucrats who are well known for being more interested in gaining political clout and moving up along the political hierarchy than maximizing shareholder value. An extensive corporate pyramid in this case may even operate in shareholders' favor since it allows the state to more effectively delegate the firm's decision rights to firm managers, separating firm management from political intervention. Fan et al. (2013) propose this political economy perspective to explain the formation of pyramids in state-controlled firms in China. They find that managerial professionalism, employment efficiency, and total factor productivity of local state-controlled listed firms are higher when their ultimate owners use more extensive pyramidal structures.

As the motives behind the use of pyramidal structure may differ between the private firms and SOEs, the effects of pyramidal structure on firm valuation differ too. Before I discuss these effects, I would like to first build our understanding about how extensively the pyramidal structure has been used by the Chinese listed companies. To do so, I take the results from my joint research with Yuande Zhu and Ying Zheng. Table 5.1 presents these results, in which the central government-controlled SOEs, local government-controlled SOEs, and private firms are discussed separately.

A careful examination of Table 5.1 reveals several findings. First, we find that the privately controlled firms tend to have a lower OC and a higher Wedge, suggesting that in China private owners build more extensive corporate pyramids than the state does. The average OC over 2001—2008 for the privately controlled listed firms is 0.647, which is much smaller than that of the central state-controlled firms (0.859) and the local state-controlled firms (0.924). The average Wedge for the privately, central state-, and local state-controlled firms are respectively 0.12, 0.058, and 0.031. The former is much larger than the latter two. These results strongly suggest that the deviation of control right from the ownership right due to the use of pyramidal structure is much more severe among the privately controlled firms in China.

Second, although the sample period covers only eight years, we observe notable changes in Chinese listed firms' ownership structures over time. For privately controlled firms, the average OC increases steadily from 0.579 to 0.709 and the average Wedge decreases monotonically from 0.142 to 0.103. In the meantime, neither the OC nor Wedge of the central government-controlled firms changes much over time. Notably, the

Table 5.1 Pyramidal structure of Chinese listed firms: 2001–2008

	2001	2002	2003	2004	2005	2006	2007	2008	Total
Panel A: Central state-controlled listed firms									
# of firms	199	210	230	232	239	244	264	280	1898
Layer	3.734	3.757	3.774	3.819	3.887	3.898	3.939	4.000	3.860
Control rights	0.484	0.489	0.476	0.472	0.461	0.431	0.434	0.435	0.458
Ownership	0.432	0.435	0.416	0.410	0.400	0.374	0.377	0.377	0.400
OC	0.883	0.871	0.852	0.846	0.850	0.859	0.861	0.855	0.859
Control rights—ownership Wedge	0.052	0.054	0.060	0.062	0.060	0.058	0.057	0.059	0.058
Panel B: Local state-controlled listed firms									
# of firms	660	662	640	644	619	571	568	569	4933
Layer	3.136	3.160	3.211	3.244	3.278	3.317	3.347	3.404	3.257
Control rights	0.483	0.483	0.479	0.473	0.458	0.416	0.416	0.422	0.455
Ownership	0.463	0.459	0.451	0.441	0.424	0.380	0.378	0.381	0.424
OC	0.955	0.945	0.934	0.926	0.918	0.908	0.900	0.898	0.924
Control rights—ownership Wedge	0.020	0.024	0.028	0.032	0.034	0.036	0.038	0.040	0.031
Panel C: Privately controlled listed firms									
# of firms	129	178	237	317	332	377	435	474	2479
Layer	3.698	3.753	3.654	3.546	3.593	3.531	3.421	3.344	3.522
Control rights	0.355	0.341	0.347	0.353	0.346	0.343	0.360	0.370	0.354
Ownership	0.212	0.196	0.216	0.225	0.219	0.225	0.256	0.267	0.234
OC	0.579	0.567	0.603	0.623	0.621	0.642	0.699	0.709	0.647
Control rights—ownership Wedge	0.142	0.144	0.132	0.128	0.127	0.118	0.104	0.103	0.120

Source: Liu et al. 2012

average OC of the local state-controlled firms decreases steadily from 0.955 to 0.898 and the average Wedge increases from slightly over 0.02 to 0.04. Furthermore, although the level of OC (Wedge) is still significantly lower (higher) for privately controlled firms than that of central state-controlled firms and the local state-controlled firms, the decrease in Wedge and the increase in OC suggest that private firms' use of corporate pyramids attenuates over time. However, while private owners in China appear to be streamlining their ownership structures, thanks to a series of corporate governance initiatives introduced since 2001, local state owners appear to be building more extensive corporate pyramids. This contrast is intriguing and calls for more investigation.

This difference between the private firms and SOEs suggests that private owners and the state in China respond to changing economic and institutional conditions in different ways. Further analysis shows that institution quality affects the pattern and evolution of privately controlled and local state-controlled pyramids in opposite ways. Private owners build more extensive corporate pyramids when they are subject to less market and legal discipline and more political discretion, whereas government owners build more extensive corporate pyramids when they are subject to greater market and legal discipline and less political discretion. And more importantly, the pyramidal structures maintained by private owners tend to unravel when institution quality improves. We, however, find exactly the opposite for local state-controlled firms.

Economic Effects of Pyramidal Structure

The pyramidal structure allows the ultimate controller to control a large amount of assets with a small amount of capital. Clearly, this is very likely associated with some types of agency problems. La Porta et al. (1999), Claessens et al. (2000), and Lemmon and Lins (2003), using the examples from the emerging markets, provide supporting evidence that the deviation of control rights from ownership rights is associated with worsening firm performance.

In the paper by Qiao Liu, Ying Zheng, and Yuande Zhu (Liu et al. 2012), we find that there is a significantly negative relation between the extent of corporate pyramid measured by OC and Wedge, and firm performance measured by market-to-book ratio or return on equity (ROE), among privately controlled listed firms. However, the separation between the control rights and ownership rights, resulting from the use of corporate pyramids, enhances local state-controlled listed firms' stock market performance and operating performance. On the latter point, the Chinese experience is quite unique. This, together with an earlier finding that the use of pyramidal structure by SOEs is more popular when the institutional infrastructure is more robust, seems to suggest that pyramidal structure-enabled longer control chains effectively separate corporate management from political interventions, which contributes to the enhancement of firm performance.

While the private firms and the state firms build up pyramids out of completely different incentives, an emerging trend in the Chinese stock market is the rise of private firms. As such, one can safely predict that private firms will eventually exceed SOEs to dominate the Chinese stock market. Given this projection, examining the pyramids built by private firms would be more insightful in terms of understanding the future dynamics of corporate China.

Figure 5.3 presents the ownership structure of Fosun Group in 2009, one of the largest private groups based in Shanghai. Fosun Group was founded in 1994 by Guangchang Guo and Xinjun Liang, together with another two colleagues at Fundan University, where Guo and Liang once studied and then worked. In slightly more than 20 years, Fosun Group has developed into a large conglomerate with businesses ranging from real estate, pharmaceutical, insurance, steel, shopping malls, healthcare, and tourism, to fashion and luxury goods.

As shown in Fig. 5.3, Fosun Group's ultimate controller, Mr. Guo, who owns 58 percent of Fosun International Holding Group, has craftily used the pyramidal structure to organize Fosun's very diversified business portfolio. Take Nanjing Iron & Steel, a company listed in the Shanghai Stock Exchange with stock code 600282, as the example. Calculations show that Fosun International Holding's ownership in Nanjing Iron & Steel is 24.52 percent. However, through pyramidal structure, Fosun International Holding controls 62.69 percent of the total votes of Nanjing Iron & Steel. OC, a variable measuring the extent of pyramidal structure, has a value of 0.39. This suggests that Fosun International Holding uses 39 percent of investment to gain 100 percent of control over Nanjing Iron & Steel. For the largest shareholder, Mr. Guo, OC has a value of 0.24, suggesting that pyramidal structure has allowed Mr. Guo to secure his control over large amounts of corporate assets with a minimal amount of capital investment. Notably, in the case of Nanjing Iron & Steel, it takes 11 layers (including the two ends) for Mr. Guo to ensure his control over the listed vehicle.

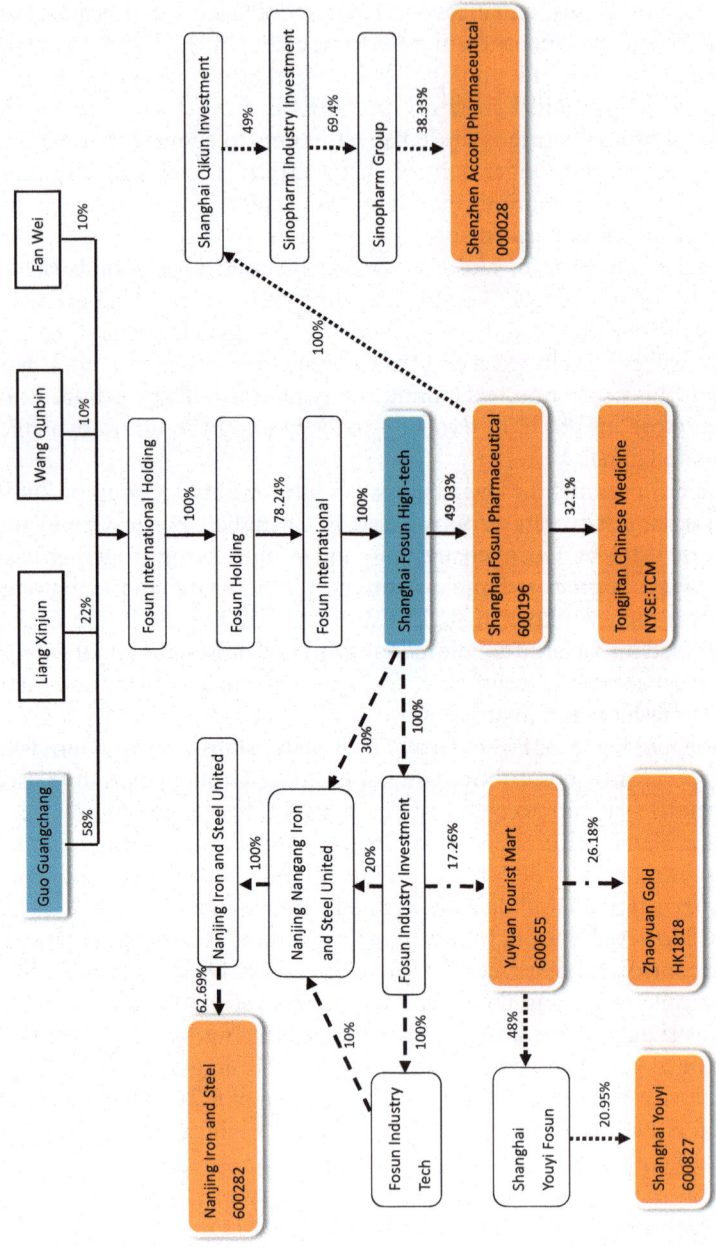

Fig. 5.3 The Fosun Group in 2009
Note: Firms in *orange* are listed companies.
Source: Liu et al. (2012)

Cases like Fosun Group are not rare. Figure 5.3 shows that pyramidal structure has been widely used by both private firms and SOEs. In the next five to ten years, private firms may gain more ground. Since there is a negative relation between private firms' ROIC and their use of pyramidal structure, understanding the underlying rationales and searching for ways to unravel private firms' pyramidal structure become the key.

Several underlying mechanisms likely drive down ROIC of firms with an extensive use of pyramidal structure. With a complex ownership structure like the one in Fig. 5.3, the group is not transparent. Loss of transparency gives the ultimate controller more freedom to make decisions in his own interests. If the decisions are against the interests of other shareholders, then the classical agency problems emerge. Also, when the ultimate controller employs an extremely complex organizational structure, there will be a tremendous amount of "related party" transactions within the group, which further increase the opaqueness of the group. In addition, imbalances between a firm's cash flow rights and control rights may be associated with over-leverage. To maintain a complex organization and diversify into other businesses, the group needs to make numerous investments, and tend to borrow more from financial intermediaries. Even worse, under the pyramidal structure, the subsidiaries may borrow debt in the name of the group or based on the guarantees offered by the group. Take the Korean chaebols, which have extensively used the pyramidal structure, as the example. In 1996, right before the eruption of the Asian financial crisis, the average debt-market equity ratio for 30 chaebols reached 600 percent. The run-away debts eventually got these seemingly unstoppable conglomerates into trouble.

There are some potential virtues associated with pyramidal structure. Pyramids enable a controlling shareholder to establish an internal capital market within the group.[28] The effective functioning of this internal market may help overcome external financing constraints and lower the cost of capital. In addition, pyramids allow the controlling shareholders to control a large amount of assets with a small amount of capital. This type of "leverage," from the ownership perspective, reduces the amount of invested capital. All else held fixed, pyramidal structure may even help boost ROIC. The trouble here, however, is that one cannot hold all else fixed. With pyramidal structure, the ultimate controller may aggressively pursue his own interests at the expense of other shareholders, which leads to lower ROIC, as plenty of empirical evidence has shown. The overall effect of pyramidal structure on firm value hence may be negative.

Since the Asian financial crisis, the pyramidal structure has been widely viewed as a major micro-level reason that triggered the crisis. In 1994, before the outbreak of the crisis, Nobel Laureate Paul Krugman published an article titled "The Myth of Asia's Miracle" in *Foreign Policy*. In this article, Krugman predicted that Asian economic miracle would be over soon. Reason? He pointed to the severe moral hazard risk in those Asian conglomerates. He argued that those Asian corporate giants, fueled by bank loans, had strong motives to make rampant investments. However, merely depending on investment but not ROIC, Asian business groups would ultimately encounter debt repayment problems. It turned out Paul Krugman was right.

Another unwelcome consequence of the extensive use of pyramidal structure is income inequality. It is not immediately clear how much of the rise of income equality in China can be attributed to the widespread use of pyramidal structure by corporate owners. Fast-growing economies like China typically go through a period of rapidly rising inequality as the new urban population see their incomes grow faster than the rural population, thanks to higher levels of productivity in manufacturing. However, income inequality in China rises much more rapidly than what the economic fundamentals could justify. Unlimited use of pyramid structure by corporate owners may have facilitated the emergence of many large business groups in the Chinese economy, with some of them even breaking into the *Fortune* Global 500 list. Pyramidal structure allows very few corporate owners to gather wealth rapidly and legitimately, which further worsens the income inequality situation in China.

Notably, a high level of income inequality by itself need not be a source of concern. In the past 35 years, China—a dynamic and fast-growing economy—has had a high level of income equality, but this does not appear to be a constraint either on economic growth or on average living standard. Income or wealth inequality becomes a serious concern once the economy is losing its dynamism and slowing down, which would very likely be the case faced by China in years to come.

A Short Conclusion and Rambling Thoughts

Corporate governance with Chinese characteristics, especially concentrated ownership structure and extensive use of pyramidal structure by corporate owners, enables many corporate empires to rise rapidly in the Chinese economy. This in turn facilitates these corporate owners' control over major parts of the economy. The presence of corporate empires with tight control over key resources in an economy exacerbates the unleveled competition between these corporate giants and other firms, squeezes the space of SMEs for survival and further development, and stifles individuals' drive for innovation and entrepreneurship.

Imagine that there is a 22-year-old university graduate. He can find a job in a famous business group with his career path clearly set out—stable return and low risk. The alternative is to join a startup with an uncertain future or start his own business with even more uncertainties. If he knows that the powerful empires can nail his small startup anytime, what is the point of running the risk of working for a small startup with no hope? When the best college graduates in China take pride in working at big companies such as PetroChina, ICBC, China Mobile, or even Alibaba, how can we find China's Steve Jobs, Bill Gates, Elon Musk, and Mark Zuckerberg? If China is determined to achieve its economic transformation from size-oriented growth to quality growth, China has to transform the mindset of those large companies that are aggressively pursuing operation scale rather than profitability and ROIC.

"To cross the river by feeling the stones" has served as an important guiding principle for China's economic reform. Now the Chinese firms are deep in the water and can no longer feel the stones in their next move. This is game-changing—the important and urgent change for corporate China to make is to learn how to swim. Change mindset, get ready for discomfort, and develop skills in managing the transition to a new path.

NOTES

1. See Southern Weekends, "The punishment on *Wanfu Biotechnology*, a joke!" (May 24, 2013).
2. Other reasons such as abnormal financial reporting and warnings initiated by the audit firms can also trigger the ST designation.
3. See Bai, Chong-en, Qiao Liu, and Frank Song, "The value of corporate control: evidence from China's distressed firms," 2004b, University of Hong Kong working paper.
4. Note that the ST firms have 24 months to turn profitable. They are delisted otherwise. Therefore, 24 months is the legitimate time frame for an ST firm to turn its performance around.
5. As I showed in Chap. 3, the average ROIC of the listed companies in China between 1998 and 2012 was only 3 percent.
6. See, for example, Liu (2006).
7. See Liu et al. (2012).
8. See Jensen and Meckling (1976). Jensen (1986) expands the argument in Jensen and Meckling (1976).

9. This expropriation takes a variety of forms, for example, excessive executive compensation, loan guarantees for, and transfer pricing between, related companies, and dilution by new share issues. Johnson et al. (2000) use the term tunneling to describe the transfer of resources out of firms for the benefit of controlling shareholders. Evidence from the Asian financial crisis indicates that tunneling is a serious agency problem in emerging markets.

10. See p.17 of Becht et al. (2003).

11. Ibid., p.18.

12. See Bai et al. (2004a).

13. See Bai et al. (2004b).

14. This is a reproduction of Fig. 5.1 from Liu and Lu (2007).

15. Ibid.

16. See Cha (2001).

17. See, for example, Clarke (2003).

18. See, for example, LLSV (1997, 1998, 2000, 2002).

19. See Pistor and Xu (2005).

20. See, for example, Shleifer and Vishny (1998).

21. See Demsetz and Lehn (1985).

22. See Bai et al. (2004a) and Liu (2006).

23. See Liu et al. (2012).

24. Note that if the two numbers do not add up to 100, it means that the rest of the firms are controlled by shareholders other than the state or families, or their ownership structure is dispersed and no shareholders own more than 10 percent of the shares.

25. In normal cases, a controlling shareholder can control a firm with less than 50 percent of ownership. For a better understanding, I assume that the controlling shareholder owns 50 percent plus one share of the firm. This arrangement ensures that the controller has majority votes under his control.

26. See, for example, Johnson et al. (2000), Bertrand et al. (2002), Bae et al. (2002), and Claessens et al. (2002).

27. Bertrand et al. (2000) provide evidence that pyramidal structures allow controlling shareholders to expropriate minority shareholders. La Porta et al. (2002) find a positive relationship between firm valuation and the cash flow rights owned by controlling shareholders and a negative relationship between the separation of control and cash flow rights and firm valuation. Claessens et al. (2002) find that the control-ownership wedge resulting from the use of pyramidal structures is associated with firm value loss, suggesting that entrenched owners with few cash flow rights are more likely to divert corporate resources. Both Johnson and Mitton (2003) and Lemmon and Lins (2003) report evidence that during the Asian financial crisis, firms with more extensive corporate pyramids suffered a greater loss in firm value.

28. For supporting evidence, see Khanna and Palepu (2000).

CHAPTER 6

The Perils of Diversification

In 2015, the Chinese economy reported a 6.9 percent of GDP growth rate, below 7 percent for the first time since 1991. Yet bank loans increased by 15.4 percent. The credit growth continued to outstrip the economic growth, suggesting that the credit-fueled and investment-led Chinese economy is somehow losing steam. As a result, China's overall debt-to-GDP ratio has followed an upward trend, increasing from 160 percent of annual output in 2007 to about 282 percent of GDP by 2014.[1] A rapid increase in debt in such a short space of time obviously is not good news for companies that have long relied on cheap and easy credit to rapidly build up their operation scale. In September 2015, China National Erzhong Group Co., a listed central government-controlled SOE producing smelting equipment, defaulted on its debt. Of course, it was eventually bailed out by its parent company and did not lose face. One month later, Sinosteel, one of China's *Fortune* Global 500 companies, had to delay its payment on a bond. To break into the *Fortune* Global 500 company list, Sinosteel pursued an aggressive diversification strategy and eventually made it. With 86 subsidiaries, Sinosteel's businesses range from metal, trading commodity derivatives, and international trade to finance. Its quick surge has been fueled by bank loans and assisted by investment opportunities inherent in a fast-growing economy. However, as the rate of economic growth declines, high corporate debt becomes a severe burden. The company's balance sheet deteriorated rapidly. Before it defaulted on its debt, Sinosteel had been on a losing track for several years.

© The Editor(s) (if applicable) and The Author(s) 2016
Q. Liu, *Corporate China 2.0*, DOI 10.1057/978-1-137-55089-7_6

Stories like those of Sinosteel and Erzhong are not rare. Diversification has been a myth for almost all Chinese companies, state owned or privately owned. For example, the Fosun Group in Shanghai, which I have discussed in Chap. 5, has craftily employed the pyramidal structure to build an extremely complex diversified business portfolio. "China Energy; Global Resources," a slogan promoted by Fosun in recent years, embodies Fosun's strategic thinking that has guided a number of high-profile cross-industry and cross-border investments. Ping An Group, the largest privately owned financial services company in China, has its eye on the "universal banking" model once hailed by Citigroup, JP Morgan, and HSBC. Through huge investments in commercial banking, investment banking, wealth management, mutual funds, and peer-to-peer lending platforms, Ping An Group has developed itself into a financial conglomerate with licenses and permits to offer all financial services and products not prohibited by Chinese regulators.[2]

From the 1960s to the 1980s, diversification strategy and conglomerates had been praised by many management gurus as the highest form of capitalism.[3] The Japanese keiretsu and Korean chaebol had followed suit and built up their own sprawling conglomerates. The conglomeration trend waned entering the 1990s, especially after the 1997–1998 Asian financial crisis—it was widely believed that the root cause of the Asian financial crisis was excessive investment and the resulting high leverage by those Asian conglomerates.

Is diversification positively or negatively associated with sustainable firm performance measured by ROIC? Does diversification conjure up a bright future that matches corporate China's mission to surge rapidly in the global markets? Given that diversification is deeply immersed in the minds of Chinese executives and corporate founders, we have to thoroughly understand the net effects of aggressively pursuing conglomeration in China.

TOO BIG TO FAIL?

The most common motive for corporate diversification is that it is believed to be able to reduce firm risk, thus helping to improve firm value. Diversified companies are safer and likely more adaptable to constantly changing business conditions. However, skepticism on the virtues of diversification has never ceased. In particular, people have long found that the stock market gives conglomerates a value discount. In fact, over the past three decades, an important finding in the empirical corporate finance research is the so-called diversification discount or "conglomerate discount," which refers to the fact that a diversified company is worth less than a portfolio of comparable single-segment firms. Nowadays, whenever the term "conglomerate" comes up in conversation, "conglomerate discount" immediately enters the discussion. The presence of "conglomerate discount" seems to strongly suggest that conglomeration is more likely to be associated with reduced firm value.

"Diversification discount" has been widely corroborated by academic research using data from different countries and different time periods. In their studies on US listed companies (excluding financial services and utilities firms), Lang and Stulz (1994) and Berger and Ofek (1995) respectively find that firms with diversified business portfolios have on average a 10 percent of discount in their market value. That is, if these conglomerates re-organize their businesses into separate and focused corporate entities, their shareholders will achieve a gain of 10 percent.

While the evidence of diversification discount has been quite robust, for quite some time, people believe that it only applies to industrial companies and non-financial services providers. In the 1990s, large financial institutions began to promote the universal banking model. The lines between commercial banks and investment banks were blurred. Financial conglomerates such as Citigroup, JP Morgan, HSBC, and Royal Bank of Scotland surged as formidable competitors in almost all areas of financial services. Economists Ross Levine and Luc Laeven, in their 2007 *Journal of Financial Economics* paper, provide empirical evidence showing the presence of diversification discount among financial institutions. Financial conglomerates' pursuit of the universal banking business model was trendy during the 1990s and 2000s and contributed tremendously to financial institutions' rapid increase in size in a short space of time. However, the fact that most were traded in the stock market at a discount had been largely ignored. In the wake of the 2008–2009 global financial crisis, financial conglomeration has been associated with terms such as "Too big to fail," "the agency problems," and "opaqueness." Both academics and policy-makers believe that diversification should be held accountable for the outbreak of the crisis.

Academics are still working hard to fully comprehend the sources of value loss or gain, if any, due to corporate diversification. One commonly accepted explanation, as proposed in Lang and Stulz (1994) and Berger and Ofek (1995), is that conglomerates tend to make less efficient investments, which causes lower ROIC and value loss. As a result, diversified firms' stocks are typically traded at a discount. As a further support for the inefficient investment proposition, Lamont (1997) and Shin and Stulz (1998) find that inefficient or poorly performing divisions of conglomerates are subsidized by well-performing divisions. Such within-group subsidies are largely inefficient, which also causes value loss. Scharfstein (1998) provides evidence suggesting that the investments of small divisions are not sensitive to their own-division cash flow, in comparison to stand-alone firms, consistent with the inefficient investment proposition. Habib et al. (1997) present a model in which splitting a firm along industry lines into separately traded firms leads to more informative stock prices. More informative prices improve the quality of managers' investment decisions and reduce uninformed investors' uncertainty about asset values. In the same vein, in one of my 2008 papers,[4] I explicitly assume that stock price conveys valuable information to the management. I show that the value loss from diversification is a function of stock price informativeness. More informed stock trading leads to a more efficient investment and a smaller diversification discount. Research along this line of reasoning strongly suggests that divestitures or spin-offs can boost firm value.

A second explanation for the diversification discount is that the conglomerates have higher required returns than the stand-alone firms. Therefore, the conglomerate firms are valued less. Lamont and Polk (2001) find that the higher required returns can account for approximately half of the empirically observed diversification discount. However, they have not explored what causes the different expected returns among firms with varied diversification discounts.

There are many studies that question whether diversification discount is indeed resulting from inefficient investment. One issue that has arisen in assessing the value loss from diversification is that the decision to diversify is also endogenous. The failure to account for the endogeneity of diversifying decisions may lead to incorrect inferences. For example, Campa and Kedia (1999) find that when they control for the endogeneity of the diversification decision, the discount due to diversification declines significantly and even disappears in some specifications. Graham et al. (2002) study the conditions of business units of multi-segment firms before conglomeration. They find that the firms that are added to the conglomerates experience poor and deteriorating financial performance prior to being acquired. About half of the value loss in conglomerates occurs simply because the parent adds an already "undervalued" unit. Whited (2001) finds evidence that disputes the argument that the diversification discount is caused by inefficient investment. She attributes the false relation between inefficient investment and diversification discount to the failure to correct the measurement errors in Tobin's q as a proxy for investment opportunity.

Given the heated debates on the net value effect of conglomeration, whether diversification leads to value loss is still an unsettled issue.

IS DIVERSIFICATION A TRAP?

Business diversification became a trend in the 1960s, when a number of large companies emerged as corporate giants through aggressive M&As or organic growth. Companies such as General Electric (GE) and Johnson & Johnson engaged in different industries and achieved quick breakthrough in operation scale and profitability. In the case of GE, its conglomeration strategy was built on the strong belief of its founder, Thomas Edison, that electricity would transform the everyday world. Beginning with electric bulbs and fans, GE went on to develop a full range of electric appliances before becoming an industrial and financial conglomerate.[5]

GE's diversification strategy was imitated by many in the USA and then by firms in other parts of the world, such as group companies in Japan and South Korea. In view of the enormous economic achievements scored by Japan and South Korea and the rise of Japanese and Korean firms in the global markets, diversification gained widespread popularity in emerging markets including, for example, Malaysia, Thailand, and India. For quite a while, the Korean chaebol model seemed to have provided a viable path for emerging market companies to grow rapidly.

The 1997–1998 Asian financial crisis triggered extensive reflections on the virtues and vices of conglomeration. Although dubbed financial crisis, the Asian crisis in the 1990s was believed to be a corporate crisis and its root cause was high leverage ratio and low ROIC in the corporate sector. As Paul Krugman strongly argued,[6] the Asian financial crisis was essentially a crisis of Asian conglomerates. Before the crisis, those conglomerates had been busy with forging corporate empires through large amounts of investments. Fueled by bank loans, they entered new industries, and ferociously expanded their business scope.

In Fig. 6.1, which is a reproduction from my joint research with Douglas Arner and Paul Lejot,[7] I provide the debt-to-equity ratio and the number of affiliated subsidiaries of the top 10 chaebols in Korea right

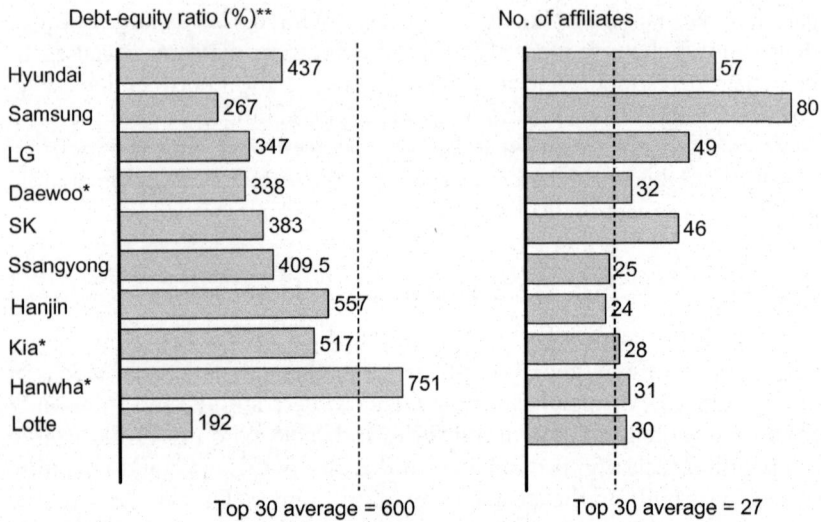

Fig. 6.1 Debt-equity ratio and the number of affiliates of chaebols
Source: Finance in Asia by Qiao Liu, Paul Lejot, Douglas Arner, Routledge, 2013

before the Asian financial crisis. All of them were highly diversified. Before the outbreak of the crisis, the top 30 chaebols in South Korea had on average 27 affiliates, and operated a wide range of businesses. In 1996, Samsung operated 80 subsidiaries, providing more than 2000 different kinds of products and services. Not surprisingly, these chaebols were highly levered—the debt-to-equity ratio of the top 30 chaebols averaged at 600 percent in 1996. In normal situations, banks can probably still arrange new loans for these conglomerates to cover the repayment of old debts. However, when encountering a rapidly deteriorating external environment, banks ran out of money. The old equilibrium was broken and most of the Korean chaebols fell into the repayment crisis.

Behind high leverage were reckless investments that had lasted for many years. In the process of becoming larger and larger, it was even more difficult for conglomerates to maintain a high level of ROIC—complex organizational structure resulted in additional layers of information asymmetry, and even more severe agency problems. Most conglomerates had done lots of things badly rather than a few things well. In the cases of the Korean chaebols, before the crisis, most of them had ROIC that failed to cover WACC. While these chaebols were growing into corporate behemoths, they failed to deliver reasonable rates of return to shareholders. The low valuation of Korean chaebols relative to their developed country peers, known as the "Korean discount," is in fact a conglomerate discount.

Of course, there are examples of good conglomerates. Over the past 100 years, GE has stood out as a great company that consistently delivers predictable earnings growth. GE's core competence is its ability to select and manage well a few sectors, and in the meantime get rid of businesses failing to generate value. In this sense, GE, like Berkshire Hathaway run by Warren Buffet and his long-term partner Charlie Munger, has been using a private equity approach to manage a sprawling corporate empire: They know what and when to enter and when to exit. Specifically, they carefully invest a few businesses and leverage their strong management skills to improve value; furthermore, they constantly adjust the component businesses of their business portfolios to ensure that only the most competitive ones will stay. Conglomeration is the result but not the reason for GE's success; the reason is the ability to select a few appropriate businesses and improve their value.

Conglomeration per se may not support value enhancement. But it is getting clearer that one should not apply diversification discount to all conglomerates. Globalization and digitations are now profoundly changing the competition landscape around the world, and there are now more examples of new value-enhancing conglomerates that bear little relation to the bloated old corporate empires. These successful conglomerates either possess managerial talents and skills that allow them to achieve rapid growth or boast of extremely talented entrepreneurs who have the ability to creatively disrupt old industries by applying new technologies and new ways of thinking. Berkshire Hathaway and GE may belong to the first group, in which management talents and skills dominate.

In the second group, Google and Alibaba are good examples. In August 2015, Google announced a big reorganization that literally transformed the company into a conglomerate. The founders of Google, Larry Page and Sergey Brin, will run a holding company called Alphabet. Google's original business—internet search and advertising—will be a subsidiary of the new entity; Alphabet also includes projects on driverless cars, medicines that will expand the human lifespan, artificial intelligence such as Alphago, which just beat one of the best Go players in the world, Lee Sedol, and so on. Alphabet's founders have sharp insights about technologies. More importantly, Alphabet is fortunate enough that its founders have both the interest and the money to apply the new technologies to the old industries.

Since getting listed in New York, Alibaba Group—the world's largest e-commerce company—has also transformed itself into a conglomerate. E-commerce of course is still Alibaba's core business—Jack Ma, Alibaba's charismatic founder, has made his ambitious plan public: "In five years, we will sell over one trillion dollars."[8] In addition to e-commerce, Alibaba has also invested in a wide range of businesses, ranging from cloud computing, healthcare, social media, and entertainment and sports, to online finance. It even purchased the *South China Morning Post*, a renowned English newspaper with a large reader base in Asia. Instead of calling Alibaba a holding company or a conglomerate, Jack Ma describes Alibaba as an ecosystem. With a strong belief that internet will change the world completely, Jack Ma has been diligently expanding the scope of his ecosystem.

Does conglomerate discount apply to Alibaba or Alphabet? These talented entrepreneurs have been bold enough to apply new technologies and new ways of thinking to disrupt traditional industries. They have been fortunate enough to boast of deep understanding of new technologies and their implications for business. Moreover, they have enough money at their disposal, which allows them to eschew short-term results and pursue long-term growth.

Few companies boast of the management skills that GE, Berkshire Hathaway, and others have developed over time; even fewer companies have visionary founders like Larry Page, Sergey Brin, and Jack Ma. For an average company, while well-managed conglomeration could be value added, staying focused may be a more feasible option and a safer bet.

THE CHINA PRACTICE

Chinese companies are steadfast upholders of the conglomeration strategy. Over time, both SOEs and private companies have experienced a continued increase in the number of business segments. The conglomeration incentives are particularly acute among the SOEs as a result of soft budget constraints. With easy credit from state-owned banks, SOEs go to great lengths to expand their business territories. Of course, the aggressive pursuit of diversification by SOEs, which uses up a great deal of resources and capital, oftentimes fails to produce desirable results.

Three reasons explain why SOEs can hardly escape the trap of the conglomeration discount. First, SOEs in general are strongly motivated to pursue scale. Being ranked among the *Fortune* Global 500 or China's top 500 is usually an important indicator used to assess SOEs' performance.

Most rankings take sales, assets, or employment, the usual measures of firm size, as the assessment criteria, which provides strong incentives for SOEs to expand their business scope through investments.

Second, as I have discussed in Chap. 5, the institutional foundations for China's economic development are weak. There is a lack of effective corporate governance mechanisms to discipline SOE managers and mitigate potential agency problems. Investments carried out by SOEs are more likely driven by managerial rent-seeking incentives. When a company can gain a large amount of funds from the state-dominated financial system at favorable rates and it does not worry about the debt repayment, investing as much as possible is a natural choice.

Third, most SOEs operate in industries with high barriers to entry, where competition tends to be weak. In addition, SOEs enjoy preferential policies, lower cost of capital, and government bailouts when they are in financial trouble. All these enable many SOEs to enjoy quite stable profits, especially when the economy is booming. When a company has in its hand a large amount of cash, the free cash flow problem proposed by Michael Jensen (1986) may prevail. If a company continues to make many inefficient investments, it will eventually run into debt repayment problems. Over time, we are seeing the pile-up of corporate debts, especially among the state sector, which has a lot to do with the above three reasons.

Private companies' diversification can be understood as a kind of market behavior. By diversifying into industries they are allowed to enter, private companies can quickly accumulate assets under management, hire more people, and likely pay more tax. All of these can appease local politicians' desire to boost local economic growth. Reciprocally, they can get better treatment in terms of funding, business permits, land use rights, and favorable tax breaks. Scale, in some sense, has firmly occupied the minds of corporate founders in China. Many of them view GE and Hutchison Whampoa as role models and vow to become the GE or Hutchison Whampoa of mainland China.

It would be insightful to quantify the extent of corporate China's diversification over time. While it is not feasible to conduct such analysis for corporate China per se, we can measure the degree of diversification among the listed companies. Figure 6.2 presents the average segments China's listed companies had during the period from 2004 to 2010.

As shown in Fig. 6.2, multi-segment organizational form has been quite common in the universe of Chinese listed companies. Over time, the average number of business segments exhibited an upward trend, suggesting

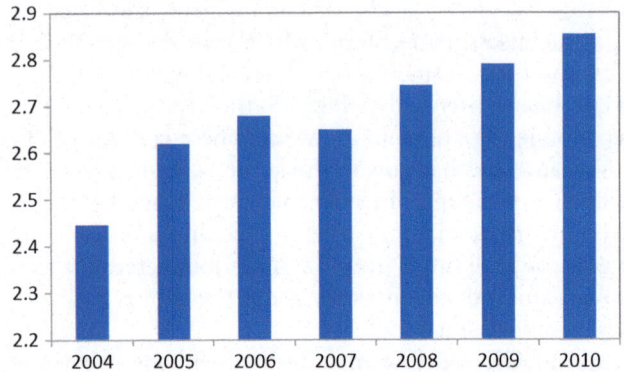

Fig. 6.2   Chinese listed companies' business segments, 2004–2010
Source: Wind database; author's calculation

that the Chinese listed companies had become more diversified. In 2004, an average Chinese listed company had 2.45 business segments. This had increased to 2.85 in 2010. A simple calculation of the average business segments may be biased. One may argue that the newly public firms may have more business segments, which biased the result upward. In unreported analysis, I excluded the newly listed companies and only focused on firms that were already public in 2004. From 2004 to 2010, the average business segments increased from 2.45 to 3.18. Conglomeration had been a trend.

The increase in business segments reflects two things. First, Chinese listed firms are largely size-oriented. Expanding into new industries facilitates the growth in firm size. Second, most listed companies in China lack clearly spelled out long-term strategies. They tend to invest in the industries that seemingly deliver good returns. For example, almost all central government-controlled SOEs have dedicated subsidiaries focusing on real estate development during China's housing market boom. Similarly, private groups had also found real estate development tempting, and this was part of the reason for the high leverage ratio among China's private groups.

Finance is another example. As a result of high barriers to entry and regulated interest rates, financial institutions normally enjoy quite handsome profits. Investing in the financial services sector has always been tempting. As the licenses are tightly controlled by the government, owning commercial banks was feasible only for very few large SOEs. But almost all large SOEs and private groups have investments in alternative financing vehicles such as small loan companies, trust companies, leasing companies, and even peer-to-peer lending platforms. Diversification or conglomeration, during economic boom, helps improve these companies' profit. But the lack of deep understanding of the nature of finance from time to time causes unnecessary and poorly managed risk exposure, especially during economic downturns. Diversification represents much of what is believed to be wrong with corporate China—they always put size ahead of profit.

Is diversification associated with enhanced return on invested capital (ROIC)? If the answer is yes, then diversification, as a tempting and well-received corporate strategy, should be applauded. If the answer is no, then diversification would only create bloated behemoths, whose ROIC cannot cover cost of capital, giving rise to conglomerate discount.

I studied all of the Chinese listed companies (excluding financial and utilities firms) from 2004 to 2010. I particularly examined how these firms' ROICs were related to the number of business segments they boasted of. Figure 6.3 presents the results of my analysis. Specifically, I classified the Chinese listed companies into five categories, based on the number of business segments these firms had developed over time. Group 1 represents the companies that focus on one product or service; Group 2 refers to the listed companies with two major business segments; Group

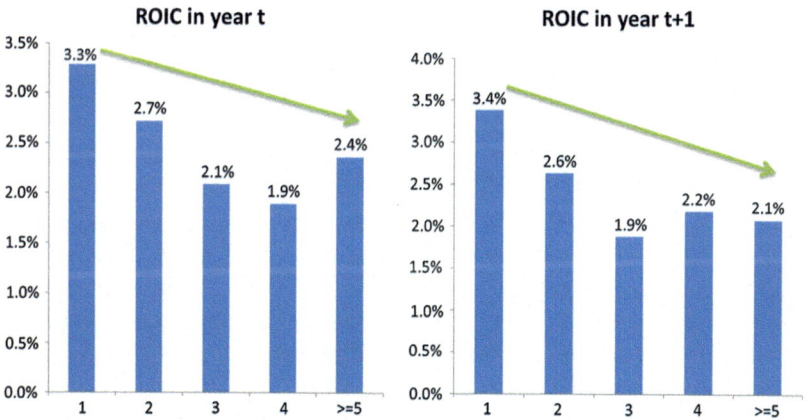

Fig. 6.3   ROIC and the number of business segments
Source: Wind database; author's calculation

3 consists of the listed companies with three major segments, and so on. Group 5 deserves a few more words—it comprises the listed companies with five or more business segments. For each group, I computed the firm average ROIC in the current year (year t), and in the next year (year t + 1).

Figure 6.3 shows the results. When the number of business segments increases, the Chinese listed companies' ROIC does not increase accordingly. In fact, ROIC declines steadily with the increase of the degree of diversification. When I extended the analysis to the relationship between the number of segments and firms' ROIC in year t + 1, I found the same results. For a specialized firm, that is, a firm with only one business segment, its ROIC averaged at 3.3 percent during the period from 2004 to 2010. When the number of business segments increased to five or more, these firms' average ROIC dropped to 2.4 percent. Diversification leads to bloated corporate dinosaurs, but not high-performing conglomerates in the universe of Chinese listed companies.

While diversification has been feverishly pursued by Chinese companies, my analysis above shows that diversification indeed facilitates the quick expansion of scale, but there is no proven evidence that it enhances firm value. To a certain extent, my presented evidence even suggests that diversification is detrimental to a firm's value creation. Recall my discussions about Fig. 3.7 in Chap. 3. In China, within-industry ROIC variance is much larger than between-industry ROIC variance of ROIC. For an average company, rushing into a new industry with an eye on its seemingly attractive investment opportunities may be illusionary. A company specializing in its own industry and excelling in execution may achieve a much higher ROIC. In any case, the Chinese data suggests that for the majority of Chinese listed companies, diversification might be just a myth.

KUNLUN ENERGY: FOCUS IS BEAUTIFUL

Kunlun Energy Company Limited (Kunlun Energy hereafter), headquartered in Hong Kong and with shares listed on the main board of the Hong Kong Stock Exchange (stock code: 0135.HK), is an international energy company controlled by PetroChina. The main business activities of Kunlun Energy are the exploration and development of oil and gas fields in mainland China, Kazakhstan, Oman, Peru, Thailand and Azerbaijan, and the end-users sale of natural gas in mainland China.

As a subsidiary of PetroChina, Kunlun Energy is an important value segment of the natural gas industry chain of PetroChina—the natural gas downstream end-users sale business. Kunlun Energy has a clear strategic positioning—it is committed to becoming the largest company engaged in the end-users sale of gas in China. Kunlun Energy's current strategy is to promote the development of the natural gas end-users sale business, focus on the liquefied natural gas (LNG) business, implement the "substitution of oil with natural gas" strategy, and develop a high-end market for the applications of natural gas.

To evaluate Kunlun Energy's capital market performance, I first compare its stock market performance with that of international peers and the overall market. Figure 6.4 presents the share prices of Kunlun Energy, PetroChina (A), PetroChina (H), the Hang Seng Index, and the Hang Seng Oil and Gas Index from November 2007 to November 2011.[9] To better illustrate the dynamic changes of stock prices for the companies, I reset the stock prices in November 2007 to be 100.

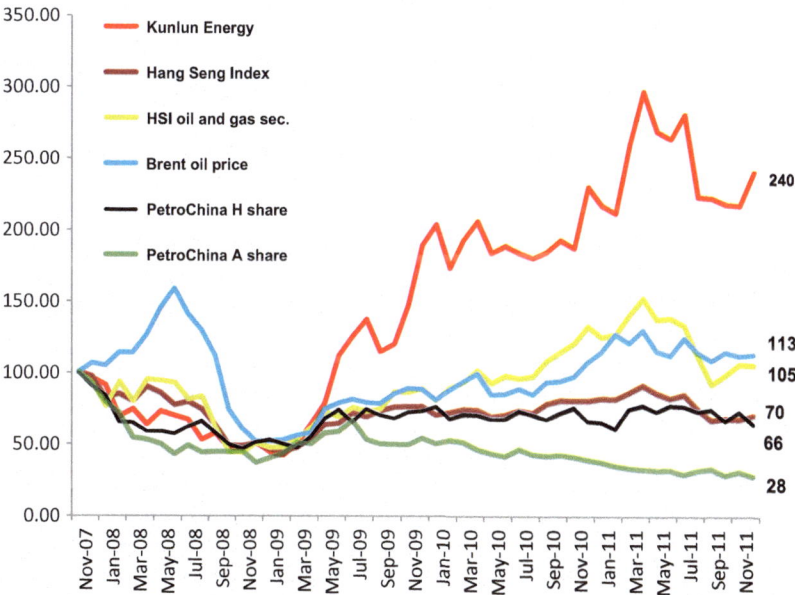

Fig. 6.4 The stock price of Kunlun Energy: Nov. 2007–Nov. 2011
Note: The stock prices and index levels in November 2007 are reset to be 100.
Source: Author's calculation

   As shown in Fig. 6.4, over the four-year period, Kunlun Energy outperformed others by a large margin. While the stock price of its parent company in the A-share market (PetroChina A share) dropped from 100 in November 2007 to 28 in November 2011, the stock price of Kunlun Energy actually increased from 100 to 240. Kunlun Energy also outperformed the market, captured by the Hang Seng Index, and the industry peers, measured by the Hang Seng Oil and Gas Index.

   As a subsidiary of PetroChina, Kunlun Energy had registered a capital market performance much different from that of its parent company, PetroChina. A careful study of the stock price dynamics and the operation of Kunlun Energy shows that the following three reasons largely account for the differences: (1) Kunlun Energy has a specialized strategy with a focus on natural gas end-users sale; Kunlun Energy's business model is thus clear and easier to understand by the market; (2) The operating performance, measured by ROIC, has been solid for Kunlun Energy; and (3) Kunlun Energy had a clear-cut stock market positioning.

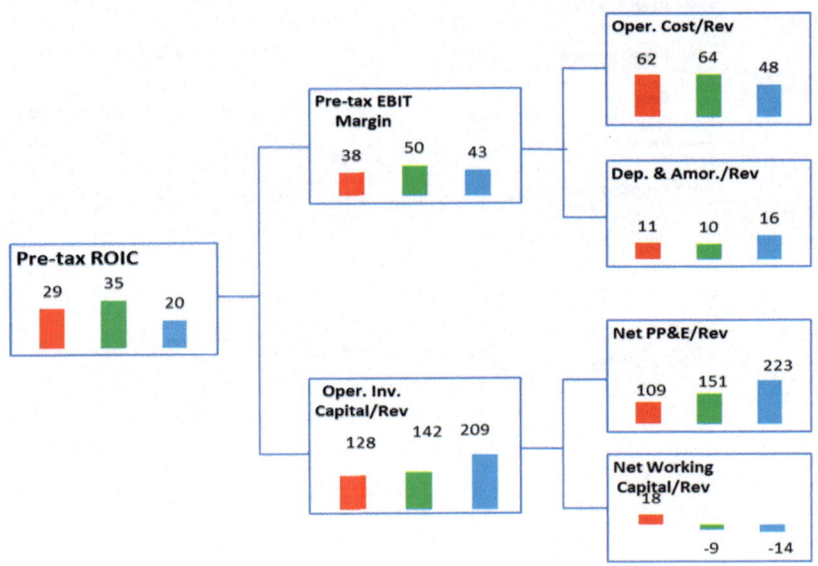

Fig. 6.5   Pre-tax ROIC of Kunlun Energy: 2009–2011
Source: Author's calculation based on information from Kunlun Energy's annual reports

In Fig. 6.5, I calculate Kunlun Energy's ROIC from 2009 to 2011. I also decompose ROIC into different components according to its definition. A careful study of Fig. 6.5 yields several interesting findings. First, Kunlun Energy achieved a relatively high level of ROIC during 2009 to 2011. The pre-tax ROIC over the three years ranged from 20 to 35 percent. Second, the invested capital-to-sales ratio had stayed at a high level from 2009 to 2011. It even increased to 209 percent in 2011, suggesting that to get a $1 sale, Kunlun Energy needs $ 2.09 capital in its operation. Although Kunlun Energy is competing in a capital-intensive industry, because of its relatively high profit margin, its ROIC had been quite impressive. Third, the case example of Kunlun Energy shows that large-scale capital investments can still get along with high ROIC, as long as the profit margin is high enough.

Figure 6.5 strongly suggests that the excellent ROIC performance by Kunlun Energy had played a decisive role in explaining Kunlun Energy's strong stock market performance. In unreported analysis, I also studied the correlation between Kunlun Energy's stock returns with the stock market returns, measured by the returns on the Hang Seng Index or the Shanghai Composite Index. I found that their correlation level was very low. In other words, using the market returns to explain the stock returns of Kunlun Energy, I found a very small R square. According to Roll (1988), low R square suggests that more firm-specific information on Kunlun Energy has been impounded on its stock prices. This implies at least two possibilities. First, Kunlun Energy's corporate strategy and operating results are transparent and have been fully appreciated by the investors. Second, Kunlun Energy had communicated very well to the investors. In either case, the firm value could be improved accordingly.

I apply another approach to study how a focused business model helps Kunlun Energy unlock firm value. In Fig. 6.6, I provide the strategic control map of the global oil and gas industry. The strategic control map is a two-dimensional diagram with the horizontal axis capturing firm size (measured by the total amount of invested capital) and the vertical axis capturing the ratio of enterprise value (EV) to invested capital. The ratio of EV to invested capital measures a firm's capital market performance.

Based on different combinations of the values of the two variables, there are four areas in Fig. 6.6. A company appearing in the northeast area has on average more invested capital and a higher EV-to-invested capital ratio. The company is dubbed industrial shaper, suggesting that it is a

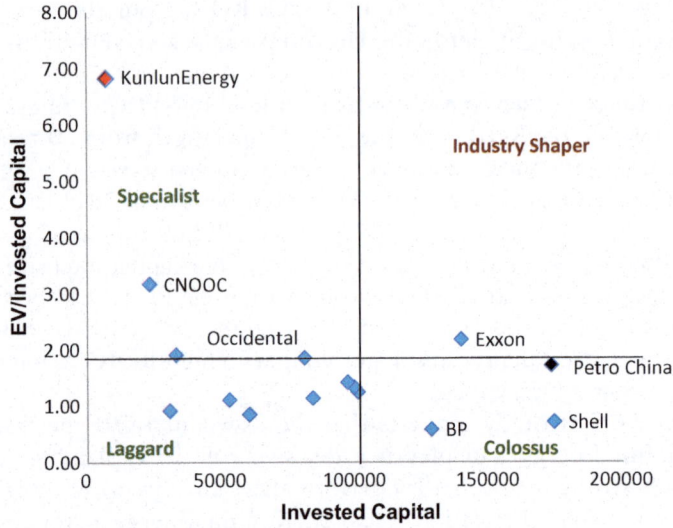

Fig. 6.6 Strategic control map, 2010
Note: unit: US$ million.
Source: Author's calculation based on the data from Compustat

leading firm in the industry; a firm appearing in the southeast area is large by size but its capital market performance is unimpressive. The company is hence dubbed colossus, suggesting that it is huge but does not necessarily generate value; a firm in the northwest area is dubbed specialist, suggesting that the firm may have a focused business line and this business has been quite profitable. That is, the firm is very good at what it has chosen to do. Finally, the firm appearing in the southwest area is dubbed laggard, suggesting that the firm has been lagging behind on both dimensions (size and value creation)—it is facing a high probability of going bankrupt.

The positioning of different firms in the same industry illustrates these firms' strategic problems and sheds light on their available strategic options. As shown in Fig. 6.6, Kunlun Energy is a typical "specialist," strongly suggesting that the company's business model has been fully appreciated by the market. Despite its relatively small size, Kunlun Energy has been highly valued by the capital market—the capital market has a preference for specialized companies because they are more transparent and can easily maintain a high level of ROIC. Being focused has brought to Kunlun Energy an obvious valuation premium.

To summarize, Kunlun Energy's strong market performance was mainly due to (1) good operating performance as reflected by its high ROIC; and (2) explicit and favorable capital market positioning. The capital market experiences of Kunlun Energy shed a lot of light on the Chinese companies aiming at diversifying their business portfolio. First, ROIC, not operation scale, eventually brings value premium; second, an explicit business scope and specialized business operation help a company gain a comparatively favorable capital market positioning; and third, if a company's investments accord with its strategic direction, a capital-intensive business model can also co-exist with a high level of ROIC.

I would like to elaborate on the third point a bit. Kunlun Energy is competing in a capital-intensive business. In past years, it has engaged in a series of acquisitions to build up its core competence in natural gas. It is a conventional wisdom that the success rate of mergers and acquisitions is not high, especially in China, where institutions for value-oriented M&As are not complete and many deals are still driven by companies' opportunistic motives.

Kunlun Energy is an exception. The company has a clear acquisition strategy—targeting assets or companies that can help it build up operation scale and competitive advantages in natural gas end-users sales. As such, the deals conducted by Kunlun on average were well received by the capital market. I employ an event study approach to examine the stock market reactions to Kunlun Energy's acquisitions in 2009 and 2010. In Table 6.1, I list all of the acquisitions made by Kunlun Energy in these two years. For each deal, I compute and list in the last column the three-day cumulative abnormal returns (from day −1 to day +1). In calculating abnormal returns, I use the stock market returns as the benchmark returns.[10] If there is a positive abnormal return, then it suggests that the transaction creates value and therefore the market positively reacts to the news; if the abnormal return is negative, it suggests exactly the opposite.

As shown in Table 6.1, most of the transactions conducted by Kunlun Energy involved using cash to purchase assets on natural gas and related assets. Out of nine deals, six received positive stock market reactions. When I calculate the average cumulative abnormal returns for all of the transactions conducted by Kunlun Energy, I get 3.85 percent, which is both statistically and economically significant, suggesting that the stock market reacts to the transactions conducted by Kunlun Energy in positive ways. The market value of Kunlun Energy has risen considerably because of these acquisitions.

Table 6.1   Kunlun energy's acquisitions in 2009 and 2010

Date	Acquisitions	Three-day abnormal returns[a] (%)
January 9, 2009	Acquired 97 % ownership of Xinjiang Xinjie Co., Ltd. with RMB 330 million	−1.42
February 16, 2009	Acquired 51 % ownership of China Natural Gas Corporation Ltd. with RMB 440 million	12.38
September 30, 2009	Acquired 51 % ownership of Qingyang Xinda Technology and Engineering Co., Ltd. with RMB4.7 million	8.98
October 21, 2009	Acquired 49 % ownership of China City Natural Gas Investment Group Co., Ltd. with RMB 620 million	5.01
May 17, 2010	Acquired 55 % ownership of Jiangsu LNG with RMB500 million	2.91
June 22, 2010	Acquired 51 % ownership of Sichuan Chuangang Fuel Gas with RMB160 million	−2.96
November 9, 2010	Acquired 75 % ownership of Dalian LNG with RMB 2 billion	0.27
November 26, 2010	Acquired 51 % ownership of Langfang Tiancheng Natural Gas with RMB410 million	10.86
December 31, 2010	Acquired 60 % ownership of Beijing Natural Gas Pipeline Co., Ltd. with RMB18.9 billion	−1.38
Average		3.85[b]

Source: Literature search and author's calculation

[a]Three-day abnormal returns (from day −1 to day +1)

[b]Statistically significant at the 5 percent level

CHINA RESOURCES ENTERPRISE[11]

China Resources Enterprise (stock code: 0291.HK, CRE hereafter) is the subsidiary of China Resources Holdings, one of the largest central government-controlled SOEs in China. CRE is one of the listed companies of China Resources Holdings. It is by itself a conglomerate with businesses spanning retailing, beverages, food processing, textiles, and real estate in mainland China and Hong Kong. Its core assets include a 51 percent share in China Resources Snow Breweries Co., the largest brewing company in China and a joint venture with SAB Miller. SAB Miller currently holds 49 percent shares in China Resources Snow Breweries Co.

Despite the fact that CRE runs a wide range of businesses, it has two main business segments: bricks and mortar and beer. CRE is the first listed company of China Resources Holdings and it is a Hang Seng Index constituent stock. For quite a long time, it has been one of the best performing blue chips in the Hong Kong Market. From May 2006 to April 2011, CRE's total returns to shareholders (TRS) averaged at 19 percent per year, beating retailers such as Wal-Mart (5 percent), Gap (7 percent) and Carrefour (−5 percent). However, compared to beer companies, CRE's stock market performance was somewhat unimpressive during the same time period. Although CRE's annual TRS (19 percent) was higher than that of Carlsberg (14 percent), Anheuser-Busch InBev (15 percent), and Heineken (7 percent), and on par with that of Yanjing (19 percent), one of the top three breweries in China, it was worse than the stock market performance of SAB Miller (21 percent) and its main Chinese competitor, Qingdao Beer (36 percent).

How can we assess CRE's stock market performance? As a conglomerate with multiple core businesses, the results crucially hinge on how we perceive CRE: Is it a beer brewery or a retailer?

To get the answer straight, I first treat CRE as a bricks and mortar retailer. Figure 6.7 compares the ROIC of CRE with that of two leading global retailers—Wal-Mart and Colruyt. To better understand what had caused the differences in the ROIC of the three companies, I also decompose ROIC into different components along profit margin and capital turnover.[12] As shown in Fig. 6.7, in 2010, CRE underperformed both Wal-Mart and Colruyt by a large margin—the pre-tax ROIC of CRE was only 5 percent, which was about one-third of that of Wal-Mart and a tiny fraction of that of Colruyt. When I analyze the sources of ROIC, it is found that the key factor causing differences in ROIC is the invested capital-to-revenue ratio. The ratio is 68 percent for CRE, and it is only 30 percent for Wal-Mart and 16 percent for Colruyt. A further analysis shows that high fixed assets–to-revenue ratio is the main reason that CRE has reported high invested capital-to-revenue ratio—CRE has employed much more capital in its operation than the other two companies. Note that because of the capital-intensive nature of CRE's business, it has a higher level of depreciation, which further erodes CRE's profit margin.

As Fig. 6.7 shows, when one views CRE as a retailer, CRE is not a great value creator. Still, CRE had reported a relatively stronger market performance than the other two retailers, which is puzzling. The potential explanation for this is that investors had counted on the high growth rate

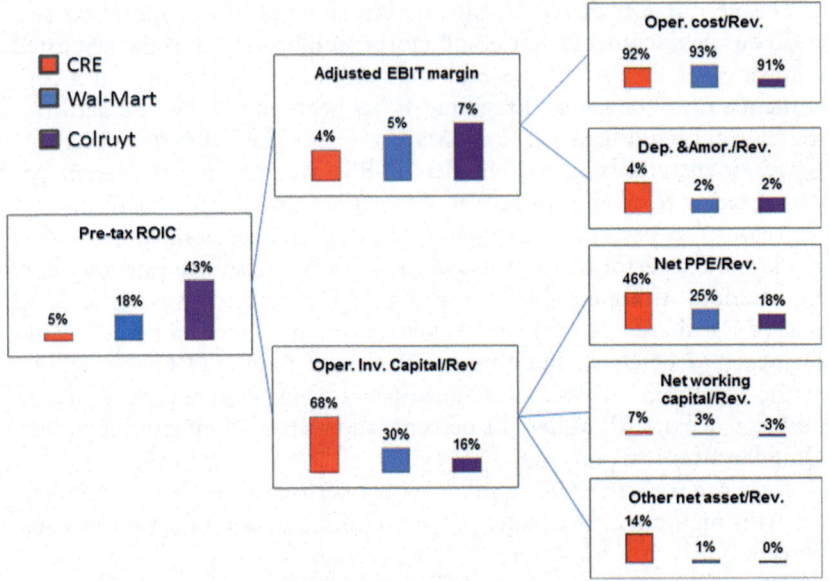

Fig. 6.7 The ROIC analysis of CRE, Wal-Mart, and Colruyt, 2010
Source: Author's calculation based on data from Datastream

of consumption in China. They also believed that CRE had successfully found its footing in the retailing business in China. They have cast their confidence votes on CRE's future.

What would happen if one were to perceive CRE as a beer company? In Fig. 6.8, I compare CRE's ROIC with that of Qingdao Beer and Yanjing—the trio are the three largest beer producers in China and account for more than 40 percent of the Chinese beer market. As shown in Fig. 6.8, CRE underperformed both Qingdao Beer and Yanjing on ROIC: the pre-tax ROIC of CRE was only one-fifth of that of Qingdao Beer and a half of that of Yanjing in 2010.

Here comes the puzzle: CRE had underperformed its benchmarks in both the retailing and beer businesses, but CRE had managed to perform well in the stock market. Clearly, the pricing of the stock of CRE had been driven by investors' positive expectation about its future growth potential. Once CRE fails to deliver such expectations to shareholders, its market performance could deteriorate rapidly.

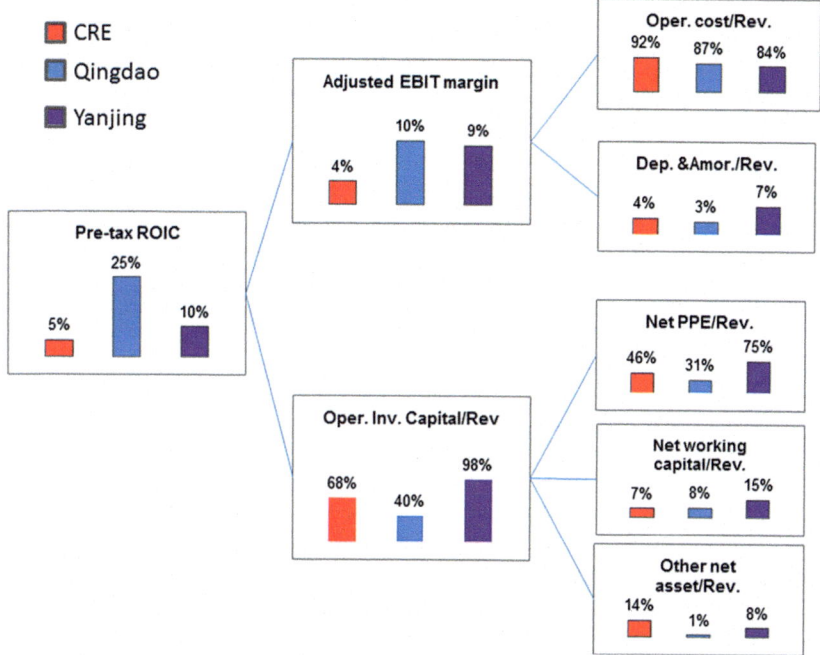

Fig. 6.8 The ROIC analysis of CRE, Qingdao Beer, and Yanjing, 2010
Source: Author's calculation based on data from Datastream

For a conglomerate like CRE, its stock market positioning is unclear. When investors price the CRE stock, should they price CRE against a retailer such as Wal-Mart or a beer company such as Anheuser-Busch InBev? Despite its strong capital market performance, poor market positioning may still bring a valuation discount. In an unreported analysis, I break CRE into three stand-alone segments: retailing, beer, and food. I assume that each segment is a separate company with its firm value determined by the industry average EV/EBIT multiple, where EV stands for enterprise value and EBIT stands for earnings before interest expense and tax. After I sort out the imputed firm value of the three segments, I sum them up. I find that the sum of the three parts has been 180 percent larger than the actual firm value of CRE. That is, having three segments under the same umbrella creates a huge valuation discount. If CRE can be broken into three separate stand-alone entities, more market value could be unleashed.

The Most Recent Developments

In the process of my writing the book, CRE conducted a series of ownership restructurings. Specifically, the conglomerate decided to focus its business on beer. On August 3, 2015, China Resources Enterprise held a special shareholder meeting. At the meeting, shareholders approved the plan proposed by the management team to sell all of CRE's non-beer businesses to CRE's parent company, the China Resources Holdings (The Group). As such, CRE would be able to focus on beer. On October 12, another special shareholder meeting was held. At the meeting, shareholders voted to change the name of CRE to China Resources Beer (Holdings) Company Limited (CRB).

Through these transactions, the original CRE had finally shifted its business focus to beer. The new entity, known as CRB now, is a specialized beer producer with 98 plants in 25 provinces. The company's total capacity, as of end 2015, reached more than 20 million hectoliters. CRB also owns Snow, the bestselling beer in the world, and had a market share of 23.2 percent in China. When consumption becomes the key theme for the Chinese economy in years to come, the new company will be well positioned to tap into the ever-increasing consumption wave through its focused strategy.

NOTES

1. See "The China effect on global innovation," McKinsey Global Institute (2015a).
2. There are three main regulatory authorities in financial services, the Chinese Banking Regulatory Commission (CBRC), the Chinese Securities Regulatory Commission (CSRC), and the Chinese Insurance Regulatory Commission (CSRC).
3. Note that in this book I use diversification and conglomeration interchangeably.
4. See Liu and Qi (2008).
5. See The Economist, "From Alpha to Omega" (August 15, 2015d), for an insightful discussion about the recent examples of conglomeration.
6. See Krugman (1994).
7. See Liu et al. (2013).
8. See The Economist, "Click to mortar" (August 15, 2015).
9. I chose November 2007 as the beginning period because PetroChina issued A-shares in the Chinese stock market in that month. Thus, we can

compare PetroChina's A-share market performance with that of Kunlun Energy.

10. The results remain intact if I use CAPM or other asset pricing models to compute the benchmark returns.

11. My analysis of China Resources Enterprise (CRE) uses data up to 2011. What happened to CRE after 2012 largely confirmed the policy suggestions based on my analysis.

12. As I only use the data in 2010 to analyze the differences in ROIC, the results should be taken with caution. Of course, when I extend the analysis to other years, the results remain largely intact. For brevity, I do not report them in the book.

CHAPTER 7

Shake Up the Foundations

The Chinese economy is now confronted with various severe challenges. China is aging. And this is eroding the demographic dividend which has greatly supported China's industrialization and economic takeoff during the early stage of China's reform era. By 2015, there were already 220 million people over 60 years in China. The number is increasing by 8.5 million every year. By 2015, 16 percent of the population in China was over 60 years and 10.5 percent were over 65 years. In the meantime, labor costs are also increasing, thanks to fast economic growth and rising living standards. China's average hourly rate quadrupled over the first decade of the twenty-first century, from $0.6 in 2000 to $2.4 in 2010. Compared to countries such as Vietnam, Bangladesh, and Indonesia, cost is no longer a competitive advantage enjoyed by the Chinese manufacturing firms.

The impact of rising labor cost varies across different industries, and even different firms within the same industry. For industries in which Chinese firms have a relatively shorter value chain such as shoes and clothes, the impact of rising labor cost tends to be large. For example, Adidas had shifted all manufacturing bases out of China to countries like Vietnam. For industries in which corporate China has a longer value chain, the impact is relatively small. China will remain an important manufacturer for the world, but the Chinese manufacturing firms will have to re-skill themselves to adapt to the changing industry dynamics, and prepare themselves for the disruptive thrusts of new technologies and business model innovation.

© The Editor(s) (if applicable) and The Author(s) 2016   155
Q. Liu, *Corporate China 2.0*, DOI 10.1057/978-1-137-55089-7_7

The investment-led growth model is not sustainable. The credit-fueled growth model has resulted in widespread high leverage among the corporate sector. The debt-GDP ratio by corporate China had reached 125 percent as of June 2014, a level much higher than that of the OECD countries. Many manufacturing sectors, especially steel, coal, and aluminum, are fraught with overcapacity. The Chinese government has proposed "the one belt, one road program," and aims at replicating the investment spree in infrastructure and property that China has experienced and found valuable in countries involved. This may help absorb excess capacity in many sectors, but it will take time to see some real effect.

MORE A MARATHON THAN A SPRINT

Let us revisit the growth identity I introduce in Chap. 1: *Growth rate = Investment Rate × ROIC*. As I have discussed, the end scenario of the Chinese economy ten or fifteen years down the road crucially hinges on the aggregate level of return on invested capital (ROIC) of the economy. To achieve an improved ROIC at the aggregate level, China needs to fix the micro-foundations of its economy and improve the ROIC of the Chinese companies.

The importance of ROIC can be further illustrated by the following analogy. Consider two companies growing at 10 percent a year. Company N earns a 20 percent ROIC, and Company O earns 10 percent. The company earning a 20 percent return, that is, Company N, would need to invest only 50 percent of its profits each year to grow at 10 percent, while the company earning a 10 percent return (Company O) would need to invest 100 percent of its profits. So a higher return on capital leads to higher cash flows available to distribute to shareholders at the same level of growth, which means high value for shareholders.

Company O represents old China—the businesses that emerged in China in the past three and a half decades, including automobiles, steel, chemicals, mining, oil and gas, paper, telecommunications, utilities, and so on. Their ROIC used to be high. With China's industrialization almost coming to a close, their ROIC started to decline. They therefore need even larger amounts of capital expenditure to generate further growth. Company N represents new China, that is, the emerging businesses with high ROIC, including pharmaceutical, technology, and so on. Since a company's rate of growth and returns on capital determine how much it needs to invest, Company N can invest less capital and still achieve the same profit growth as Company O does. The takeaway from this example is: Improving traditional businesses' ROIC and encouraging the emergence of new businesses with higher ROIC is the key to sustaining China's economic growth in the future.

Placing an emphasis on ROIC is the key theme permeating this book. However, compared to scaling up operation through investment, improving ROIC is much more difficult. Indeed, transforming corporate China from big to brilliant is a daunting task calling for a large number of indispensable elements, both outside and inside individual firms, to be well in place to make it happen. These elements include a level playing field, a shift in the ultimate goal of firm operation from size to value creation, reconfiguration of the economic landscape (from investment-led economy to consumption-driven economy; from labor- and capital-intensive businesses to intellectual capital-based businesses), innovations in both business models and technologies, and world-class execution, to name just a few. The journey lying ahead is more a marathon than a sprint.

How can corporate China transform from the O-type mentioned above to the N-type? In a sense, the factors that greatly helped the Chinese companies quickly build up their scale are also the factors handcuffing them to become truly great. To accomplish corporate China's unfinished mission, one needs to re-assess the exact factors enabling Chinese firms to achieve a quick breakthrough in the early stage of China's reform era. China-specific institutions are the most important things to look to.

INVESTING IN INSTITUTIONAL INFRASTRUCTURE

To many, China has achieved its economic miracle in the absence of enabling institutions including well-defined and protected private property rights, effective financial intermediation, and rule of law.[1] While most thinkers of our time praise the relevance and importance of institutions to economic development,[2] the economic rise of China still poses a puzzle for many. Indeed, since the outset of opening up and economic reform in the late 1970s, the Chinese government has persistently imposed tight restrictions on resources (labor and capital) mobility.[3] In addition, local protectionism and trade barriers across regions impede interregional flow of goods.[4] However, the Chinese economy has maintained a strong growth momentum despite all these institutional distortions.

There is plenty of evidence showing that poor institutions distort the allocation of resources and adversely affect ROIC. I have discussed this issue in Chap. 4. In a recent paper, Hsieh and Klenow (2009) investigate the impact of factor misallocation across firms within four-digit manufacturing industries on aggregate total factor productivity (TFP) in China and India. They find that a more efficient factor allocation contributed to around two percent a year aggregate TFP growth in China's manufacturing sector between 1998 and 2005. Holz (2009) also found that there had been a significant increase in interregional trade accompanying a reduction in barriers.

Reform in the banking system dating from the late 1990s, including the development of an inter-bank market, also allows a more efficient regional allocation of capital through the inter-bank market and other channels, which improves the efficiency level of resource allocation in the Chinese economy. Obviously, enhancing institutions helps improve ROIC.

The levels of economic development and institutions are uneven across different regions. We can also use variation in levels of institutions across regions to identify the impact of institutions on ROIC, and present a more compelling case that good institutions are conducive to the enhancement of ROIC. In the paper introduced in Chap. 4 (Liu and Siu 2011), I used the discount rate inferred from actual capital expenditures to measure ROIC perceived by firm managers when making investment decisions. With such an investment-based discount rate in hand, I examined its relationship with regional institution variables and found a positive relationship between the two, which suggests that better institutions help improve ROIC.

Specifically, I hypothesize that regions with well-functioning institutions tend to see better investment decisions at the firm level. I use the NERI index compiled in Fan and Wang (2006) to measure the regional level of institutions. Fan and Wang (2006) examined the extent of marketization in each province or province-equivalent municipal cities by focusing on the following five aspects: (1) the relations between the local government and local markets; (2) the significance of non-state sector in the local economy; (3) the development level of product markets; (4) the development level of factor markets; and (5) legal environment, law enforcement, and the development of market intermediaries. The weighted average of scores on the five aspects is computed and used to capture the regional institution level. Not surprisingly, coastal provinces (e.g., Zhejiang, Guangdong, Fujiang, and Jiangsu), Beijing, Shanghai, and Tianjin have scored quite high on NERI, suggesting that they have institutions that are more conducive to market-based transactions.

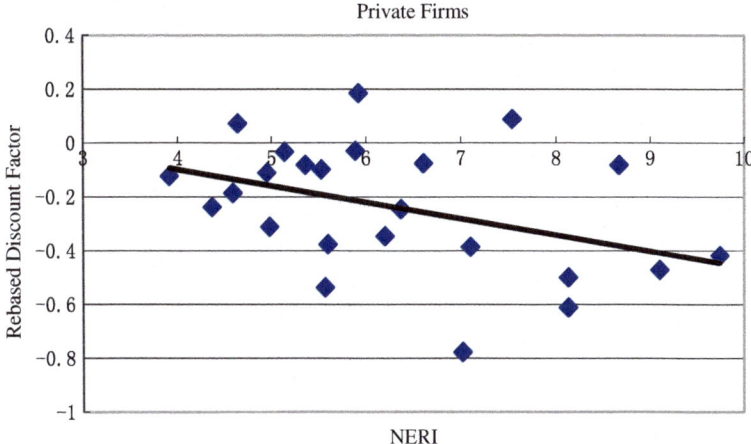

Fig. 7.1 The relationship between the NERI index and discount factor at province level: private firms in China
Source: Author's analysis. See Liu and Siu (2011) for details about the empirics

As shown in Fig. 7.1, I found a significant negative relation between investment-based discount factor and the NERI score among the private firms in China. Note that discount factor is negatively correlated with discount rate (i.e., the relation between the discount factor and the discount rate is as follows: discount rate = 1/discount factor − 1). What I present in Fig. 7.1 suggests that there is a positive correlation between institutions and ROIC.

To get a better sense of the economic significance of the impact of regional institutions on ROIC, I note that the slope in Fig. 7.1 takes the value of −0.061. This suggests that a one unit increase in a region's institution level led to a 6.1 percent decrease in its private firms' effective discount factor, a roughly 6 percent increase in the discount rate inferred from capital expenditure (investment-implied ROIC). For example, the NERI score of Shandong Province is 7.1, while the NERI score of Jiangsu Province is about 8.1. If Shandong can improve its institutions to the level of Jiangsu, then an average private firm in Shandong can harvest a 6 percent increase in its ROIC.

Figure 7.2 repeats the analysis for SOEs across different provinces. Again, I found a significantly negative relation between firm-level ROIC and regional institution level measured by NERI. The slope based on the

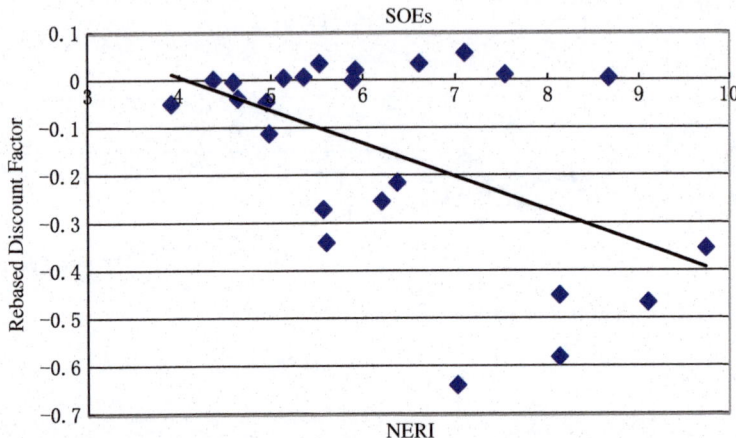

Fig. 7.2 The relationship between the NERI index and discount factor at province level: SOEs in China
Source: Author's analysis. See Liu and Siu (2011) for details about the empirics

regression is even steeper among SOEs, suggesting that enhancing institutional level would generate an even greater and more positive effect on SOEs' ROIC. As the state sector still dominates the Chinese economy, the fact that establishing market-oriented institutions helps improve SOEs' ROIC significantly has particular meaning.

China-specific institutions, including political tournament based on economic performance, tight restrictions on labor mobility both within and between provinces through the household registration system (the hukou system), and strict control over the allocation of capital through the persistent use of a moderate degree of financial repression policy, undoubtedly spur the improbable surge of the Chinese companies in their operation scale. But they severely distort the factor markets and result in massive misallocation of resources in the real economy, which to a great extent explains the paucity of great companies with strong ROIC performance.

Given distorted institutions, a very natural choice for a Chinese firm is to pursue short-term interest by taking advantage of the loopholes in the existing institutional arrangements. Perceiving "institutional arbitrage" as the basic approach to conjure up winning business models provides the strongest motives for many firms to seize those transient time windows, and chase easy, quick, and, sometimes dirty, money. Accordingly, we see many short-lived zombie companies in the Chinese economy but very few great companies.

During China's reform era, China has invested tremendously in building skyscrapers, expressways, high-speed railways, subways, and fancy plazas and shopping malls. Indeed, the infrastructure for economic development has been well in place, thanks to over 30-year heavy investments fueled by bank loans. However, to help corporate China achieve its transformation from "big" to "great," China has to increase investment in another kind of infrastructure—institutional infrastructure. In this respect, the following three areas need to be addressed: (1) governments, especially local governments, need to fundamentally change their role from economic decision-maker to rule-setter and public service provider; (2) the existing financial system needs to be reformed to greatly improve the efficiency of financial intermediation; and (3) an open and fair environment needs to be created to promote innovation and entrepreneurship.

FROM VISIBLE HAND TO INVISIBLE HAND

Guess which region owns the most *Fortune* Global 500 companies in China? Is it Guangdong (including Shenzhen, one of China's most prosperous special economic zones), the most economically developed province in China? Or Jiangsu, which boasts of the same size of economy as Guangdong? The answer, which may surprise some, is Beijing, the capital and political center of China. Out of China's 106 *Fortune* Global 500 companies (including 8 companies from Hong Kong and Taiwan), more than 50 are headquartered in Beijing, including 3 of the world's 10 largest companies—Sinopec, PetroChina, and State Grid—and financial institutions such as ICBC, ABC, BOC, and CCB. Guangdong, which takes the lead position in economic size, only has 6 *Fortune* Global 500 companies, whereas Hong Kong, an international financial center, only has two companies in 2015. By 2014, 90 out of 110 central government-controlled SOEs were headquartered in Beijing, where more than 60 percent of the country's financial assets, 50 percent of the listed companies' registered capital, and 53 percent of the country's bond issuances cluster.

Headquartered in Beijing, these Chinese companies are not far away from the center of political power in the country. It is therefore easier for them to leverage all sorts of political resources to do business. This undoubtedly manifests the strong influence of the government on economic affairs, and the pivotal role played by the administrative power in allocating resources in China.

Think about another example: The very existence of China's five-year plan itself is indicative of how the government's visible hands profoundly affect the economy. In 1953, China launched its first five-year plan, which charted a course for economic development. Since then, every five years, a new five-year plan has been drafted to set specific production and over-all economic growth targets. China's newest plan, the 13th five-year plan, which covers the five-year period from 2016 to 2020, will kick off in 2016. It clarifies many of China's medium-term priorities, indicating where the government wants to take various industries and the whole society. Accordingly, local governments set their own targets, and adjust their rhetoric and policies to fall in line with the grand plan set by the central government; banks allocate funds to industries the plan has chosen to boost; and companies, both state owned and private, change their business strategies to grab investment opportunities listed in the plan.

Every year, the World Bank publishes a report assessing the ease of doing business across different countries. In its newly released 2015 report, China has been ranked 90th, out of 189 economies on the list. According to the survey taken by the research team behind the report, it takes an average of 11 procedures and 33 days to start a business in Beijing, while the OECD average is 5 procedures and 9 days.[5] Although China's premier Li Keqiang has repeatedly urged the government to cut red tape, it may take longer than expected to see the result. For now, the visible hand of the government can be seen everywhere.

Helping Hand or Grabbing Hand

What economic role do governments play? This has been an unsettled issue that is still causing endless debates in the academic research and the policy arena. Adam Smith emphasized the role of the marketed-based price system. The invisible hand of the market can effectively allocate resources among competing ends to achieve a competitive equilibrium. The first welfare theorem states that any competitive equilibrium leads to a Pareto-efficient allocation of resources. And the second welfare theorem states that any efficient allocation can be sustained in a competitive equilibrium. The two theorems are the building blocks of neo-classical economics and are believed to have fully embodied the spirit of Adam Smith's "invisible hand" thesis: Let the markets fully function and the resulting outcome will be the most efficient.

However, the examples of market failure abound as the real world is riddled with frictions and distortions that have been assumed away in theory—imperfect markets, information asymmetry, moral hazard problems, and so on. The laissez-faire market economy from time to time leads to economic stagnation, unemployment, income inequality, speculative bubbles, monopoly, environment problems, and financial crisis. In contrast with the "invisible hand," the advocates of the "helping hand" emphasized the role of governments in economic development. Government intervention into economic activities can better allocate resources, fix the problems in the markets, and thus, promote economic development.

The "helping hand" hypothesis is built on the assumption that the government can best represent the benefits of the whole society, and its ultimate goal is to achieve maximal social welfare. For quite a long time, there had been heated debates between the advocates of the "invisible hand" and the "helping hand." There were also many social experiments conducted in different countries and during different time periods. To a certain extent, the bulk of the economic history of the twentieth century could be written around policies and experiments associated with these two views on government.

Yes, there are plenty of examples of market failure. But government failure is by no means rare. Widespread corruption, inefficient state sector, wasteful investments, and shameless exploitation of underrepresented groups by the privileged few, among many others, sound an alarm bell for advocates of the "helping hand." In a totalitarian society, the government may well represent the interests of the dictator; in a democratic society, the government likely represents the interests of the voters, who help them win the election.

In "The Calculus of Consent," the late political economists James Buchanan and Gordon Tullock point out that to curry favor with supporting groups, the government has incentives to exploit those failed minority groups through punitive transfer. On this point, the government acts as an agent who serves the interest of the principals such as dictators, or selected voters. The principal-agent problems that usually apply in the corporate setting may apply to the political arena as well. Treating the government as an agent allows us to better understand incentives and behavioral patterns of the government, and design better public governance mechanisms to discipline it.

Here comes the problem: If the government does not represent the interests of the whole society, can we still rely on the government to achieve a social optimum? Even worse, if the government acts as an agent of a certain interest group, the visible hand of the government may very likely be a grabbing hand.[6] That is, the government only makes decisions to benefit the interest group it represents rather than the general public. As such, the most natural rationale behind government decisions is rent-seeking. The government is incentivized to deliberately generate rent-seeking opportunities for the interest group to grab. In "*economics of shortage, the*" economist Janos Kornai points out that the commonly experienced shortage of goods and services in socialist countries was man-made. With shortage, those privileged groups would have a final say about how to ration goods and services, which gives them rent-seeking opportunities in the form of taking bribe, distributing scarce resources to people who can meet their special interests.

Taking cues from the "helping hand" hypothesis, China had adopted a planned economy approach to develop its economy until 1978, when China launched economic reform. Before 1978, the Chinese government simultaneously played multiple roles in the economy: the central planner, regulator, and active participant in economic activities. During China's reform era, China gradually introduced the market-based price system into economic activities and developed a mixed type of economy, which combines the features of both a planned economy and a market economy.

The proactive involvement of the government in economic matters is one of the reasons that China achieved an economic miracle in the early stage of the reform era. The political tournament based on economic performance, as I have discussed extensively in Chap. 1, provides local governments with strong motives to focus on local development. However, when China shifts the focus of its economic growth from investment-led to consumption and efficiency-driven, the helping hand of the government becomes less impressive.

In the Chinese context, government being a strong economic decision-maker leads to two distortions. First, the investments made by the government and fueled by bank loans are largely inefficient; and second, government involvement in market competition may very likely distort the price system, which eventually causes inefficient allocation of resources. On the first distortion, let me use the analysis of local government debt (as shown in Fig. 7.3) to illustrate the inefficiency of investments driven by local governments.

As discussed in Chap. 1, the Chinese growth story can be characterized as a combination of political centralization and economic decentralization. Under economic decentralization, the political tournament among local governments provided local officials with strong incentives to develop the

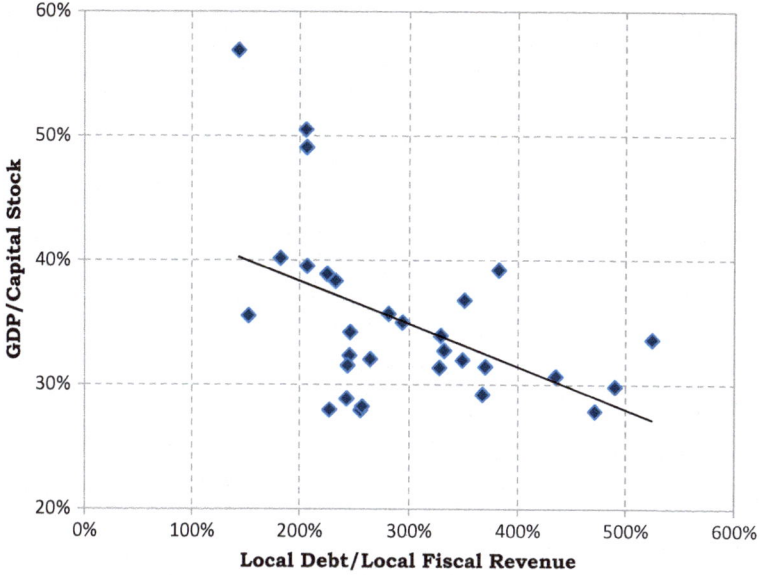

Fig. 7.3   Local investment efficiency versus local government debts
Source: Author's calculation

economy, especially in the early stage of China's reform era when product markets and indispensable elements for a fair market competition were absent. Competition among local governments in some sense substituted for market competition.

The tax reform conducted in the early 1990s changed the split of the tax revenues between the central government and local governments. Relative to local governments' ever-increasing expenditures, fiscal revenue at their disposal was not enough—the gap has been largely filled by revenues from land sales and/or local government debts.

Nevertheless, the ROIC of local government investments may not be high enough to cover the cost of funding as a result of moral hazard and soft budget constraint problems. Local governments hence have to rely on new debts to cover the repayment of old debts. Over time, local government debts pile up. As of June 2013, the total amount of local government debts had reached RMB 18 trillion.

In Fig. 7.3, I show that the pile-up of local government debts has a lot to do with a low level of investment efficiency at the local government level. Particularly, I use the debt-to-fiscal revenue ratio to measure the leverage ratio of a certain province or province-equivalent municipal city (horizontal axis); I use the local GDP-to-local capital stock ratio to measure investment efficiency. Here, local capital stock is calculated as the sum of the previous 20 years' fixed-asset investments depreciated at an annual rate of 5 percent.[7] Clearly, at the province level, there is a significantly negative correlation between local investment efficiency and local government debt. The provinces with high investment efficiency tend to have lower levels of government debt-to-fiscal revenue ratio. The local government debt issue in China, unlike what the policy-makers firmly believe, is not an issue of size or scale—it is an issue of how local debts have been used and whether they have been used efficiently.

On the second distortion, if the government also participates in market competition, then a level playing field can no longer be taken for granted , especially when effective public governance mechanisms are missing. When the state sector dominates an economy, the prices formed in the market may be biased and cannot effectively guide the allocations of resources. As a result, the overall efficiency level of the economy would be compromised.

In 2014, for the first time in the history of the People's Republic of China, the central government revised the Budget Law and gave ten selected provinces and cities the green light to issue their own debts. This experiment provides an ideal setting to study how the prices of local government debts were formed and whether the prices were efficient.

Table 7.1 presents the results of the experiment, in which the differences between the local government debt rate and the treasury rate with the same maturity are compiled.[8]Intriguingly, as shown in Table 7.1, most

Table 7.1 Differences between local debt rate and treasury rates (June–September 2014)

Area	5-year maturity (%)	7-year maturity (%)	10-year maturity (%)
Guangdong	0.00	0.01	0.00
Shandong	−0.20	−0.21	−0.20
Jiangsu	0.03	0.00	−0.01
Jiangxi	0.02	0.02	0.02
Ningxia	0.00	−0.02	0.01
Qingdao	0.00	0.04	0.05
Zhejiang	0.01	0.01	0.01
Beijing	−0.01	−0.01	−0.01
Shanghai	0.03	0.02	0.04

Source: Compiled by the author based on publicly available information

local government debts have an interest rate on par with or even lower than that of treasury bonds with the same maturity. For example, in the case of Shandong Province, the local debts with 5-, 7-, and 10-year maturities had yield rates 20, 21, and 20 basis points lower than those of the treasury bonds with the same maturities. Does Shandong province have better credit ratings than the People's Republic of China?

What follows is a preliminary analysis of the Chinese local government debt market. Investors in local government debts are mainly the local branches of large state-owned commercial banks such as ICBC, Bank of China, China Construction Bank, and Communications Bank, where the local governments deposit their fiscal revenues. When bargaining with these financial institutions about the prices of local government bonds, fiscal revenue deposits, which could easily amount to more than RMB 10 billion, can be very powerful bargaining chips tightly held by local governments. Anecdotes have shown that the more concentrated the fiscal revenue deposits in the state-owned banks, the more powerful the local governments are in the process of bargaining for favorable debt rates.

With the cost of local government funding so severely distorted, how could one expect the local government to be an efficiency-driven economic decision-maker?

Reconfiguration of the Government

The government being an agent or rent-seeker will inevitably give rise to various agency problems. The central or local governments, both of which have their own built-in interests, may take actions that are beneficial to themselves only. Interpreting the government as an agent or a rent-seeker can generate a rich set of policy implications. First, it helps to better understand how existing game rules were formulated—the existing public governance system is at best a bargaining result between the government and interest groups that may have hijacked the government. It cannot be perfect from a social welfare maximization point of view. Second, it provides valuable insights on how to reform the existing system to better reflect the interests of the public. This requires deep institutional reforms that can solve those agency problems. The likely starting point is to limit the influence of interest groups behind the government. A practical approach may be to let the market play a decisive role in allocating resources.[9]

Chinese governments have to learn to have their grabbing hands tied up, and change their role from active interventionist to rule-setter and rule-defender. In doing so, the governments need to take the following initiatives. First, they should stop driving economic growth through their investments. After decades of high-speed economic growth, the market mechanisms have expanded considerably and are playing increasingly important roles in allocating resources among competing ends in the economy. Chinese companies have also reshaped their expectations about governments—what they need are level playing fields and effective public governance rather than hard-charging competitors endowed with many privileges.

Second, on a related point, the government should make it very clear that its role is to set rules and maintain a fair and transparent environment for the market-based mechanisms to work. The ongoing reforms, including privatizing the state sector, letting the market play a more decisive role in allocated resources, and reforming the production factor markets, should be furthered. Without full-fledged reforms in these areas, a market-based environment for fair competition cannot be formed. The government's policy preference should tilt in this direction.

Third, the government should be committed to cutting corporate tax, and taking initiatives to define and protect private ownership and property rights. High tax affects corporate China's competitiveness and holds it back from actively taking on productivity. Poor protection of property rights erodes private entrepreneurs' confidence in an extremely uncertain time, dwindles their investment incentives, and discourages them from eschewing short-term benefits for long-term development.

Good Finance versus Bad Finance

The key to China's future economic success is ROIC. When China runs out of the "demographic dividend" and the credit-fueled growth model becomes unsustainable, leveling up TFP will become the most feasible source of China's future economic growth. In this setting, China needs a new generation of finance to facilitate the metamorphosis of its corporate sector.

The role of finance is to produce trade and settle financial contracts among the participants of economic lives that can be used to pool funds, share risks, transfer resources, produce information, and provide incentives. Effective financing should provide a strong support for the real economy. The current financial system in China, which I label "finance 1.0," is associated with three fundamental flaws, namely, inefficient financial intermediation, suboptimal structure, and poor financial services coverage.

On the first point, because of long-standing interest rate regulation,[10] for quite a long time, the interest spread between the deposit rate and lending rate had been maintained at somewhere around 3 percentage points in China. In the first half of 2015, the finance industry's share of GDP reached more than 9.5 percent in China. The incomes received by financial intermediaries such as commercial banks, investment banks, and others types of financial intermediaries measure the aggregate costs of financial intermediation—they are in essence the sums of all interest spreads and non-interest fees paid by economic participants (i.e., firms, households, and governments). The financial industry's share of GDP captures the profitability of the financial industry. Higher profitability is essentially a curse on the real economy. In the first half of 2015, to generate one dollar of financial asset in the form of either debt or equity in China, the real economy needs to shoulder a financing cost of more than 9.5 cents.

Thomas Philippon, a finance professor at the Stern School of Management at New York University, studies the US finance industry's GDP share in the past 130 years. He offers compelling evidence that the US finance industry's GDP share grew slowly from 2 percent to 6 percent from 1880 to 1930; it shrank to less than 4 percent in1950, thanks to the Great Depression. It increased again after 1980, and reached its peak—close to 8 percent right before the 2008–2009 global financial crisis—then declined to about 7 percent in the wake of the global financial crisis. Despite the fact that the finance industry's GDP share in the USA has varied dramatically in the past 130 years, Thomas Philippon points out that most of the variation can be explained by corresponding changes in the quantity of intermediated assets—financial intermediation has constant return to scale and an annual cost of 1.5 to 2 percent of intermediated assets in the USA[11]

Compared to the USA, where financial intermediation is much more sophisticated and efficient, the Chinese financial industry's GDP share of 9.5 percent is simply too high. An average interest spread of 3 percent suggests that intermediation in China has an annual cost of 3 percent of intermediated assets; compared to 1.5 to 2 percent in the USA, financial intermediation is simply too expensive in China.

On the second flaw of Finance 1.0—suboptimal structure—it is worth noting that the Chinese financial system is bank-oriented. As of 2014, the total amount of financial assets concentrated in the banking institutions had reached RMB 160 trillion, [12] accounting for more than 70 percent of China's total financial assets. As a result, risks incurred in the process of financial intermediation and real economic activities tend to concentrate in the banking system. This, on the one hand, greatly increases the systemic risk within the banking institutions; on the other hand, it dwindles the importance of the capital markets.

On the limited financial services coverage, it is well known that in China only a small portion of the corporate sector and households can access products and services provided by China's financial system. The number of registered firms (including individual firms) has reached over 50 million. Out of 50 million firms, less than 10 percent have access to a banking system. According to the IMF, as of 2007, there were only 1.3 bank branches per 100,000 people in China; the number was 36.3 in the USA, and 49.4 in Germany. Obviously, a large part of the Chinese economy has been left out of services provided by the formal financial system.

The aforementioned flaws are largely associated with the financial repression policy adopted by the Chinese government during the reform era to speed up China's industrialization. While financial repression has spurred the rapid growth of the Chinese economy and has given birth to many large companies, its adverse effects are also piling up.

Why Does More Money Not Flow from Low-ROIC Sector to High-ROIC Sector?

Capital tends to flow from areas with lower returns to areas with higher returns. This is the nature of capital. However, University of Chicago economist Robert Lucas raised a puzzling question in 1990: Why does more money not flow from rich countries to poor countries? According to Lucas, money should flow from developed countries to developing countries simply because developing countries boast of higher marginal returns of capital as they are still in the early stage of industrialization and capital tends to be scarce. The rule of diminishing return of capital thus applies here—developing countries would gain enormously from a little more capital investment. [13]

However, what Lucas found was that the amount of capital flowing from developed countries to developing countries was much smaller than expected. Although not specified by Lucas, researchers following Lucas have suggested a number of factors that may account for the Lucas puzzle, including segmented global financial markets, restrictions imposed by sovereign governments on cross-border capital flows, high transaction costs, and so on. Such imperfections in the real world greatly limit the free flow of capital. Since the publication of the Lucas article in 1990, both globalization and digitalization have escalated. According to the theory of neo-classical economics, when globalization and technologies advance, transaction costs will be significantly reduced. As a result, capital flows from developed countries to developing countries should increase. But people have seen a completely opposite movement—a large amount of capital is still flowing from developing countries to developed countries. The USA, the world's largest economy, is also the world's largest debtor. Aggressively pursuing an export-led strategy, China has over time accumulated close to US$ 4 trillion of foreign exchange reserves.[14] However, the majority of the foreign exchange reserves have been invested in the markets in the USA and other developed economies. Former IMF chief economist Raghuram Rajan and his coauthors Eswar Prasad and Arvind Subramanian called this reversed movement of capital across borders "the Paradox of Capital."[15]

In China, because the economy is still expanding, there are numerous investment opportunities, especially in the newly emerging industries that are consumption-related. In 2015, the service sector's GDP share exceeded 50 percent for the first time. Despite strong growth in services, compared to 70 to 80 percent of GDP share by the service sector in most developed economies, investment opportunities in China's services sector are plentiful. The room for further capital investment in these areas is huge. However, the lion's share of China's foreign exchange reserves has been allocated in the developed economies rather than in China's much needed sectors.

In addition to the reversed capital flow across borders, the paradox of capital also shows up in another form in China—the capital tends to flow to the areas where ROIC is low. Specifically, capital formation tends to concentrate in the state sector, although this yields lower investment returns, as I have shown in Chap. 4 of this book. From the perspective of the state-owned banking institutions, allocating capital to the state sector is natural and can be easily warranted. Investment projects conducted by large SOEs are implicitly guaranteed by the paternalistic governments. Lending to the state sector is safer. In the meantime, because interest rates are still strictly regulated in China, the interest rate spreads have been quite stable and have been maintained at around 3 percentage points for most of the past 15 years. This provides the banking sector with strong incentives to lend to the state sector, which boasts of a combination of stable return and low risk.

In Chap. 4, I analyze the distribution of corporate ROIC across different ownership types, and show that SOEs in China on average have ROIC that are 4 to 6 percentage points lower than that of the non-state sector. Given the difference, in theory, the money should shift away from the state sector and move to the more profitable non-state sector. In reality, we have observed the exactly opposite scenario. Especially since 2009, as the result of a series of government initiatives to stave off the adverse impact of the global financial crisis, huge amounts of money were pumped into the less efficient state sector. Before 2008, there were no noticeable differences in debt-to-asset ratio between SOEs and non-state firms: For China's more than 200,000 "above scale" manufacturing companies, the average debt-asset ratio was around 60 percent for both SOEs and non-state firms before 2008. However, we observed a divergent pattern beginning in 2009. While the debt-asset ratio of SOEs continued to spike and approached 65 percent, the debt-to-asset ratio of non-state firms had declined steadily. As of 2013, there was an almost ten percentage point difference in debt-asset ratio between SOEs and non-state firms already. Multiple reasons can be drafted to explain this divergence. Since 2009, many large projects initiated by the government to boost the economy have concentrated in the state sector, including SOEs and local governments with the support of banking lending. In addition, many investments conducted by the state sector were not profitable. Using new debts to cover the repayment of old debts leads to the pile-up of debts in the state sector.

ROIC is not a key indicator that banks would pay much attention when making lending decisions. When interest rates are regulated and private capital is not allowed to freely enter the banking sector, lending to SOEs or local governments is the most natural decision. Though interest spread does not vary much across different types of firms, as borrowers, SOEs and local governments are much safer because the paternalistic governments can always act as the last resort. More than 70 percent of China's banking lending has gone to the state sector, despite its low ROIC.

The money swarming into sectors with lower ROIC results in the pile-up of debt in certain areas of the economy, and has further aggravated the overcapacity problems in various parts of the Chinese economy, when those less favored sectors in the economy (i.e., SMEs and private companies) are still plagued by external financing constraints. The essence of "the paradox of capital" is financial repression.

Finance 2.0

Only when capital can flow freely from low-ROIC to high-ROIC areas can finance facilitate the emergence of truly great companies in China. This calls for a complete overhaul of China's existing financial system. China needs to deepen the reforms of its financial system by enhancing the efficiency of financial intermediation, optimizing the structure of the financial system, and improving the coverage of financial services. In short, China needs good finance.

What characterizes good finance? Since the 2008–2009 global financial crisis, policy-makers and economists have called for a series of reforms with the tone of "making finance boring." Finance is good in the sense that it is able to link the end supplier and the end-user of funds in simple, direct, and effective ways. "Simplicity," "Directness," and "Effectiveness" are hence criteria for judging whether a finance is good or not. To make finance simple, direct, and effective, cutting off unnecessary layers between the two ends of financial intermediation is a must. This calls for more effective ways to resolve information asymmetry between the end-user and end supplier of funds, and align the incentives of intermediaries. The current financial system is becoming a bad finance simply because there are too many intermediate layers between the two ends of finance. The presence of so many layers in between makes the financing process opaque and costly. The fact that the GDP share of the finance industry in China amounted to more than 9.5 percent during the first half of 2015 is a compelling piece of evidence showing that China needs a completely different sort of finance—Finance 2.0!

Finance 2.0 ideally should follow the features below. First, Finance 2.0 should be more efficient in allocating scarce funds among competing ends. It should be able to address the Chinese version of "the paradox of capital," and, broadly speaking, it should facilitate the improvement of Corporate China's ROIC. Second, Finance 2.0 should reach out to more people and more firms, especially underprivileged people, and SMEs who have long suffered from stringent external financing constraints. Finance is for everyone, not just a select group of people or entities. Third, Finance 2.0 should help reduce the reliance of the Chinese economy on the banking sector. As of end 2014, out of RMB 180 trillion worth of financial assets in China, more than 70 percent was generated by the banking sector. The corporate bond market and stock market only account for a small fraction of China's overall intermediated assets. With such a suboptimal structure, a disproportionate amount of risk has concentrated in the banking sector, which makes the whole financial system extremely fragile. Finally, Finance 2.0 should work effectively to contain risks, improves people's consciousness of risks, and enhance their understanding of the nature of finance and the difference between good finance and bad finance. More importantly, Finance 2.0 should provide people with better and more reliable information.

How can China get to Finance 2.0? The key lies in institutions. China needs to develop solid institutional infrastructure to ensure that the new generation of financial intermediation will be simple, direct, and effective. To do so, China needs to resolve the bottlenecks that are holding back the development of good finance. On institutional infrastructure, the following are indispensable ingredients necessary for a more effective finance. First, China has to work hard to build up a complete set of laws and regulations governing the financial system. Currently, the China Banking Regulatory Commission (CBRC), the China Securities Regulatory Commission (CSRC), and the China Insurance Regulatory Commission (CIRC) govern China's banking sector, capital markets, and insurance industry, respectively. However, the "one stop shop" universal banking model has gained huge popularity in China, and financial transactions are getting more and more sophisticated. Separate financial supervisory bodies may leave loopholes in financial oversight. Going forward, it is urgent for China to consolidate the regulatory authorities, and to build up a complete, effective, and, more importantly, innovation-tolerant regulatory framework. While all-inclusive monitoring and regulation will definitely stem the vitality of the economy, lax regulations and accompanying "regulatory arbitrage" make the whole financial system frail. Monitoring and regulation can generate lasting effects only if they are more direct and more transparent. On this point, getting rid of those middle layers and having one consolidated regulatory body that oversees the whole financial system is the way forward.

Second, developing a sizable and well-functioning capital market is of huge importance. Like any big and sophisticated economy, China needs a healthy stock market. For investors from households to pension funds, stocks should, in theory, provide a better return over time than banking deposits, and government bonds. For companies, equity financing is an important alternative to bank loans, helping reduce their reliance on debt. Moreover, the scrutiny and rules that come with a share listing should also help improve corporate governance, and, consequently, ROIC.

Before the stock market crash in June 2015, China was inching toward reforms that would fix the distortions in the market. A program launched in 2014 connected markets in Hong Kong and the mainland market. Though subject to strict quotas, this program promised to introduce more of an institutional presence on China's exchange, which helped reduce the pricing distortions. More progress should be made on the IPO process. China has been using the approval system to screen listed companies ever since the reopening of its stock market in the early 1990s. The registration system should be implemented to allow more private companies and growth companies to go public, giving firms more control over the timing and size of their listing (see Chap. 5). Meanwhile, the delisting system should be strictly enforced to improve the quality of the listed companies in China's A-share market. Regulators should also step up supervision of insider trading.

Third, the government should allow the market to play more decisive roles in allocating resources and furthering financial development. In short, the government should cede control over finance. The implications here are twofold: interest rate deregulation, and permitting new entrants (especially from the technology sector and from abroad) into financial services. On the first point, China urgently needs a market-based term structure to reflect the real cost of financing and more effectively allocate funds. On the second point, allowing private capital to enter the finance industry brings a new breed of competition and nurtures potentially more efficient and innovative ways of intermediation.

Finally, China needs to strike a good balance between formal finance and informal finance. Informal finance such as pawn shops, underground financing platforms, and, now, internet financing platforms including P2P lenders, to a certain extent, improves access to finance for SMEs and underprivileged individuals and households. Proponents of the informal sector weigh in on its positive role, epitomized by Hernando De Soto in *The Mystery of Capital*: "The formals themselves first give informality room to develop." Indeed, informal finance surged in China mainly because the formal financial system failed to service the real sector in simple, direct, and effective ways, which leaves a lot of room for informal financial intermediaries to blossom. However, in the absence of regulations and appropriate legal protection when disputes erupt, informal finance unavoidably is associated with problems such as cheating, flying lending rates, and a high level of non-performing debts. Without any doubt, informal finance has complemented the poorly performing formal finance. But it does not provide the answers to structural problems associated with the overall financial system. The final solution should be strengthening China's institutional infrastructure so that informal finance will surface and eventually be integrated into the formal system. It is time to push these initiatives forward.

The Enduring Power of Entrepreneurship

After studying and working in the western world for 15 years (5 years at UCLA and 10 years in Hong Kong), I was about to make a decision on whether to return to Beijing in 2010. As a researcher on the Chinese economy and Chinese finance, returning to the mainland was not a hard decision—you want to be where the activities are in order to better understand those activities. Almost six years has passed since I moved to Beijing, and I can still feel the excitement of seeing the Chinese economy power ahead like a high-speed train. There are bumpy roads ahead and the train may have to slow down a bit to avoid derailing, but China remains the growth engine of the world.

I always remember a scene that occurred several years ago. At about four o'clock in the morning of a winter day, I walked out of a bar in Sanlitun, an area where Beijing's late-nighters hang out. Cold and half drunk, I decided to walk for a while before hailing a cab. I passed by the gate of a newspaper building, in front of which about 20 young newsboys gathered, taking instructions from a young team leader. It was still dark. But at this time, more than one million people were already up, delivering newspaper and milk, carrying vegetables from outside the town to bazaars in every corner of the city, preparing breakfast at small food shops all around the city. They used their hard work to hail the arrival of a new day. The 20-plus young and enthusiastic faces have ever since stuck in my memory. They came to Beijing from the countryside to search for opportunities that could change their fate. Years later, some of them may become real estate agents or sales representatives; they may further their education and find an office job, or open their own companies. Of course, not all of them will be equally successful. But coming to cities like Beijing is one important step—people living in cities enjoy better education and income, more accessible medical services, and higher living standards.

Indeed, what these aspiring young people pursue is better access to opportunities so that they can advance themselves during an extremely uncertain era. Building an equal and transparent system to protect these young people's aspirations for better lives, and enable them to transcend social ladders and be the masters of their own fates, is the foundation for China's sustainable growth and for the emergence of great companies in China.

The Micro-Foundations of the Economy

After China emerged as the world's second largest economy and its largest growth engine, people started to compare the Chinese economy with the US economy. On the surface, the Chinese economy has lagged behind the US economy for two reasons. First, although the GDP growth rate dropped to below 7 percent in 2015, the economic growth rate in China still more than doubles that of the USA. Second, with more than $3.4 trillion of foreign exchange reserves in hand, the Chinese government remains the largest creditor of the US government.

As a corporate finance researcher, when I assess the two economies, I am more inclined to compare their balance sheets. The level and structure of debts and the quality of assets speak louder. Households, financial inter-mediaries, non-finance firms, and governments are the main economic participants in an economy. The interactions among the four types of economic agents decide the future dynamics and the health of an economy. Checking their respective balance sheets sheds light on how things are at work.

Compared to the Chinese government, the US government has balance sheets with poor quality, suggested by a high-flying government debt. As of June 2014, the government debt-to-GDP ratio was 89 percent in the USA. Although the Chinese economy has also been plagued by the local government debt problem, the total government debt-to-GDP ratio is only 55 percent. Obviously, the Chinese governments are in much better shape.

The total amount of debt held by American households, as of June 2014, was 77 percent of the US GDP. In the case of China, the ratio was 38 percent. Although explanations vary, there is no denying the fact that Chinese people are more frugal and save more.

Now, let us compare the corporate sector, the micro-foundations of an economy. The total amount of debt held by financial intermediaries was 65 percent of GDP in China, while the number was 36 percent in the USA. The lower level of debt held by the financial institutions in the USA reflects two facts. First, the financial institutions in the USA have succeeded in deleveraging in the wake of the Great Recession (also known as the 2008–2009 global financial crisis); and second, the financial system in China is still bank-dominated. Therefore, the debt owned by banks tends to stay at a higher level.

The largest difference between the USA and China lies in the balance sheets of non-finance firms. The USA boasts of 128 *Fortune* Global 500 companies in 2015, and the number for China is 106. China is catching up. However, if we check on corporate profitability and the quality of firm assets, there exists a huge difference between the two countries. As of June of 2014, the ratio of corporate debt (excluding financial firms) to GDP was 67 percent in the USA. Nonetheless, the corporate debt-to-GDP ratio in China was as high as 125 percent. The Chinese firms were on average much more highly leveraged than their US counterparts. Behind the high leverage ratio of corporate China lies the fact that the majority of Chinese firms fail to deliver returns to their shareholders. As I have shown in Chap. 3, listed companies in China registered an average ROIC of 3 percent only, while their American counterparts reported an average ROIC of more than 10 percent in the past one hundred years. The three largest companies (by market capitalization) in the USA are respectively Apple, Google, and Microsoft, all of which are technology companies. The three largest companies (by market capitalization) in China's A-share market are respectively Industrial and Commercial Bank of China, PetroChina, and China Construction Bank, all of which are state owned and, more importantly, compete in state-dominated industries providing inputs of production (i.e., energy and funds). They grow quickly by benefiting from the characteristics of China's growth model—high reliance on investment and hence inputs of production such as raw materials, energy, and funds.

The competitiveness of corporate America derives from companies such as Apple, Microsoft, and Google, which are devoted to developing top-notch products or services through innovations. Behind such companies are numerous entrepreneurs and their futile or fruitful efforts. "Stay hungry, stay foolish" allows Steve Jobs and others like him to constantly transcend the boundaries of imagination, reshape the landscape, and eventually change people's lives for the better. Behind such entrepreneurs and their brave endeavors is an ecosystem that tolerates failures, and trusts the bottom-up forces—no matter how trivial they are.

In China, the top-down grand plan still plays an important, if not decisive, role in allocating resources. One of the most recent examples is China's high-speed trains, a top-down and nation-wide effort initiated by the Ministry of Railways. The government drove the innovation by spending generously on purchasing technologies from overseas partners and urging Chinese firms to tailor their offerings to local requirements through incremental innovation.

Most Chinese companies still put operating scale and firm size ahead of maximizing shareholder returns. Going all out to grab as much resource as possible has become the most viable competitive strategy. Its hidden message unfortunately is "too big to fail." For the few entrepreneurs who are innovation-minded, they find that "copy and paste" works pretty well in China. Their success often relies on their ability to take advantage of certain features of the Chinese economy—for example, the massive size of China's consumer market—which enable rapid and large commercialization of business ideas. However, a country's economic growth stems from the vigor illustrated through numerous individuals' efforts and their personal drive for better future prospects. China has benefited tremendously from unleashing individuals' creativity. The bottom-up forces have been proven to be more powerful than top-down administrative forces in incentivizing individuals and companies to focus on economic matters rather than other things.

In the narrative of Robert Solow, a Nobel Laureate in Economics, economic growth is mainly driven by labor, capital, and intermediate inputs. The residuals, which cannot be accounted for by the three factors, are labeled total factor productivity (TFP). There is plenty of evidence showing that TFP is closely related to entrepreneurship and innovation. Now, as China is running out of the demographic dividend, and corporate debt problems have made credit-fueled investments less effective, future growth can only be sustained through continuous improvement on TFP—these are the imperatives for China to promote innovation and entrepreneurship.

Hayek, Keynes, and the Law of Large Numbers

In the 1930s and 1940s, there was a fierce debate between Nobel Laureate Friedrich August von Hayek and John Maynard Keynes on whether the government or the market should play a more decisive role in allocating resources. Keynes emphasized the effective roles of government spending in pushing up aggregate demand, which eventually dragged the economy out of the trap of recession. China's rapid economic growth in the past three and a half decades offers a live example of how the government's active involvement in economic activities boosts economic growth. Hayek, adhering to the great tradition of the Austrian school, stressed the importance of individual information and local information in allocating resources. To him, in addition to capital and labor, diffused information possessed by individual consumers and producers, if aggregated, could guide the allocation of resources and lead to a more efficient production outcome.

In Hayek's view, the knowledge required to solve the problem of what to produce in an economy lies scattered—it includes information on preferences embedded in people's heads, as well as information on costs, technologies, and so on. Collecting this information without market mechanisms is both a practical and a theoretical impossibility. Hayek suggested that relative to a central planner, who only has one piece of information, market prices, which aggregate diffused information of hundreds and thousands of consumers and producers, were more informative, and could therefore better allocate resources.[16]

For Hayek, the central planner's information is less informative and less efficient in guiding the production process for two reasons. First, there is only one piece of diffused information held by the central planner, whereas the market prices are determined by hundreds and thousands of agents' selling and buying decisions. Second, even if the central planner can collect all information, human deductive rationality is simply not up to the job of understanding, predicting, and planning in a system as non-linear and dynamic as the economy. In contrast, market prices are formed based on the demand and supply of a certain product, which reflects the self-interests of the buyers and sellers. Clearly, market prices would be much more informed if the market had enough liquidity and individuals were allowed to trade so that their information could be impounded into the prices.

Chinese policy-makers tend to interpret the differences between Hayek and Keynes in an overly simplified way. The two views are placed at opposite extremes where Hayek represents the market and Keynes represents the government. I would say that China needs both Hayek and Keynes. In the early stage of China's economic development, Keynes played a more important role. And now China has to complete the transition of its growth model from investment-led to efficiency-driven. The source of growth has to shift from capital and labor input to productivity measured by TFP. Innovation and entrepreneurship are the most reliable sources of heightened TFP. The bottom-up efforts, represented by the markets and applauded by Hayek, may be more important.

The importance of Hayek may be better illustrated by applying the law of large numbers (LLN) in probability theory. LLN states that the average of the results obtained from a large number of trials should be close to the number of trials multiplied by the probability of having a success. Suppose that the chance of an R&D project yielding its desired outcome (e.g., finding a cure for cancer) is one out of one thousand. If a top-down approach is applied, for example, the project has been designated by the central government to a certain SOE, the final result may be unpleasant—with more than 99 percent of probability, no solution would be found and the project would fail. Such a small-probability event may very likely discourage any firms who are willing to try. However, if the Hayek approach is adopted, for example, the government has built an environment that encourages massive entrepreneurship and innovation. More than one thousand startups have been established and none of them is actually funded by the state. According to the law of large numbers, the expected value of having success is one. One company will definitely achieve final success, although we do not know which one out of the one thousand will be the lucky draw.

To have more successful innovations, China needs to build well-developed institutional infrastructure, create a fair, equitable, and transparent business environment, and protect and acknowledge the seemingly trivial attempts made by individuals.

The Second Demographic Dividend

It is true that China is aging and the "demographic dividend" is gradually disappearing. But at the same time, new sources of growth are being forged. As of 2030, China will boast of more than 400 million people who were born after 1990, the so-called post-1990s generation. Half of the post-1990s generation—200 million—would have completed college education and have some sort of university degree by then. Even now, China already has more than 100 million people in the labor force who have completed college education. The number in the USA is about 90 million and in South Korea, 9 million. In the history of mankind, there has never been a nation with such a highly educated labor force. Compared to old generations, the post-1990s generation in China are more prone to consumption, and are more likely to be endowed with entrepreneurial spirit. Take a recent episode as the example. On November 11, 2015, Alibaba, the world's largest e-retailer, recorded sales of more than RMB 91 billion (approximately $14.3 billion), a record for a single day anywhere in the world. And most of the buyers are the new generation of Chinese consumers.

The younger generation in China is not afraid of innovation either. Many are stretching their minds to create new business models or new technologies. Google, Facebook, Uber, Airbnb, and Amazon.com all have their Chinese versions. In fact, their Chinese counterparts tend to have larger markets given the deeper consumer base in China. For example, Didi Kuaidi (also known as Didi), a car-hailing company and China's Uber, was forged in 2015 by the merger of two rival taxi-hailing apps, Didi and Kuaidi. In less than three years (both Didi and Kuaidi were born in 2012), it has dominated China's personal transport. In 2015, Didi arranged 1.4 billion rides in China, more than Uber has done worldwide. However, Didi has gone beyond what Uber is doing. Didi allows users to select a taxi, private car, shared car, shuttle van, or bus to pick them up, or even a driver in case the user is drunk. In addition to getting people from point A to point B, Didi Kuaidi is trying to expand its business into other areas. For example, by collaborating with China Merchants Bank, Didi Kuaidi offers car loans for drivers or passengers who want to buy a car; with a large number of drivers and passengers relying on the platform to commute, Didi Kuaidi may very well develop into a social media platform as well.

China is now welcoming its second demographic dividend—emerging labor forces that are much better educated and have innovation in mind. Their rise will fundamentally change the structure of the Chinese economy, and to a great extent decide whether China can smoothly enter into the so-called new normal.

Notes

1. See, for example, Allen et al. (2005) and Xu (2011).
2. See, for example, Acemoglu et al. (2001).
3. See, for example, Brandt and Zhu (2000), Boyreau-Debray and Wei (2005), and Dollar and Wei (2007).
4. See Young (2000).
5. See "Paper tiger, roaring dragon" (*The Economist*, September 12, 2015b).
6. See Shleifer and Vishny (1998).
7. Using other depreciation rates, for example, 5 percent or 8 percent, yields the same qualitative results.
8. I was able to find local debt issuance information for nine provinces and cities.
9. In this setting, a market could be understood as an aggregation of individual decisions.
10. The Chinese government is loosening up the regulation on interest rates. Still, it takes longer time to achieve fully market-based interest rates.
11. See Philippon (2015).
12. Banking institutions include the state-owned banking institutions such as ICBC, BOC, ABC, CCB, and Communications Bank of China, joint stock banks such as the China Merchant Bank, city commercial banks, rural commercial banks, and others.
13. See Lucas (1990). Also see pp.48–49 in Rajan (2010) for further discussion on the capital paradox proposed by Robert Lucas.
14. China's foreign exchange reserves, in 2015, experienced a significant drop. As of end 2015, the total foreign exchange reserves had dropped to US$3.4 trillion. Still, China holds the largest foreign exchange reserves in the world.
15. See Prasad et al. (2007).
16. See Hayek (1945).

CHAPTER 8

The Beginning of a Breakthrough

Ren Zhengfei, the reclusive founder of Huawei, is already a living legend. Right before the Chinese New Year in 2016, a snapshot of Ren Zhengfei circulated on China's most popular mobile internet messaging app, WeChat, and got numerous likes: On the airport shuttle connecting the plane and the terminal, 70-year-old Zhengfei, without any escort, carried his own luggage just like other passengers. The person who stealthily took the photo put down "emotional" lines under the photo: "He is the founder of China's most respectable company; he could easily enjoy all sorts of VIP services but he chose not; he could be as rich as any other tycoons on the Forbes riches list but he had chosen to distribute most of his company's shares to more than 80,000 Huawei employees (out of 170,000 employees worldwide). He is the most admirable business leader in China!"

"Think of Xiaomi as a company that is bringing innovation to everyone." When interviewed by the *WIRED* magazine, Xiaomi's founder, Lei Jun, tried to explain what Xiaomi is all about: "We put an emphasis on high-quality products that help to create a connected lifestyle for everyone as we move into a new era of technological innovation. This doesn't only mean smartphones, tablets, TVs, routers—we invest in startups that form what we call an ecosystem. They make products that are sold on Mi.com, ranging from power banks to wearables to air and water purifiers, so we have hundreds of products that come together to create a lifestyle." The interview was featured as a cover story for *WIRED*'s China Special Issue, which came out in March 2016 with a big splash. Its running title on the

© The Editor(s) (if applicable) and The Author(s) 2016
Q. Liu, *Corporate China 2.0*, DOI 10.1057/978-1-137-55089-7_8

cover goes, "It is time to copy China: What you can learn from its most inventive startups."

Does China have great companies? I have tried to address this question throughout the book. Still I have not provided a definite answer. Great companies are created by great minds. Jack Ma of Alibaba once said, "You must have a dream—what if you realize it!" Xiaomi's Lei Jun refused to be called China's Steve Jobs. Ren Zhengfei of Huawei has taken a less traveled road by insisting on self-developed technologies and it eventually paid off. Wang Wei of SF Express rejected flirting with the capital market so that SF Express could focus on providing quality delivery services. *"We are all in the gutter, but some of us are looking at the stars,"* Oscar Wilde wrote in *Lady Windermere's Fan*. In this chapter, I would like to discuss the companies established by these great business innovators, who have been looking at the stars. By the standards listed in Chap. 2, Huawei, Alibaba, and the up-and-coming Xiaomi and SF express probably cannot be counted as great companies yet, simply because they have not been in business long enough. But into the next decade or so, all of them have a good chance of breaking into the very small elite club of the world's great companies.

HUAWEI: CHINA'S HOMEGROWN MULTINATIONAL[1]

Ren Zhengfei single-handedly founded Huawei in Shenzhen in 1988 with RMB 21,000 of his own money. In the very beginning, Huawei imported telecommunication equipments from Hong Kong and sold them to vendors in China. From the outset, Huawei decided to develop and manufacture its own equipments. Zhengfei's vision was to aggressively build in-house innovation capability. He was convinced that setting up joint ventures with foreign companies would not enable Chinese companies to obtain foreign technologies; on the contrary, the Chinese companies might end up losing domestic markets. Huawei's approach, according to Zhengfei, was to closely follow global cutting-edge technologies and insist on self-development, and to gain domestic market share first, and then explore international markets and compete with foreign companies.

The road taken by Huawei was fraught with uncertainties. Choosing this development strategy clearly suggests that Huawei has to sacrifice short-term benefits for long-term growth. Unlike many other Chinese firms, Huawei has taken it as an internal policy that each year Huawei must spend no less than 10 percent of its sales on R&D—in 2015, R&D

accounted for 15 percent of Huawei's total sales (RMB 60 billion). The employees involved in R&D amounted to 79,000 in 2015 and accounted for more than 45 percent of Huawei's headcount. As a result, intellectual capital is where Huawei really shines—as of 2015, Huawei had submitted 52,550 patents, among which 30,613 were international patent applications. Huawei's R&D strategy pays off.

The first in-house designs of Huawei were for basic switching components. Over time, the company had demonstrated a very steep learning curve. In less than three decades, the privately owned Huawei has grown from an importer of basic telecommunication equipment to a telecommunication equipment giant, supplying equipment and providing related services covering billions of people across the world.

Huawei started with the fast-growing domestic market, where telephone subscriptions grew more than 15 times and mobile phone subscriptions grew 500 times from 1992 to 2000.[2] By providing telecom equipment and services to the Chinese telecom carriers, Huawei's business flourished. By 2002, Huawei had overtaken Shanghai Bell, an Alcatel joint venture, to become the dominant supplier of digital switches and routers in China. As of 2005, Huawei had already captured 30 percent of China's domestic market.

Beginning in the early 2000s, Huawei had set its goal to become a global company. Huawei's cost advantage gave it an edge over other global players in defining and meeting the needs of customers. Compared to its international peers, Huawei can provide quality equipment and service for about 30 percent less. Quickly, Huawei broke into the markets in the neighboring Asian countries, and then expended to developing markets in the African and Latin American regions. In 2004, the company expanded into developed European markets, where it fully leveraged its cost advantage and won contracts from budget-constrained telecom carriers. After building up robust brand and reputation, it started to sign big contracts from major operators such as France Telecom, Vodafone, and the BT Group.[3] In 2005, Huawei's international sales had exceeded domestic sales.

By 2010, Huawei's sales had amounted to $22 billion, making it one of the three largest providers of telecom equipment in the world. As the telecom infrastructure market became saturated, Huawei moved beyond the traditional equipment market and got into smartphones, as well as enterprise. This has charted a clear transition of the company's business from telecom infrastructure to including consumer business and enterprise.

In the long run, Huawei's overall strategy is to leverage its relationship with telecom carriers to offer a broad set of enterprise products including routers, servers, and storage. Meanwhile, Huawei would tap into the smartphone and enterprise markets and build up its core competence in both segments. In 2014, Huawei reported a total sales of RMB 288.2 billion and a net profit of RMB 27.9 billion. The company was ranked 228th on the 2015 *Fortune* Global 500 company list. In 2015, Huawei continued its strong growth momentum with the total sales reported at RMB 390 billion.[4]

Huawei is known for execution efficiency. Strong execution has a lot to do with Zhengfei's military background. He instilled a unique corporate culture within Huawei, which emphasizes devotion, sacrifice, patriotism, discipline, and organizational aggressiveness. Huawei's culture is epitomized by wolves. Zhengfei repeatedly urged his colleagues to learn from the behavior of wolves: tough, aggressive, and hunting in packs. Huawei's path to globalization vividly illustrated its wolf-pack culture. In the early 2000s when Huawei set its sights on the international telecom equipment market, it had to compete with international rivals with much better credentials and a deeper and broader base of intellectual capital. Huawei employed very aggressive tactics including attractive pricing (typically 30–40 percent lower than competitors), dispatching engineers on site even after the completion of the project, providing additional products and services free of charge, hiring local personnel, and so on. These tactics worked very well. Huawei soon entered the low-end equipment markets, gradually building up partnerships with major telecom carriers around the world. Against the common perception that Chinese products were cheap and of low quality, Huawei won several big contracts with renowned global telecom carriers. By 2015, Huawei's international sales had accounted for 55 percent of its total sales. Looking back, while relatively lower labor cost and the abundance of Chinese engineers had played an important role in Huawei's success, Huawei's unique wolf-pack corporate culture was also critical.

Huawei's ROADS Strategy[5]

Huawei's strategy is evolving rapidly. Now, the company's strategy has been phrased as "R"eal-time, "O"n-demand, "A"ll online, "D"IY, and "S"ocial with ROADS as the shorthand. This new strategy largely reflects how Huawei positions its three major business segments in the medium term: telecom carrier, enterprise products, and consumer business. From the outset, Huawei provided telecom equipment and has ever since seen continuous market share gains in both fixed-line and wireless infrastructure markets. Even now its role as telecom carrier still contributes the lion's share of Huawei's revenue, accounting for 59 percent of total sales in 2015 (RMB 232.3 billion) and reporting a year-on-year revenue growth rate of 21 percent. However, as the telecom infrastructure market becomes saturated, Huawei has taken steps to shift its investment focus to the enterprise and consumer businesses.

Huawei's enterprise business contributed 7 percent of total sales in 2015. It grew by 43.8 percent from one year earlier to RMB 27.6 billion. Huawei introduces solutions and services focusing on enterprise networks, cloud computing, data center, and applications in finance, transportation, energy, power, public utilities, ISPs, and governments. With ROADS in mind, Huawei expects to form an ecosystem that can address complex client problems by using integrated solutions. Eventually, Huawei expects to make inroads into the IT hardware market and take shares from traditional IT hardware companies. With a deep and broad portfolio of patents, Huawei has been able to quickly expand its enterprise business. On enterprise business, Huawei firmly believes that by offering a broad portfolio, Huawei can significantly shake up the competitive dynamics of the IT market.

The consumer business, mainly smartphones, grew 72.9 percent in 2015 to RMB 129.1 billion, accounting for 33 percent of Huawei's total revenue. Huawei's smartphone shipments exceeded 108 million units in 2015. It was ranked the third largest smartphone manufacturer in the world, behind only Samsung and Apple.[6] Huawei's strong intellectual capital base pays off tremendously. Along with Sweden's Ericsson, Huawei is now at the forefront of research on 5G technology for the next generation of mobile phones. On the consumer business, Huawei's strategy is to continue to build premium products and focus on quality products. Huawei successfully launched Ascent Mate 7 and P8 under the Huawei brand. It has also built up an e-commerce platform as a new sales channel. Moreover, by following its success in the telecom equipment business, Huawei has moved successfully to international markets. In 2014, more than 50 percent of Huawei's smartphone sales came from overseas. In Myanmar, Huawei already dominates the mobile phone market with 50 percent of market share.

Success Factors

The privately owned and homegrown corporate giant Huawei has taken a road less traveled, which is completely different from other *Fortune* Global 500 companies in China. First, Huawei is not state owned, although its founder Ren Zhengfei's military background did bring certain value-added political support, especially in the early stage of Huawei's development. Unlike the railroad equipment industry in which China has 41 percent of global revenue and China's success is the result of the government being a purchaser and a facilitator of access to knowledge, Huawei's success in telecommunication equipment was mainly based on arduous R&D, marketing efforts, and effective execution.

Second, Huawei competes in a highly competitive knowledge-based industry in which corporate China had a very humble start. Most of the Chinese *Fortune* Global 500 companies rely on their dominant positions in the production factor markets and very high barriers to entry set by the government to succeed. Huawei relies on R&D. In 2015, Huaewei spent more than RMB 59 billion on R&D, more than that of all A-share listed companies combined.

Third, Huawei has developed into a global leader in less than three decades. In 2013, Huawei's sales reached $34.9 billion, exceeding Ericsson's $33.6 billion and becoming the world's largest provider of telecommunication infrastructure. Huawei's sales increased to RMB 288.2 billion in 2014 and RMB 390 billion in 2015. Huawei's total sales is far larger than the sum of the sales of China's three most attention-catching internet giants: Baidu.com, Alibaba, and Tencent, collectively known as BAT.

Fourth, Huawei is probably the only homegrown multinational company in China. As of 2015, more than 55 percent of Huawei's total sales came from overseas; Huawei had also developed a strong and robust base of global clients—more than 500 across 150 countries; Huawei provides telecommunication equipments that serve more than one-third of the world's population. No Chinese firm has gone this far.

Huawei's success is reflected in its ROIC. As the official version of the 2015 annual report is still not available when I write this chapter, I use Huawei's 2014 annual report, which is available from its website, to do the calculation. I extract relevant information to sketch out the return on invested capital (ROIC) of Huawei in 2014. Because Huawei is not a publicly listed company, I do not have further information to embark on a more detailed analysis. In 2014, Huawei's reported revenue was RMB 288.2 billion and its earnings before interest expense and tax (EBIT) was RMB 342 billion. Revenue growth had been strong for Huawei—from 2013 to 2014, its total sales increased by 20.6 percent. Now, let us have a look at the company's invested capital. In 2014, Huawei's working capital amounted to about RMB 89.4 billion. The total amount of fixed assets involved in operation was RMB 29.8 billion. The sum of the two yields the total amount of invested capital, RMB 119.2 billion.

Based on the above numbers, it is not hard to compute the pre-tax ROIC of Huawei in 2014, 28.7 percent. Its ROIC (after tax) was 21.6 percent, suggesting that every dollar of capital invested in Huawei's operation can generate 21.6 cents of after-tax profits. Recall that from 1998 to 2012, the average ROIC of Chinese listed companies was only 3 percent. Huawei's operating results are far better than most of the Chinese listed companies. The mysterious source of Huawei's success is high ROIC.

Analyzing the various components of ROIC sheds further light on Huawei's success. First, the profit margin of the company, defined as the ratio of EBIT to sales, was 11.9 percent in 2014. Although Huawei has been operating in very competitive markets and has been very aggressive in its pricing strategy, Huawei has demonstrated more efficient operation than its peers, with lower production costs for every dollar of sales. Operation efficiency is one important reason that Huawei can achieve a high profit margin in very competitive industries.

Second, the ratio of invested capital to sales was 41.4 percent for Huawei in 2014, suggesting that for $1 of sales, Huawei only needs to invest 41.4 cents of capital. In a capital-intensive industry that calls for huge amounts of investment in both physical and intellectual assets, Huawei has exhibited an impressive record of managing working capital and maintaining higher asset turnover ratio than its rivals. Operating with great capital efficiency, Huawei has managed to stay lean and agile.

To sum up, analyzing Huawei's ROIC, from a corporate finance perspective, shows why Huawei has managed to continuously create firm value: maintaining a strong revenue growth; achieving higher profit margin through efficient operation; and employing more idea-intensive and innovation-oriented approaches to achieve great capital efficiency in a capital-intensive business.

Four factors account for Huawei's improbable surge: a visionary leader and well-defined corporate strategy; taking value creation as the top priority; R&D spending spree; and, lastly, incentive-compatible mechanisms.

A Visionary Leader and Articulated Corporate Strategy
Huawei's success so far crucially hinges on its founder Ren Zhengfei, as evidenced by the three things Zhengfei and Huawei have insisted on from the outset. First, Huawei chose to invest in telecommunication infrastructure, a fast-growing industry that meets the needs of the increasingly connected world. Successful companies need a fast-growing market to sustain their explosive growth. Huawei's choice, probably stemming from Zhengfei's intuition, had proven to be a great one. Second, Zhengfei insisted that Huawei ought to develop its own technologies rather than following international rivals. The self-development strategy eventually paid off: with strong in-house R&D capability, Huawei has built a broader and deeper base of intellectual assets, which allows it to overtake its competitors and take the leading position in telecom infrastructure. Third, Zhengfei has instilled a unique culture within Huawei. Though one should not overstate the power of spiritual force, Huawei's wolf-pack culture allows Huawei to aggressively take domestic market share and, then, international market share.

On corporate strategy, Huawei set as its target in the very beginning that it would one day become the world's leading telecom equipment provider. Along the way, Huawei demonstrates agility in adapting to the ever-changing business environment and the disruptive forces in the market. When the growth of telecom equipment business slows down, Huawei gets into fast-growing consumer and enterprise businesses. Such a dynamic portfolio of business segments ensures that Huawei's fast growth can be sustained because when traditional growth engines have lost steam, new growth engines step in to keep the company's strong growth momentum. On this point, Huawei is a perfect living example of the practical insights raised in the 2000 bestseller *The Alchemy of Growth.*[7]

Investing in R&D
While the competitiveness of companies can be affected by factors such as industry structure, costs of production factors, and government policies, R&D based innovation is a primary and robust source of firm growth. In his internal speeches, Zhengfei repeatedly emphasizes the importance of building strong in-house R&D capability. Huawei has made it a strict rule that the company has to spend at least 10 percent of its revenue on R&D. This is atypical in China as an average SOE spends less than one percent of sales on research and development.

To support the company's R&D strategy, Huawei recruits aggressively at the best engineering schools in China. Out of Huawei's 170,000 employees, more than 95 percent have a college degree. In 2015, more than 45 percent of Huawei's employees were involved in R&D. Huawei has built 16 R&D centers across the world. They are located in China, Germany, Sweden, Russia, and India, among others. As of end 2015, Huawei had submitted more than 83,000 patent applications. Huawei's strong patent portfolio has exhibited tremendous advantages because Huawei can make additional innovations based on existing intellectual capital and trade its patents to get access to other innovations. Although it emphasizes organic growth, Huawei also uses mergers and acquisitions to advance its technologies. A recent example is that in 2014 Huawei acquired a UK firm, Neul, to strengthen its position in the growing market for the Internet of Things.

Take Value Creation as the Top Priority
In the early stage of its development, Huawei developed its unique competition tactic—serving the clients' interests as the top priority. This was probably just a marketing gimmick as Huawei needed to do more for its clients so as to win contracts. However, Huawei benefited tremendously from practicing this client-oriented approach. Zhengfei later made it an iron rule within Huawei that serving the interests of the clients is the top priority.

Huawei is not a publicly listed company. Although Ren Zhengfei is the sole founder of the company, over time he has distributed almost all of his shares to employees. Now, more than 80,000 Huawei employees collectively own 98.6 percent of the company. Zhengfei only owns 1.4 percent of the company he single-handedly founded. In the past 15 years, many investment banks have courted Huawei. But Zhengfei has been quite firm—Huawei will not go IPO. To him, being a listed company would unavoidably compromise Huawei's mission of creating value for clients and employees.

Notably, Huawei emphasizes creating value for both clients and employees. The latter group consists of the *de facto* shareholders of Huawei. The meaning of value creation at Huawei is hence twofold: creating value for both the clients and the shareholders. From this perspective, Huawei has put a broader sense of value creation far ahead of increasing market share and operation scale.

Incentive Mechanisms

Every year Huawei hires 5000 to 6000 new employees, the majority of whom are rookies from technology universities and the rest are experienced. Huawei has orchestrated a rigorous system to evaluate the performance of both experienced and new employees. "Up or out" has been strictly enforced within the company. An outstanding employee has a compensation package consisting of three components: basic salary, bonus, and shares. The last two components are far larger than the basic salary. On this front, Huawei's result-driven evaluation system is compatible with the wolf-pack culture strongly advocated by Ren Zhengfei.

Huawei's improbable surge in a highly competitive industry may not be replicated by others. Still, uncovering the underlying factors that are driving Huawei's strong ROIC performance sheds light on the Chinese companies struggling to be great—getting into fast-growing industries; investing in intellectual assets; and achieving both operation efficiency and capital efficiency.

ALIBABA GROUP

September 19, 2014 was a special day for Hangzhou-based Alibaba Group: With $25 billion in IPO proceeds, Alibaba inaugurated the largest IPO ever in the American history. The media, investors, and the public applauded Alibaba's achievements within only 15 years, and called its quick rise as one of the most significant miracles in business history. For Alibaba's charismatic founder, Jack Ma, having a successful public floatation was only the beginning. "We want to live for at least 102 years!" he says on many occasions. Alibaba was born in 1999. If Alibaba could live for more than 102 years, it would become one of very few Chinese companies whose lives span 3 centuries—from the twentieth century all the way to the twenty-second century.

E-Commerce Juggernaut

Jack Ma founded Alibaba with the support of a group of friends and followers in 1999 in Hangzhou, a city bursting with entrepreneurial energy. From the outset, Jack Ma has made Alibaba's mission very clear: to create an internet platform to assist small and medium-sized enterprises (SMEs) in selling their products and services. Jack Ma said: "There are more than

400 million SMEs in China. Many of them operate in fragmented markets, with limited access to communication channels and information sources that would help market and promote their products. A critical difficulty is that many SMEs have no way to evaluate the trustworthiness of their trading partners."[8] Alibaba was born to lend its helping hand.

Alibaba's first website was English-language Alibaba.com, a global wholesale marketplace, that is, a business-to-business (B2B) exchange for SMEs to find overseas trading partners. At the same time, Alibaba Group launched a China marketplace (now known as 1688.com) for domestic wholesale trades.

Hundreds of thousands of small enterprises have been empowered by Alibaba's various platforms. While Alibaba's B2B business went well, to compete with eBay, Alibaba launched its online shopping website Taobao Marketplace in May 2003. At the time, eBay had turned out to be a great success in the Chinese market. But Jack Ma insisted that Taobao could instill more Chinese elements since Alibaba, as a Chinese company, had deep a understanding of Chinese consumers and their consumption behavior. Taobao Marketplace, right from the beginning, was positioned to carry out B2C (business to consumer) and C2C (consumer to consumer) exchanges for Chinese retailers and consumers. Alibaba has since focused on unmet needs in the Chinese retailing business, where a highly fragmented brick and mortar retail business offered limited choices to customers.

In December 2004, Alibaba introduced Alipay ("payment treasure"), an escrow service designed to eliminate the settlement risk among trading partners. Alipay was initially promoted as a third-party online payment platform for the Taobao shopping site, allowing customers to keep their money in Alipay until confirming the receipt of goods from sellers and guaranteeing refunds to customers who lost money in insecure transactions. Using Alipay, a buyer deposited payment for an outstanding order in an Alipay account; Alipay informed the seller when it received the funds, and the seller then shipped the goods. When the buyer informed Alipay that the merchandise had arrived, it instructed its bank to release the funds to the seller. Alipay turned out to be critical for Taobao's fast growth. It effectively resolved the potential settlement risk among buyers and sellers, which was extremely valuable in a market where the creditworthiness of trading partners is unknown. As of 2015, Alipay has more than 400 million active users.[9]

The retail industry in China has been highly fragmented, which limits choices available for consumers, especially those who live in small cities and the countryside. Across retail categories, Chinese industry is also far less concentrated than in other economies, which means that consumers in many places have access only to local stores. The online bazaar developed by Alibaba helps solve these problems and boost the efficiency in China's retail sector.

In April 2008, Alibaba introduced Taobao Mall (now known as Tmall. com), a dedicated platform for third-party brands and retailers, to complement Taobao Marketplace. In March 2010, Taobao Marketplace introduced online group buying marketplace juhuasuan.com. In April 2010, Aliaba.com officially launched AliExpress to enable exporters in China to directly transact with consumers around the world.

In addition to the retailing business, Alibaba also proactively looks for expansion opportunities. It has made rapid moves into adjacent sectors including financial services, big data, cloud computing, and social media, to name just a few. On finance, Jack Ma spun off Alipay, the most valuable asset and pioneering payment system originally belonging to Alibaba Group, and established Ant Financial to provide financial services around Alipay's more than 400 million users. Ant Financial includes Alibaba's small business lending, consumer finance, internet insurance, and money market funds. On cloud computing, Aliyun was established in 2009. Now, Aliyun is China's biggest cloud provider and Jack Ma has planned to spend a billion dollars for Aliyun to go global.

Since launching its first website in 1999, Alibaba Group has gradually grown into a global leader in online and mobile commerce. Today the company and its affiliates operate leading online wholesale and retail marketplaces as well as internet-based businesses ranging from advertising and marketing services, electronic payment, and cloud-based computing to network services and mobile solutions. Alibaba is the world's largest e-commerce platform. In 2013, all marketplaces of Alibaba Group reported a gross merchandise volume (GMV) of $249 billion, more than double that of Amazon.com. In fact, Alibaba sold more than Amazon. com and eBay combined. The GMV of Alibaba Group continued to grow and it increased to $394 billion in 2014 and $469 billion (more than RMB 3 trillion) in 2015. As of June 30, 2014, Alibaba had 279 million active buyers (the number of active buys further increased to 407 million by end 2015) and 8.5 million active sellers. With more than 1 billion product and service listings, Alibaba Group processed 14.5 billion orders in 2014.[10] Alibaba had also recorded more than RMB 91 billion in sales on its platform in just 24 hours in its 2015 "single day" promotion.

In just 15 years, Alibaba Group has developed into the world's largest e-commerce platform and one of the largest companies in the world (by market capitalization). While the scale and dynamism of the Chinese consumer market has provided a powerful advantage for Alibaba, its business model and several strategic moves have been critical.

Alibaba's Business Model

Unlike its closest rival Amazon.com, Alibaba has adopted an online marketplace model. A simple way to describe this model is that Alibaba does not sell; it only provides an online bazaar for sellers and buyers to trade. In some sense, Alibaba could be viewed as an e-commerce infrastructure provider, which distinguishes its business model from that of Amazon. com. Examining Alibaba's fee-charging model illustrates the nature of its business model. In the earlier stage, Alibaba mainly engaged in B2B business. For clients using Alibaba.com to trade, the company collected membership fees, and also charged fees for online marketing services. When Alibaba Group introduced Taobao Marketplace, its fee structure changed accordingly. For Taobao merchants, using Taobao Marketplace is free. However, if a merchant wants to have additional services, they have to pay to become a premium member. Alibaba thus charges two types of fees: online marketing services and storefront fees. For merchants on Tmall Marketplace, Alibaba charges commissions too.

The ecosystem that Alibaba has tried very hard to build has been expanding very quickly, especially after its IPO in September 2014. Still, Alibaba's fee structure remains largely intact. Not all GMV that occurred in the Alibaba ecosystem could be counted as Alibaba's revenue. Only a fraction of GMV would translate into Alibaba's sales. This conversion rate is usually called monetization rate. Since 2012, Alibaba has achieved a blended monetization rate (PC and mobile combined) ranging from 2.18 to 3.05 percent. This explains why Alibaba is not a *Fortune* Global 500 company despite the fact that it generated a GMV as high as $349 billion in 2014—a company needs to generate at least $23.7 billion in sales to be included in the 2005 *Fortune* Global 500 list.

To prepare for public floatation, Alibaba made many investments to grab mobile commerce opportunities. In addition to providing shopping and payment services, these newly added Alibaba ecosystem members provide a wide range of services including browse and search (UC web), location-based services (AutoNavi), entertainment (Youku Tudou), and social media (Weibo). Through these online platforms, Alibaba aims to further increase user acquisition and engagement, improve customer experiences, and expand the products and services offered. As such, Alibaba would eventually increase the monetization rate of mobile GMV, which is significantly lower than that of non-mobile.

Alibaba is evolving into a conglomerate. Over time, its business portfolio has expanded rapidly. It has invested heavily in technology and data platforms including big data (e.g., deep learning, high-volume process, real-time analytics), security, search, targeted marketing, database, and cloud computing. The ultimate goal of these investments is to improve the monetization rate.

Taking ROIC as a metric to assess Alibaba's operating performance, one can immediately spot a number of advantages that are inherently associated with Alibaba's business model. Figure 8.1 presents the ROIC of Alibaba Group from 2011 to 2015. Clearly, Alibaba reported very strong ROIC performance over the five-year time period. In 2013, before its IPO, Alibaba reported an overall ROIC of 108 percent, meaning that $1 capital invested in the operation of the Alibaba Group had generated $1.08 after-tax profit. After IPO, in 2015, the overall ROIC of Alibaba Group still remained at 85 percent. Recall that the average ROIC of the Chinese A-share companies from 1998 to 2012 was only 3 percent. If Alibaba is able to maintain such a high level of ROIC for a long enough time, say, 102 years as Jack Ma has wished, Alibaba may very likely be the greatest Chinese company ever.

What are the sources of Alibaba's high ROIC? First, unlike Amazon. com and JD.com, Alibaba adopts the online marketplace model. There are no inventory costs for Alibaba. Note that in retailing business, inventory costs typically account for the majority of a company's working capital. As shown in Fig. 8.1, the working capital-to-sales ratio was fixed at 10 percent for Alibaba, which may look high. However, the company did not have any inventories, account receivables, or account payables. The only item that could be classified as working capital is operating cash—here I have made an assumption that the operating cash-to-sales ratio is 10 percent for Alibaba.[11] If I make an extreme assumption that all of Alibaba's cash and marketable securities are required for its operation, the level of working capital will increase noticeably. ROIC based on this extreme assumption is still very high.

Second, the marketplace model can also effectively reduce the operating costs. Most traffic on Taobao Marketplace is organic, which significantly

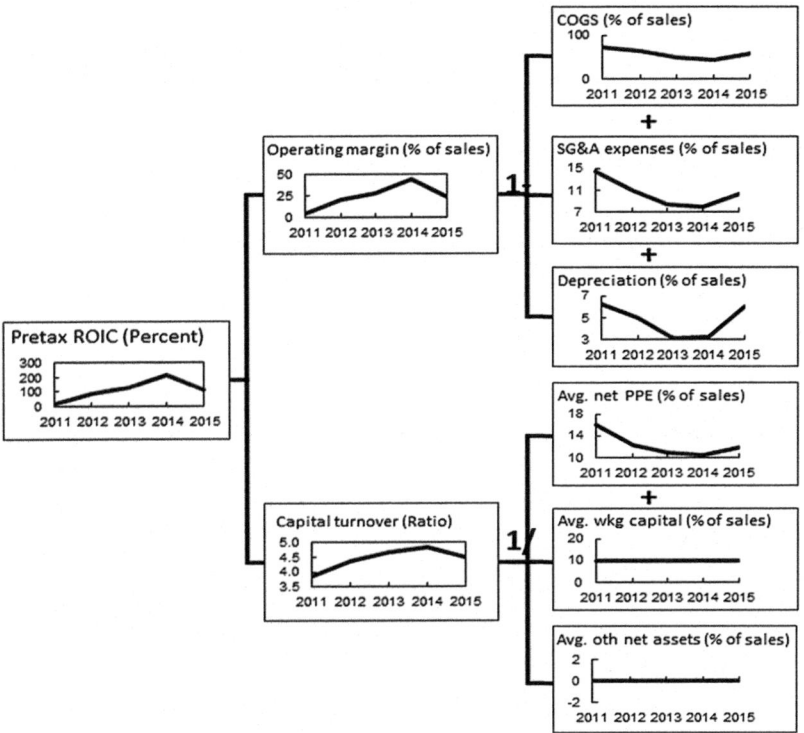

Fig. 8.1   Alibaba's ROIC: 2011–2015
Source: Author's calculation based on public data

reduces the user acquisition costs. In addition, the millions of merchants on various Alibaba marketplaces are natural buyers of Alibaba's marketing services, which makes large sales force and marketing expenditures unnecessary. Alibaba's operating margin, measured by the EBIT-to-sales ratio, was quite high. In 2014, it reported an operating margin of 44 percent. Although the margin dropped to 24 percent in 2015, it is still higher than other retailers given that the Chinese economy had significantly slowed down.

Third, Alibaba follows a light-asset strategy. Although the company has spent a lot on technology and data platforms, and building its own logistical system, Alibaba is still quite "light." Checking the company's balance sheets in the past five years, combined with a little algebraic help, one can easily find that in 2015 (after IPO), Alibaba's net property and equipment stood at slightly over RMB 9 billion, and its invested capital—the total amount of capital applied to Alibaba's operation—was only RMB 17 billion. As a result, almost all accounting items that would lead to a higher ROIC have values on Alibaba's side—lower depreciation, higher revenue-to-invested capital ratio, and so on.

Having analyzed Alibaba's sources of high ROIC, I would like to point out two notable features regarding Aibaba's post-IPO balance sheets. First, as of 2015, Alibaba had RMB 122 billion in cash and cash equivalents, which can be largely attributed to close to RMB 160 billion in IPO proceeds (approximately $25 billion) raised by Alibaba during its public floatation in 2014. For example, the total amount of cash and cash equivalents was less than RMB 37 billion in 2013, after a huge dose of strategic and financial investments. For corporate finance researchers or corporate governance advocates, so much cash on a firm's balance sheet is surely not a welcome sign. The familiar "free cash flow problem" raised by Michael Jensen may cause concerns about Alibaba's growth opportunities and future profitability.[12] Second, as of 2015, Alibaba had accumulated RMB 52 billion in equity investments. Most of this has been spent on facilitating the construction of Alibaba's ecosystem. Still, one cannot help ask whether those investments really help Alibaba enhance its monetization rate during the mobile era, when potential disruptors can come from anywhere.

Why Alibaba? Why Jack Ma?

What secrets lie behind Alibaba's quick surge? Given its current momentum, can Alibaba evolve into a world-class company? In a way, Alibaba's success is a testimonial to the formula of success, "You got to be right person to show up in the right place and at the right time!"

Several reasons may account for Alibaba's huge success. Most notably, Alibaba operates in a fast-growing market during its fastest-growing period. China, which contributes more than 95 percent of Alibaba's total sales, presents itself as the largest e-commerce opportunity in the world. First, China is going through an arduous transition from an investment-led economy to a consumption-driven economy. As of 2013, consumption only accounted for 36 percent of GDP in China, whereas this figure was 67 percent in the USA. Increasing consumption provides tremendous opportunities for Alibaba. Second, McKinsey & Company, a consulting firm, defines the mainstream consuming class in China as households with disposable income of RMB 103,000 to RMB 222,000 ($16,000 to $34,000). According to McKinsey's estimate, since 2000, more than 100 million Chinese households have joined the mainstream consuming class. As disposable income has increased at 10 percent per year in real terms over the past decade, it is expected that the mainstream consuming class would reach 200 million by 2025, which poses a huge commerce opportunity.[13] Third, China is seeing a rapidly growing penetration of both internet users and mobile internet users (46 percent and 37 percent respectively as of 2013). In the meantime, the penetration of online shopping has also increased dramatically—by end 2013, online shoppers had reached 49 percent of the total population in China. Now, online shopping only accounts for 10 percent of China's retail: the room for further growth is huge.

From the outset, Alibaba had adopted a business model that was conducive to enhancing ROIC. Over the past 16 years, although Alibaba's business model has evolved rapidly, its core value proposition—making business easier for both customers and small enterprises—has not changed. Alibaba's online marketplace model had allowed it to generate positive cash flow three years after its birth. This is extremely unusual for an e-commerce company. Think about Amazon.com or JD.com, which are still struggling to make a profit years after their IPOs. Alibaba's asset-light and idea-intensive business model distinguishes it from other Chinese corporate giants, who place scale expansion far ahead of ROIC.

Alibaba and Jack Ma have been extremely lucky as well. The Chinese consumer market is deep and highly segmented, Alibaba has benefited tremendously from the scale economy and scope economy provided by this market. China had more than 40 million registered SMEs by end 2014, employing over 500 million people.[14] There were many e-commerce startups competing with Alibaba in the early 2000s. Why did Alibaba stand out while others failed? Working hard to acquire users, improving users' experience, enlarging the scope of products and services, and shifting from B2B to B2C and C2C have all played significant roles. Of course, at the core of Alibaba's 16-year journey is an audacious pursuit of value creation, which has been reflected in Alibaba's sustained high ROIC.

Can Alibaba endure over 102 years, as Jack Ma has wished? Despite its huge success, the road ahead is still uncertain. Nowadays, greater variability in corporate performance is becoming a global trend. As an idea-intensive and asset-light company, high growth rate is crucial. As the Chinese economy has significantly slowed down, can Alibaba maintain its strong growth momentum? The online bazaar model brings cost advantage and enhances

ROIC noticeably. However, it also poses difficulties for Alibaba to control for the quality of goods and services simply because Alibaba does not own the sellers. How to build trust, or how to overcome distrust, between the sellers and buyers remains a challenge.

Jack Ma and his partners are trying to diversify their investments through aggressive mergers and acquisitions and organic investment in financial services (e.g., Ant Financial), newspapers, movies, sports, healthcare, and so on. Can these investments be as profitable as Alibaba's asset-light online marketplaces? How would Jack Ma and his partners take care of risks associated with financial services in the case of Ant Financial? Finance is a capital-intensive business. How much of Alibaba's "light asset" spirit could spill over to finance? How can Alibaba increasingly create value from brands and innovative ideas by getting into the new industries such as finance and healthcare?

Alibaba is unavoidably getting bigger. However, size does not guarantee Alibaba's market position for long in a fast-moving industry such as e-commerce. Alibaba is also getting heavier. Now, Alibaba is also investing to building warehouses, which may transform Alibaba's nature as an asset-light company. China's inefficient logistics network has forced Alibaba to build its own network. Cainiao, a consortium that runs a digital platform linking more than a dozen logistics providers, 1800 distribution centers, and more than 100,000 dispatch points, was established in 2013. Building up Cainiao requires a huge amount of capital investment. More importantly, Alibaba is going offline too. In 2015, Alibaba made a $4.6 billion investment in Suning, one of China's leading electronics retailers. According to the agreement signed by Alibaba and Suning, Suning will open an online storefront on Tmall; meanwhile, Alibaba would be able to use Suning's well-developed delivery network, and Alibaba's online shoppers can pick up and return their online purchases at Suning stores.[15]

Jack Ma wants to develop Alibaba from a pure shopping platform into a broad-based ecosystem providing all sorts of online services. To achieve this ambition requires huge amounts of investment. In this process, can Alibaba's higher ROIC be sustained?

THE UP AND COMING...

Companies like PetroChina, Sinopec, State Grid, and ICBC have been responsible for the vast bulk of China's economic advances during the early stage of China's reform era. Their capital-intensive nature and influence on the economy and other firms is reminiscent of the legacy of using massive investments to drive economic growth. As the Chinese economy enters the "new normal," the source of China's future growth ought to come more from other places. The improvement of total factor productivity (TFP) has been singled out as the source of future growth. Conceivably, corporate China will go through a transition from capital-intensive to intellectual capital- and knowledge-intensive. Alibaba, Huawei Technologies, and others are pioneering this transformation. Their success has fully demonstrated how business strategies and rigorous executions centering around ROIC can leapfrog the Chinese firms to the frontline of global competition.[16]

Besides Huawei and Alibaba, I will discuss two up-and-coming companies, Xiaomi.com and SF Express, in the next section of this chapter. The two companies share several similarities: first, both have been riding on the booming Chinese economy and the very deep and broad Chinese consumer market; second, both companies have stringently placed their emphasis on quality and client experiences, which distinguish them from their closest peers; and third, both have successfully built up an ecosystem, which hosts a wide range of end-users and service providers. Their platforms are now providing a wide variety of services including logistics support, online payment, and even financial services. They are well positioned to become China's world champions in years to come.

While I focus on Xiaomi and SF Express, I must point out that there actually are many up-and-coming Chinese companies—the list of potentially great Chinese companies could be long, including JD.com, DJ, Ant Financial, and Didi Kuaidi

The Xiaomi Frenzy

Xiaomi stands out on the up-and-coming list. In only five years, Xiaomi has built a base of 160 million phone users, entered markets such as Indonesia and India, and challenged western assumptions about how Chinese tech companies think. In addition, raising $1 billion through private placements in December 2014, Xiaomi was valued at $45 billion and has become one of the most lucrative startups in the world.

Founded in April 2010 by Lei Jun, a vocal and passionate entrepreneur, Xiaomi did not launch its first smartphone model, Mi 1, until August 2011. The company's sales increased rapidly—Xiaomi sold 7.2 million phones in 2012; the next year this increased to 18.7 million; and in 2014 it sold 61 million and reported $12 billion in revenue. It has grown at triple-digit rates to become the world's third largest smartphone maker, after Samsung and Apple, even though it does not sell phones in Europe or the USA. Despite the fact that Huawei, another Chinese company, overtook Xiaomi's position in 2015, the rise of Xiaomi, for many, was explosive and miraculous. Dubbed China's Steve Jobs, Xiaomi's charismatic founder Lei Jun once said, "*Even a pig can fly if it is in the middle of a whirlwind.*" For him, mobile internet is right in the middle of a whirlwind.

Xiaomi's Business Model
Although Xaiomi sells smartphones and other electronic gadgets, most still view Xiaomi as a *mobile internet company* rather than a hardware producer due to its unique business model. Xiaomi's businesses range from hardware, software, and internet content, to social networking, backed by the MIUI operating system—a refined user interface (UI) for Andriod smartphone users. Xiaomi launched the MIUI operating platform in 2010, long before its first smartphone model was up for sale. MIUI is a highly customized Android ROM with a focus on ease of use, openness for customization, and weekly upgrade with new features and performance optimization based on the improvement suggestions made by its users.

A unique feature of Xiaomi's innovation is keeping in close touch with consumers on social media and through direct online polling to determine what innovations to take. Specifically, Xiaomi turns to online communities to solicit design ideas and product feedback, provides product and service updates, and announces future products. With its online community of "Mi fans," Xiaomi extracts information about product features and improvements that will resonate with users; it uses the group's insights to build improvements into new versions of its operating system MIUI on a weekly basis. Xiaomi, as of 2015, had allegedly amassed more than 100 million "Mi fans."

Another critical part of Xiaomi's business model is that it aims to sell high-quality smartphones at lower prices—at just above cost—and make money from selling additional services. Xiaomi's marketing is done almost entirely through social media and/or word of mouth through "Mi fans," which keeps its advertising costs at very low levels. Meanwhile, Xiaomi only releases a few new models every year, so each model remains profitable for a longer time. Xiaomi has also nurtured dozens of startups to make smart appliances, ranging from routers and air and water purifiers, to home security cameras that connect with its phones. With the margins on hardware manufacturing declining, Xiaomi seeks to add value through its additional value-added services on content—its customized UI and self-developed or co-developed mobile apps/platforms have boosted consumer awareness of Xiaomi and its products, allowing the company to develop its own distinct user community.

Xiaomi has developed into a leading mobile internet firm in China, which, as a software and content provider, is making a deliberate entry into hardware—smartphones first, then Xiaomi TV, and then other devices that could be connected through the Xiaomi ecosystem. This vertically integrated model pioneered by Xiaomi allows software companies to sell hardware at or below cost in order to attract users and generate recurring revenue from content. For Xiaomi to fly, escalating its ecosystem of content and apps is a top priority.

Xiaomi's ROIC

Xiaomi is not a listed company. I do not have detailed income statements and balance sheets to compute its ROIC and assess the performance of the ROIC contributors such as profit margin and capital efficiency. However, several components of Xiaomi's business model are inherently associated with higher ROIC, which explains the quick surge of Xiaomi in an extremely crowded and highly competitive industry. First, Xiaomi spends very little on marketing and distribution channels. About 55 percent of Xiaomi's sales are made directly online, and 15 percent through Mi.com, the third largest e-commerce site in China, which incurs lower retailing and management costs.

Second, Xiaomi has been implementing an effective way to manage its working capital. Before releasing a smartphone model, Xiaomi would pre-sell the new model directly online, which significantly reduces the amount of working capital required. Xiaomi sells more smartphones per model. So far, each model of Xiaomi has had more than 10 million shipments. With high shipment volume and visible demand, Xiaomi could aggressively negotiate with component vendors for volume discounts. Xiaomi has thus lowered production cost, thanks to high shipment volume per model. In the meantime, Xiaomi's has lowered R&D cost because of high volume per model.

Third, on a related note, Xiaomi has developed a new kind of internet-enabled ecosystem: one that turns customers into "fans" who co-design and then evangelize products; that transfers market-demand risk to small hardware startups in which it tactically incubates; and that significantly reduces costs by minimizing inventory and optimizing supply chains in fresh ways.

Fourth, Xiaomi's low hardware margin can be compensated by selling services, content, and accessories.

Will Xiaomi Be a Great Company?

Up to this point, Xiaomi, a five-year-old startup, selling more than 61 million smartphones in 2014, reporting revenue of $12 billion, and being valued at $45 billion, has been extremely successful. If Xiaomi can keep this momentum for another five years, it will very likely achieve Lei Jun's dream of "connecting everything!" However, keeping a triple-digit growth rate, as Xiaomi did in 2014, or even a double-digit growth rate might be a daunting task. First, the market observers and Xiaomi's competitors all ask some variant of the same question: Is it sustainable for great phones to be sold at substantial discounts? Without doubt, Xiaomi's e-commerce model, which saves retail distribution costs, and disruptive pricing tactics, which generate buzz for its phones, allows Xiaomi to sell smartphones at much lower costs. However, Xiaomi's success cannot escape the notice of its competitors. Huawei and Samsung have also started building their own online communities of fans.

Second, although Xiaomi claims repeatedly that Xiaomi is going after big data, services, and content for revenue, it takes time. Now Xiaomi still has to rely on selling hardware such as smartphones for revenue. Can Xiaomi sustain its high sales growth rate? To sustain strong growth, going global is necessary. However, it may take a longer time and smarter maneuvering for Xiaomi to tap into foreign markets such as India and Brazil.

On a related note, Xiaomi is only five years old. Unlike Huawei and Lenovo, who boast of a broad portfolio of patents, Xiaomi lacks deep intellectual assets such as patents and brands that are internationally recognized. This may constrain the company's growth momentum. In 2015, Xiaomi failed its target of selling 80–100 million smartphones. As a result, doubts about the robustness of Xiaomi's business model are mounting. Lei Jun obviously has his hands full with all kinds of challenges.

SF Express

SF Express was established in 1993 by Wang Wei, who has been known to be very secretive. Before founding the company, Wang Wei worked as a laborer for his uncle in Hong Kong. Upon establishment of SF Express, he started to deliver goods and documents in small parcels between Shenzhen and Hong Kong. After more than 20 years' development, SF Express has developed into China's leading private express delivery company. Now, SF Express has 290,000 employees, more than 12,000 transport vehicles, 18 cargo planes, and 9100 branches inside and outside mainland China. SF Express is not listed and according to its founder, Wang Wei, it does not have an IPO plan yet. Although financial information about SF Express is scarce, living in China, especially in cities, one can easily feel the existence of SF Express—every day, more than 12,000 transport vehicles with the SF Express logo are on the road. In 2012, SF Express' operating revenue exceeded RMB 12 billion.

SF Express' business model has several features. First, it adopts a direct operating model. In the early stage of the company's history, SF Express had tried the franchise model. SF Express soon found that this model resulted in poor management and low quality of services. Also, it was difficult for SF Express to standardize operations in transportation and delivery, and to carry out other value-added businesses. In 2000, SF Express started to streamline its business model. Two years later, the company completely abandoned the franchise model and shifted to a direct operating model.

Second, SF Express is the first air express company in China. During the SARS epidemic in 2013, the airline industry suffered a severe recession. SF Express seized the opportunity of low freight rates and signed a contract with Yangtze River Express for five cargo planes. SF Express started planning for its own air carriers in 2005. On December 31, 2009, SF Airlines completed its first trip. As of end 2014, the company owned 18 cargo planes.

Third, SF Express ventured into cold chain through sfbest.com in 2012. It first focused on high-end room temperature food and then ventured into low-temperature fresh food.

Fourth, in May 2014, SF Express launched "Heike" stores across China, in an effort to tackle the problem of the last mile. Now there are more than 3000 Heike stores in China. SF Express hopes to bridge the online and offline channels of logistics and information exchange through its physical sites—"Heike" stores. SF has invested a tremendous amount of capital in Heike, although the results were somewhat disappointing in the beginning.

Fifth, SF Express also has its eye on international markets. The company launched its cross-border e-commerce platform sfbuy.com in 2014. In January 2015, SF launched its cross-border B2C platform, sfht.com—it directly purchases goods from overseas suppliers through SF Express' global supply chain and stores the goods in own warehouses. Delivery could be made in five working days.

SF Express is now developing an integrated ecosystem consisting mainly of logistics, information, and capital. The company has secured the third-party payment license, and license for bankcard-acquiring service. The company launched SF Pay services. With SF Pay, SF Express is well positioned to provide services such as payments, bank transfers, placing express orders, wealth management, and online shopping. SF Express is now cooperating with financial institutions to provide credit cards and supply-chain finance services. SF Express is the only delivery company in China that has established a closed-loop ecosystem that has courier, cold chain, overseas shopping, offline convenience stores, and financial services provided around its third-party payment license.

SF Express has benefited greatly from the profound changes that China has experienced during its reform era. China's reform and opening up policies have led to an expansion in import and export trade, generating the earliest demand for deliveries. In 1985, China Post, a central government-controlled SOE, established EMS, which had remained the only delivery operation in mainland China for a long time until SF express was established in Guangdong and STO Express was established in Shanghai, both in 1993.

The express delivery business, especially in the private sector, has experienced strong growth from the outset, thanks to the quick surge of e-commerce in China. In the late 1990s, the rapid penetration of the internet gave birth to e-commerce. E-commerce has developed rapidly in China for several reasons. First, China is a nation with 1.37 billion people, and population density is high, especially in cities. E-commerce platforms can easily achieve scale economy. Second, the traditional brick and mortar retail sector in China was highly segmented. E-commerce, with its scale effects, may improve the efficiency of the retail sector. According to a CICC study,[17] the scale of online shopping transactions had experienced explosive growth, from RMB 5.6 billion in 2007 to RMB 2.8 trillion in 2014, implying a CAGR of 75 percent. The delivery business benefited from the rapid growth of e-commerce in China. From 2007 to 2014, the volume of deliveries increased from 1.2 billion pieces to 14 billion pieces, suggesting a CAGR of 42 percent. The revenue of delivery companies increased from RMB 34.3 billion to RMB 204.5 billion.[18]

The high growth of the delivery business is likely to continue in China. First, the potential for online consumption remains huge. The surge of mobile internet further strengthens the trend. Second, the structural transformation of the Chinese economy also provides huge upside potentials for the delivery business. As of 2015, the tertiary sector had contributed more than 50 percent of GDP in China. The knowledge-based and high-valued added industries will become more important in years to come, and they pose stronger demand to delivery services. Third, although China's per capita utilization of delivery services had increased from 1.1 pieces to 6.8 pieces in 2013, it was only a quarter of that of the USA, suggesting significant room for future growth.[19]

SF Express has charted a convincing course. As China's leading express delivery company, it has potential to develop into a great company. First, SF Express is operating in a fast-growing Chinese market, which ensures its high growth rate. Second, SF Express has demonstrated well-devised strategy and strong execution. Its direct operating model, clear focus on the medium-end market for documents and small parcels rather than large and heavy cargo, and performance-based incentive mechanisms enable SF Express to outperform its immediate competitors. Third, SF Express has established an integrated system of logistics, cash flow, and information collection. This closed-loop ecosystem can nurture many growth areas including big data, e-commerce, supply-chain finance, and other value-added services.

Notes

1. Literally translated, Huawei means "China achievement." The name of the company illustrates the vision of its founder, Ren Zhengfei: to build a great and world-class Chinese company.
2. "Huawei enters the United States," July 2013, Case W13306 published by Ivey School of Management at the Western University, Canada.
3. Ibid.
4. The 2015 annual report of Huawei is not available yet. The sales in 2015 were taken from Huawei's official website (http://www.huawei.com/cn).
5. Huawei's new company slogan, which accords with its corporate strategy, is "Open ROADS to a better connected world!"
6. The operating and financial results for 2015 were taken from the CEO of Huawei Mr. Ping Guo's public speech. The transcript of the speech (in Chinese) can be downloaded here: http://www.huawei.com/cn/news/2016/1/huawei-xiaofeizhe-yewu-2015nian-chao-200yi-meiyuan.

7. See Baghai, Mehrdad, Stephen Coley, and David White, "The Alchemy of Growth: Practical Insights for Building Enduring Enterprise," 2000, Da Capo Press.

8. Quoted from Harvard Business School case "Alibaba's Taobao (A)" (9-709-456), July, 2009.

9. Alipay was divested from Alibaba Group in 2010 in a very controversial case. It is now the core part of Ant Financial, a financial conglomerate established in November 2014 by Jack Ma and his Alibaba management team. Alipay continues to support the transactions on the Alibaba ecosystem through contractual arrangements.

10. Refer to Alibaba's road show presentation for detailed operation and financial results.

11. Note that for industrial companies, it is common to assume that operating cash-to-sales ratio is 2 percent. As Alibaba is a retailing business, which demands more operating cash, I assume the operating cash-to-sales ratio to be 10 percent.

12. See Jensen (1986).

13. Data source: McKinsey Global Institute, "The China effect on global innovation" (October 2015a).

14. Ibid.

15. For further reading, see *The Economist*, "Clicks to bricks" (August 15, 2015c).

16. In this book, I do not provide much discussion on Tencent and Baidu. com, both of which are technology companies and have demonstrated their potential to become industry shapers.

17. See "Research on unlisted company," CICC, October 2015.

18. Ibid.

19. See "The Postal Industry Development Statistics Communiqué," 2014.

CHAPTER 9

Conclusion: How Can Chinese Companies Be Truly Great?

Chinese companies have already blown their fanfare for the second "Long March"—a game-changer with a shifting focus and a new set of game rules. Whether corporate China can successfully move its primary focus from scale to value creation and translate such changes into a higher level of ROIC will directly decide whether the Chinese economy can accomplish its long overdue transition from investment-led to efficiency-driven and whether China can escape the unanticipated "mid-income trap." Of course, one can always argue that the causality between owning a handful of great companies and achieving sustainable economic growth in the Chinese context can easily go either way. Still, the evidence on the importance of having a large number of great companies is mounting, as I have shown in previous chapters of the book.

Unlike the reform and opening up policies that were initiated by the central authority more than three and a half decades ago, making China's companies great can no longer rely on a top-down approach. The top-down approach, which uses mandates, government subsidies, discriminatory financial support, and other administrative measures to coerce the size-minded Chinese companies to put value creation ahead of operation scale, is not working its magic. The breakthrough can only be achieved through the bottom-up efforts by existing corporate incumbents or by more innovation-savvy entrants like Huawei, Alibaba, Xiaomi, and SF Express.

China is already the world's second largest economy and boasts of more than 20 percent of the world's largest companies. While Chinese

© The Editor(s) (if applicable) and The Author(s) 2016   211
Q. Liu, *Corporate China 2.0*, DOI 10.1057/978-1-137-55089-7_9

companies have experienced a remarkable rise, their profit margins are declining. To sustain China's economic growth and meanwhile accomplish the transformation of its economic growth model, China needs a new breed of companies, which take value creation as top priority and boast of competitive business models and excellent operation results. I expect the metamorphosis to take place in two potential areas. First, the old behemoths in the traditional capital-intensive industries will leverage the opportunities provided by globalization and digitization to leapfrog to the frontiers of new technologies and continue to improve their ROIC. Second, entrepreneurs and younger generation corporate founders cluster in Zhongguancun (Beijing), Shenzhen, and Hangzhou, and so on. They are the more audacious and agile innovators, who can skillfully harness new technologies such as robotics, 3D printing, driverless technology, new materials, and reusable energies to improve operation efficiency and develop high-end new products and services.

In either case, I do not have many successful case examples to share yet. The great companies of China are still on the road. In Chap. 8, I discuss Huawei, Alibaba, Xiaomi, and SF Express, all of which are truly exceptional in their own ways. While they are profoundly shaking up the microfoundations of the Chinese economy, none has been in operation long enough to claim that they are truly great. Nevertheless, their success so far has pointed to a few guidelines that may provoke one's thinking about how to make firms great in China: getting into a fast-growing market, focusing on quality and productivity, and being innovative in either technologies or ideas. All of them can eventually translate into higher return on invested capital (ROIC).

If the above formula works, then out of tens of millions of Chinese companies, there will be a fair number of truly great companies, as suggested by the law of large numbers (LLN). However, we are not seeing this happen. Pondering the odds, one may question whether the China-specific institutions and growth strategies have shaped corporate China's behavioral patterns in such a way that they just do not care about value creation. As this is likely true, the efforts to make Chinese companies truly great have to go beyond firms. As I have argued in Chap. 7, improving institutions and changing growth models may be equally or even more important.

The following eight aspects, some at the macroeconomic and institutional levels and some at firm level, are indispensable for corporate China to re-align their incentives and adapt their behavior so that they can move in the direction of making themselves truly great. Although the eight aspects are not mutually exclusive—they are in fact interrelated—they collectively provide an enabling formula that can make a Chinese company truly great. If these elements, outside or within firms, are well in place, then, as LLN suggests, having some truly great Chinese companies is one sure thing. As Albert Einstein once said, "*Things should be and must be as simple as possible, if not simpler.*" The eight must-does I discuss below provide enough guidance for the emergence of great Chinese companies.

Transform the Chinese Growth Model

One of the analytical frameworks I have repeatedly stressed in this book is the growth identity: *Growth Rate = Investment Rate × ROIC*. While both investment rate and ROIC can drive a nation's economic growth, China has relied more heavily on investment rate in the past. Under an investment-led growth model, a company's obsession with size and speed is all-encompassing. The Chinese economy had grown so fast that almost everything a company produces can find a buyer, regardless of quality. This has created strong incentives for short-term gains over long-term value creation. The situation was typically worse when companies were owned by the state. As the soft budget constraint problem prevails among SOEs, getting as much bank lending as possible to invest is always a dominant winning strategy.

However, corporate debt has been piling up and overcapacity has been everywhere. China now needs to rely more on ROIC to sustain its growth. China's future growth will have to stem more from the improvement in total factor productivity (TFP), which can translate into higher ROIC. Along with the economic transition, intellectual capital-based companies and idea-intensive companies will surge—pursuing higher ROIC is in their genes. For the traditional Chinese economy—the capital-intensive industries—the Chinese government launched in 2015 an ambitious plan dubbed "Made in China 2025," which will employ multiple measures to encourage Chinese manufacturers to upgrade their factories and to become a greener and more innovative "global manufacturing power" by 2025. I expect to see significant improvement in ROIC in traditional businesses along the way.

Changing the growth model and transforming corporate China from big to great are two sides of the same coin. Only when the micro-units of the economy can extensively improve their ROIC can the aggregate ROIC of the Chinese economy be significantly improved. China's structural economic transformation is tightly bonded with corporate China's rise to greatness. People have to change their belief that the fast growth of the Chinese economy can be taken for granted. In fact, rapid economic growth is not guaranteed if the economic foundations are becoming less stable. Only through grass-roots efforts that enhance corporate China's ROIC can another wave of economic growth become feasible.

REDEFINE THE ROLE OF THE GOVERNMENT

For many, China has been practicing a state capitalism in which the state and the party are omnipresent in the economy and their roles are enshrined in the law. Indeed, China's economic miracle has been the result of large-scale state planning and intense government intervention. Investments fueled by the state-owned banks and carried out by SOEs or local governments were one of the building blocks of China's miraculous economic expansion. However, capital spending by SOEs and the governments has been on a steady decline in recent years. But the state firms still monopolize industries providing production factors such as funds, energy, and commodities. SOEs, although they contribute less than one-third of total value added in China, have received more than half of bank lending. Local governments have also been heavily involved in investments, resulting in over RMB 20 trillion in local government debt.

Investments by SOEs or the government are inherently associated with lower ROIC. In Chap. 4, I present robust empirical evidence showing that state firms' ROIC on average is 4 to 6 percentage points lower than that of non-state firms, suggesting a huge waste of both capital and labor. More importantly, government investments tend to crowd out more efficient investments made by private firms, posing severe opportunity cost. Under the "new normal" growth era in China, ROIC will be the key to sustaining China's future growth. Therefore, it is a must for the government to exit the monopolized industries and loosen up the restrictions on private capital in industries where private capital has been banned.

The majority of future growth will stem from the improvement in total factor productivity that is closely tied to innovation and entrepreneurship. The government should scale down their economic function and let the market play a decisive role in allocating resources. Firms with strong value proposition, unique product offerings, and targeting a broader group of customers should be better positioned to monetize the macro-shifts during the new era. What the government can do best is to level the playing field by ending granting subsidies and privileges to state-favored interest groups. Only when the government redefines its economic role can economic growth in China be inclusive.

INTEREST RATE LIBERALIZATION

Let me return to the principle of optimal investment and financing introduced in Chap. 2: $ROIC \geq WACC$. In order to create value, a firm ought to achieve an ROIC higher than its weighted average cost of capital (WACC). However, it is important to bear in mind that this inequality will generate meaningful guidance on corporate decisions if and only if WACC is market-based; if WACC is distorted, for example, downwardly biased, this condition means nothing.

When interest rate is regulated, the regulator more likely lowers the interest rate to implicitly subsidize favored companies or entities, which are more likely to be SOEs or local governments in China. With cheap and easy credit, these entities are incentivized to make more investments. If the economy heats up, the central bank tends to ask the banks to cut back on lending. Typically, private companies without the backing of the state bear the brunt of these credit crunches. Another adverse effect due to lower interest rate is it reduces household income and may force households to save more in order to prepare for retirement. This discourages consumption and makes the Chinese economy continue to rely on investment. A vicious cycle is thus forged.

China started the process of liberalizing interest rate several years ago but still needs one critical step to bring the reform to fruition—let the market, not the regulator, decide how much interest income a financial intermediary should pay to its depositors. The regulators do not have much faith in competition and market. They are overly concerned with the possibility that with market-based deposit rate, arrogant and less nimble state banks may lose deposits to more market-oriented financial intermediaries, which are competitive and more customer-oriented.

Even though the interest rate is fully liberalized, the prevalence of the soft budget constraint problem may still distort the incentives of the state sector to make value-added investments. Think about the following question: What is the WACC perceived by a Chinese mayor when he makes investment decisions? Well, one can use the capital asset pricing model (CAPM), the Fama-French three-factor model, or other fancier models suggested by the finance textbooks to compute WACC, but the actual answer could be a simple "zero." Why? This mayor may borrow money at a very low rate from the state-owned banks and policy banks, or through local government financing platforms. If the projects go under and the debts are due, it is hard to believe that the state-owned financiers would force the local government to go bankrupt. For the mayor, the cost of the fund he perceives is indeed zero. On this point, the presence of an outsized state sector in the economy dampens the effects of interest rate liberalization.

As such, the meaning of interest rate liberalization is twofold: First, let the market decide interest rate; and second, get rid of the implicit guarantee provided by the state and make the soft budget constraint a hard constraint. The government should make it very clear that the state firms are not default-free. When the interest rate liberalization is finally achieved, banks in China will have to work harder to make profits. Borrowers, facing higher rates, will have to be more discerning about their investments. Chinese households will reap more interest incomes from their savings. We may finally see a virtuous cycle.

Fortunately, actions have been taken to set the process of liberalizing interest rates in motion. Now, banks in China have to fight harder for deposits and profitability, while the savers have a wider range of investment options than before, from money market funds and certificates of deposit to wealth management products. In March 2014, Shanghai Chaori Solar became the first Chinese company to default on China's onshore bond market. In October 2015, state-owned firm Sinosteel defaulted on a bond payment, even after the government was said to have stepped in. The implicit guarantees provided by the government may eventually be removed, although the progress might be gradual, and the process might be long.

ALLOW PRIVATE CAPITAL TO ENTER FINANCE

Since the onset of China's industrialization, the government had adopted a financial repression approach to facilitate the industrialization process. This legacy has been carried over to the present, and is still reflected in the following two aspects. First, the state-dominated financial system allocates the majority of bank lending to the less efficient but state-favored sector, which crowds out the investment opportunities in the more efficient private sector. In some sense, the private sector in China is squeezed between the state sector, which has access to cheap credit, and foreign companies competing in China, who can raise cheap money outside. Despite the fact that the private companies boast of much higher ROIC than SOEs do, very few can grow large enough to claim greatness. Second, the government has imposed many restrictions on potential entrants—it is extremely difficult for private capital to enter finance.

The finance industry's GDP share in China had reached 9.5 percent in the first half of 2015, far larger than the level in the USA.[1] This strongly suggests that the existing finance in China has failed terribly in channeling money from savers to borrowers in an efficient way. Finance in China has involved too many intermediate layers, which contribute little to the resolution of the information asymmetry problems but increase the cost of financial intermediation significantly. Corporate China, especially the private companies, can benefit tremendously from more efficient financial intermediation. Allowing private capital to enter finance would facilitate the emergence of differentiated financial services and beef up the competition among financial service providers. This, in the long term, would particularly benefit the private sector and the SME sector in China.

DEEPEN MARKET-ORIENTED REFORMS IN PRODUCTION FACTOR MARKETS

In the past three and a half decades, China has scored notable achievements in pushing forward market-oriented reforms. Now, the vast majority of prices are set by supply and demand. Although the market economy in China is still flawed and those flaws are oftentimes dubbed "Chinese characteristics," it is an indisputable fact that the bulk of the Chinese economy is a market economy. Nevertheless, in the markets of production factors and the government-monopolized markets such as tobacco, the government still meddles in many things, from the prices of oil, gas, and electricity to cost of capital.

When the state tightly controls the factor markets, there are at least two adverse economic consequences. First, the allocation of production factors would be influenced by national policies and by entrenched interest groups who may have hijacked the government. Given that, high-ROIC companies, the real growth engine of the Chinese economy, may not get full access to resources and capital for their future development, while the state-favored inefficient companies may overspend and drag down the level of ROIC. Second, the state monopolizing the factor markets also results in distorted prices. Pricing distortion leads to inefficient allocation of resources and fails to boost production efficiency. The fact that China has ended up with a scale-driven rather than an efficiency-driven growth model to develop its economy is largely due to the insufficient marketization of the production factors.

In the following section, I shift my discussion to the firm-level initiatives. Over-emphasis on scale rather than value creation, poorly conceived corporate strategy, and a lack of effective corporate governance mechanisms have all been suggested earlier in this book to explain why there are big but not great Chinese companies. The prescriptions offered below are not just painkillers—they are the cure if we take action.

BE IN THE RIGHT PLACE

One has to appreciate the empirical observation that successful companies always go after fast-growing markets. The rise of General Electric benefited tremendously from the widespread use of electricity everywhere in people's lives. The surge of Huawei has a lot to do with the strong demand for telecommunication equipment and services by telecom carriers all over the world; Huawei's current growth momentum stems more from the arrival of the mobile internet era. The success of Alibaba is largely due to the explosive growth of China's e-commerce market.

The growth engine of the Chinese economy is now changing from investment to consumption; the service sectors have for the first time contributed more than 50 percent of China's GDP in 2015. These economic megatrends are reshaping the economic landscape and spotting new growth areas for the Chinese companies.

Corporate behemoths, including SOEs and large private groups active in capital-intensive industries such as finance, energy, commodity, real estate, and low-end manufacturing, may simply stop growing, or even be forced out of business if they fail to move up the value chain. The up-and-coming companies have to understand that persistent growth can only come from fast-growing markets. In China, the fast-growing markets include healthcare, culture, high-end manufacturing, and so on. For incumbents and disrupters, going after fast-growing markets and showing up in the right place is a must.

ROIC, ROIC, ROIC

"One has to repeat important things three times." This line, widely circulated on China's most popular messaging app, WeChat, in 2015, can be applied here to highlight the most important rule for making a great

company in China. As I have elaborated in this book, the most important principle for a value-maximizing firm is to tenaciously work on ROIC—the foundational concept directly determining how valuable a company is. By presenting plenty of empirical evidence and anecdotes in Chap. 3, I have shown that ROIC squarely applies in China—the Chinese listed companies with higher ROIC tend to deliver higher risk-adjusted returns to their shareholders. For companies in either traditional or emerging businesses, putting ROIC ahead of size is the first step toward achieving greatness.

By aiming at high ROIC for a long enough time, a company prioritizes profit margin and cash flow over sales and total assets. It more likely pursues long-term benefit rather than short-term gains. It may deliberately pass up opportunities that only generate short-term returns. The company may also adopt an asset-light strategy to minimize potential disruptions and proactively create incentives for long-term value. To achieve high ROIC, the company may overcome strategic inertia and stay resilient in an uncertain time. A company needs sustainably high ROIC to survive the hits of potential depression, and escape the trap of management hubris arising during economic boom. Enhancing ROIC significantly is the greatest value redemption corporate China has to accomplish.

Promote Innovation

Winning firms are more productive. Innovation is the most reliable source of improved productivity. New cutting-edge technologies, global competition, digitalization, emerging competitors, and continuous changes in the global governance structure have made the life expectancy of a typical company significantly shorter than before. A company, if committed to being a great one, should be bold enough to promote "creative destruction" within itself by proactively spotting potential disruptive factors and disrupting itself before others do, seek the elements that can boost a company's ROIC, and incorporate them into the business model.

Chinese companies can learn lessons from Dell's experiences. Introducing the direct-sale model, Dell revolutionized the PC market and outperformed rivals on ROIC. Dell's rise benefited tremendously from the arrival of the internet era, which made it possible for it to build up an effective interface with customers. However, Dell was so profitable that it lost the urge to innovate further. Eventually, lack of innovation took its toll. Over time, more cost-effective Asian companies such as Lenovo and Acer had competed away Dell's market share. The emergence of substitutes such as tablet computers and smartphones dealt another blow to Dell. The company gradually lost its cutting edge, and slipped into mediocrity.

Sony is another example. Sony's value proposition used to be delivering to customers the most convenient and most fashionable new products. In the 1970s and 1980s, Sony was the king of innovation—Walkman once enjoyed the same worldwide popularity as Apple's iPod and iPhone do today. With success, Sony deviated from its customer-oriented and innovation-driven traditional value. It started pursuing a conglomeration strategy and made huge amounts of investments in businesses such as entertainment and properties. The company remained very profitable, thanks to its strong execution. But it gradually lost its technology savvy that had made it different from its peers. With the arrival of the internet, especially the mobile internet era, Sony totally lost its competitive edge and has been surpassed by Samsung and Apple. Sony, once a great company, is now on the brink of bankruptcy.

Stay innovative and get ready to disrupt yourself before others disrupt you. Tencent has set an excellent example for companies around the world, not just the Chinese companies. Before it launched its highly acclaimed mobile phone-based messaging app, WeChat, Tencent's computer-based messaging service, QQ, was already a huge success with more than 600 million users. Pushing WeChat out to the market would significantly erode QQ's user base and many took this as a suicidal move. However, Pony Ma, the founder of Tencent, firmly believed in the arrival of the mobile internet era, and did not want to sit on huge piles of cash, waiting for others to disrupt Tencent. As a result, WeChat was developed in three months and then launched. It has turned out to be an even greater success. As of end 2015, it has drawn 600 million monthly active users. In addition to instant messaging services, it is developing into an encompassing ecosystem that allows users to shop, book taxis and flights, transfer money online, and set up online stores. And the new features of WeChat are still growing.

If we chronicle the emergence of influential private companies in China in the past 35 years—from Lenovo, Haier, Huawei, Taikang, and Ping An Group to Alibaba, Tencent, Baidu.com, and Xiaomi.com—we observe four entrepreneurial waves during China's reform era.[2] The first wave occurred in the 1980s and gave birth to Lenovo, Huawei, and Haier; the second wave was jumpstarted right after Mr. Deng Xiaoping's "southern China tour," during which Taikang Life Insurance and many real estate developers were established and later flourished; the third entrepreneurial wave witnessed the boom and bust of the internet bubble in China and the surge of IT companies such as Baidu.com, Sohu.dom, Sina.com, and Tencent and e-commerce giants such as Alibaba and JD; finally, during the ongoing fourth entrepreneurial wave, one sees the birth of a series of mobile internet-based companies such as Xiaomi.com and Didi Kuaidi.

Companies with origins tracing back to different entrepreneurial waves have distinctive features. The success of the first and second generations of companies was largely due to the founders' courage and vision. The economic reform and opening up to the outside world unleashed Chinese people's demand for all sorts of products and services. Such demand had been repressed under the planned economy regime for more than 30 years since 1949. As long as a thing was produced, there was a demand out there. For these companies, their major concern was how to secure necessary resources to expand their operation scale as rapidly as possible. To secure resources such as land, raw materials, and bank loans, building up political connections was crucial.

Over time, market competition got tough and both the scope and scale of market-based transactions expanded greatly in China. To survive and thrive, a company, especially a private company, needed business savvy and strategic view. The third and fourth generations of companies were incentivized to learn from their western rivals—terms such as corporate strategy and business models entered the conversations of those younger founders and corporate executives. Competition and disruptive new technologies have forced many Chinese companies to constantly adapt their business to the changing business conditions. The Chinese companies have demonstrated their vibrancy and resilience in the process. If the government can embrace the bold reforms I have laid out in Chap. 7 to let Chinese companies compete on equal terms, some will rise to become truly great companies. For corporate China, this is not the best time, but this is the beginning of the best time.

NOTES

1. According to Philippon (2015), over the past 130 years, the finance income-to-GDP ratio in the US ranged from 2 to 5 percent most of the time. It jumped to more than 7 percent ahead of the most recent global financial crisis, and declined steadily to below 7 percent after the crisis.

2. The four entrepreneurial waves taking place during China's reform era were first raised by Edward Tse, a long-term consultant with Boston Consulting Group and PWC. See *The Economist*, "Back to Business," September 12, 2015a.

APPENDIX

TECHNICAL APPENDIX: SUNTECH'S ROIC

Return on invested capital (ROIC) is the ratio of net operating profit less adjusted tax (NOPLAT) divided by invested capital (IC). The concept is introduced to better capture a firm's operating performance. A simple way to compute NOPLAT is: NOPLAT = earnings before interest expense and taxe (EBIT) × (1 – the marginal tax rate). Invested capital refers to the total amount of capital employed in a firm's operating activities. It is computed as: IC = operating working capital + operating fixed assets + other long-term net operating assets, where operating working capital is measured as "operating cash + inventories + account receivables – account payables."

I use Suntech, the Chinese solar PV manufacturer discussed in Chap. 2, as an example to calculate ROIC based on information contained in financial statements. First, we start with Suntech's balance sheets, based on which we calculate the company's IC. Table A.1 presents Suntech's balance sheets from 2007 to 2011.

OPERATING WORKING CAPITAL

Operating working capital equals operating current assets—mainly including operating cash, account receivables, and inventories—minus operating current liabilities. In practice, operating cash is typically calculated as 2 percent of a company's total sales (note that when I analyze Alibaba's

© The Editor(s) (if applicable) and The Author(s) 2016   223
Q. Liu, *Corporate China 2.0*, DOI 10.1057/978-1-137-55089-7

Table A.1   Suntech's balance sheets, 2007–2011

$ million	2007	2008	2009	2010	2011
Cash and cash equivalents	521	507.8	833.2	872.5	492.4
Account receivables	268.3	259.9	423.7	534.9	480.9
Inventories	176.2	231.9	280.1	558.2	516.5
Short-term investment	61.6	5.1	201.1	15.4	37.4
Other current assets	230.4	317.2	417.9	431.4	558.8
Total current assets	1257.5	1321.9	2156.0	2412.4	2086.0
Fixed assets	293	684.5	777.6	1326.2	1569.2
Intangible assets	86.0	176.7	140.8	156.0	23.0
Goodwill	29.8	87.6	86.1	278	0
Long-term investment	1.3	275.6	305.2	599.5	463.8
Other assets	299.4	660.6	518	445	395.3
Total assets	1967.0	3206.9	3983.7	5217.1	4537.3
Account payables	116.3	255.1	390.9	627.3	762.5
Short-term borrowing	321.2	638.5	800.4	1400.8	1573.4
Other current liabilities	40.6	83.1	326.8	341.9	273
Total current liabilities	478.1	976.7	1518.1	2370.0	2608.9
Long-term debt	20.7	5.9	138	163.3	133.3
Convertible bond	423.4	812.9	516.9	551.2	580.9
Other liabilities	215.5	177	197.9	252.4	261.4
Total liabilities	1137.7	1972.5	2370.9	3336.9	3584.5
Common equity	811.4	1225.9	1598.1	1867.7	946.4
Minority investment	17.9	8.5	14.7	12.5	6.4
Total liabilities and equity	1967.0	3206.9	3983.7	5217.1	4537.3

ROIC in Chap. 8, I have assumed that Alibaba's operating cash is 10 percent of its total sales). Operating current liabilities are the liabilities generated in a company's operations including accounts payable, wages payable, deferred incomes, and income tax payable.

FIXED ASSETS

Fixed assets are a company's net plant, property, and equipment.

OTHER LONG-TERM OPERATING ASSETS

If no detailed explanations are given about a company's other long-term assets, then they could be assumed to be part of the long-term operating assets.

I do not discuss goodwill here. When calculating a company's IC, we usually consider two cases: including goodwill and not including goodwill. The latter is more common.

According to the above explanations, we can calculate Suntech's operating IC as shown in Table A.2.

Next I show how to calculate NOPLAT based on a company's income statements. Table A.3 presents the income statements of Suntech and the calculated NOPLAT between 2007 and 2011.

The two most important items for the calculation of NOPLAT are EBIT and the marginal tax rate. EBIT could be found in the income statement. For simplicity, I assume that the marginal tax rate in China is 25 percent. Table A.3 presents the process of computing NOPLAT, though the required items can be found in the income statement. It also shows the computed ROIC of Suntech from 2007 to 2011.

As shown in Table A.4, Suntech's ROIC varied significantly, ranging from −19.9 percent in 2011 to 16.2 percent in 2007. Also note that the ratio of EBIT to IC is labeled pre-tax ROIC.

Table A.2 Suntech's operating invested capital, 2007–2011

$ million	2007	2008	2009	2010	2011
Operating cash	27.0	38.5	33.9	58.0	62.9
Inventory	176.2	231.9	280.1	558.2	516.5
Account receivables	268.3	259.9	423.7	534.9	480.9
Account payables	116.3	255.1	390.9	627.3	762.5
Other operating assets	189.8	234.1	91.1	89.5	285.8
Working capital	545.0	509.3	437.9	613.3	583.6
Fixed assets	293.0	684.5	777.6	1326.2	1569.2
Other long-term operating assets	83.9	483.6	320.1	192.6	133.9
Invested capital (not including goodwill)	**921.9**	**1677.4**	**1535.6**	**2132.1**	**2286.7**
Goodwill	29.8	87.6	86.1	278.0	0.0
Invested capital (including goodwill)	**951.7**	**1765.0**	**1621.7**	**2410.1**	**2286.7**

Table A.3 Suntech's income statements, 2007–2011

$ million	2007	2008	2009	2010	2011
Sales	1348.3	1923.5	1693.3	2901.9	3146.6
Cost of goods sold	1048.1	1532.1	1264.9	2273.9	2618.4
Selling, general, and administrative costs	80.7	152.0	159.0	251.1	411.4
Research and development expenses	15.0	15.3	29.0	40.2	38.6
Other income	0.0	0.0	0.0	54.6	581.8
Earnings before interest expense, tax, depreciation, and amortization (EBITDA)	204.5	224.1	240.4	282.1	−503.6
Depreciation and amortization	20.5	41.6	66.4	84.9	141.6
Earnings before interest expense and tax (EBIT)	184.0	182.5	174.0	197.2	−645.2
Interest income	11.8	31.2	32.6	9.6	7.6
Interest expense	30.0	104.7	126.3	101.5	143.5
Income from affiliates	−0.7	0.3	−3.3	250.8	−98.7
Other income	−8.7	−76.7	11.2	−94.4	−171.3
Pre-tax income	156.4	32.6	88.2	261.7	−1051.1
Income tax	−13.2	−1.6	−2.5	−23.8	47.2
Loss from operation suspension (after tax)	–	–	–	–	−14.1
Net profit	143.2	31.0	85.7	237.9	−1018.0
Minority interest	2.7	1.4	−0.1	−1.0	−0.6
Net profit to shareholders	145.9	32.4	85.6	236.9	−1018.6
EPS before dilution	1.0	0.2	0.5	1.3	−5.6
EPS after dilution	0.9	0.2	0.5	1.3	−5.6

Table A.4 Suntech's NOPLAT and ROIC, 2007–2011

$ million	2007	2008	2009	2010	2011
Total sales	1348.3	1923.5	1693.3	2901.9	3146.6
Cost of goods sold	1048.1	1532.1	1264.9	2273.9	2618.4
Selling, general, and administrative expenses	80.7	152.0	159.0	251.1	411.4
Other operating income	0.0	0.0	0.0	54.6	581.8
Depreciation and amortization	20.5	41.6	66.4	84.9	141.6
EBIT	**199.0**	**197.8**	**203.0**	**237.4**	**−606.6**
Tax on EBIT	49.7	49.4	50.8	59.3	−151.6
NOPLAT	**149.3**	**148.4**	**152.3**	**178.1**	**−455.0**
ROIC (before goodwill) (%)	**16.2**	**8.8**	**9.9**	**8.4**	**−19.9**
ROIC (after goodwill) (%)	**15.7**	**8.4**	**9.4**	**7.4**	**−19.9**

BIBLIOGRAPHY

Acemoglu, D., & Robinson, J. (2012). *Why nations fail: The origins of power, prosperity, and poverty*. New York: Crown Business.

Acemoglu, D., Robinson, J., & Johnson, S. (2001). The colonial origins of comparative development: An empirical investigation. *American Economic Review, 91*, 1369–1401.

Alibaba Group. (2014). The road show presentation. September, 2015.

Allen, F., Qian, J., & Qian, M. (2005). Law, finance, and economic growth in China. *Journal of Financial Economics, 77*(1), 57–116.

Bae, K.-H., Kang, J.-K., & Kim, J.-M. (2002). Tunneling or value added? Evidence from mergers by Korean business groups. *Journal of Finance, 57*, 2695–2740.

Baghai, M., Coley, S., & White, D. (2000). *The alchemy of growth: Practical insights for building enduirng enterprise*. Boston: Da Capo Press.

Bai, C.-E., Hsieh, C. T., & Qian, Y. (2006). The return to capital in China. *Brookings Papers in Economic Activity.*

Bai, C.-E., Liu, Q., Lu, J., Song, F., & Zhang, J. (2004a). Corporate governance and firm valuations in China. *Journal of Comparative Economics, 32*, 4519–4616.

Bai, C.-E., Liu, Q., & Song, F. (2004b). The value of corporate control: Evidence from China's distressed firms. *HKU working paper.*

Becht, M., Bolton, P., & Roell, A. (2003). Corporate governance and control. In G. Constantinides, M. Harris, & R. Stulz (Eds.), *Handbook of The Economics of Finance* (Vol. 1A). North Holland: Elsevier.

Beinhocker, E. (2006). *The origin of wealth: Evolution, complexity, and the radical remaking of economics*. Boston: Harvard Business School Press.

Berger, P. G., & Ofek, E. (1995). Diversification's effect on firm value. *Journal of Financial Economics, 37*, 39–65.

Berle, A., & Means, G. (1932). *The modern corporation and private property*. New York: Macmillan.

© The Editor(s) (if applicable) and The Author(s) 2016   227
Q. Liu, *Corporate China 2.0*, DOI 10.1057/978-1-137-55089-7

Bertrand, M., Mehta, P., & Mullainathan, S. (2002). Ferreting out tunneling: An application to Indian business groups. *The Quarterly Journal of Economics, 117,* 121–148.

Boyreau-Debray, G., & Wei, S. J. (2005). Pitfalls of a state dominated financial system: The case of China. *NBER working paper.*

Brandt, L., & Zhu, X. (2000). Redistribution in a decentralized economy: Growth and inflation in China under reform. *Journal of Political Economy, 108,* 422–439.

Brandt, L., & Li, H. (2003). Bank discrimination in transition economies: Ideology, information, or incentives? *Journal of Comparative Economics, 31,* 387–413.

Buchanan, J., & Tullock, G. (1962). *The calculus of consent: Logical foundations of constitutional democracy.* Ann Arbor: University of Michigan Press.

Cai, H., Liu, Q., & Yu, M. (2013). Trade liberalization and corporate financing decisions. *Peking University Guanghua School of Management Working Paper.*

Campa, J., & Kedia, S. (1999). Explaining the diversification discount. *Working paper,* Harvard Business School.

Cha, L. (2001). *The future of China's capital markets and the role of corporate governance.* Luncheon Speech at China Business Summit.

China International Capital Corporation. (2015). Research on unlisted companies. October 2015.

Classens, S., Djankov, S., & Lang, H. P. (2000). The separation of ownership and control in East Asian corporations. *Journal of Financial Economics, 58,* 81–112.

Claessens, S., Djankov, S., Fan, J., & Lang, L. (2002). Disentangling the incentive and entrenchment effects of large shareholders. *Journal of Finance, 57,* 2741–2771.

Clarke, D. (2003). Corporate governance in China: An overview. *China Economic Review, 14,* 494–507.

Collins, J. (2001). *Good to great: Why some companies make the leap and others don't.* New York: Harper Business.

Collins, J., & Porras, J. I. (1994). *Built to last: Successful habits of visionary companies.* New York: Harper Business.

Cull, R., & Xu, L. C. (2003). Who gets credit? The behavior of bureaucrats and state banks in allocating credit to Chinese state-owned enterprises. *Journal of Development Economics, 71*(2), 533–559.

Demsetz, H., & Lehn, K. (1985). The structure of corporate ownership: Causes and consequences. *Journal of Political Economy, 93,* 1155–1177.

Denis, D. K., & McConnell, J. J. (2003). International corporate governance. *Journal of Financial and Quantitative Analysis, 38*(1), 1–36.

De Soto, H. (2000). *The mystery of capital: Why capitalism triumphs in the west and fails everywhere else.* New York: Basic Books.

The Economist. (2015a). Back to business. September 12.

The Economist. (2015b). Paper tiger, roaring dragon. September 12.

The Economist. (2015c). Clicks to bricks. August 15.

The Economist. (2015d). From alpha to omega. August 15.

The Economist. (2015e). Just a little bit richer. April 4.

The Economist. (2016). Grossly deceptive plans. January 30.

Fama, E. F. (1970). Efficient capital markets: A review of theory and empirical work. *Journal of Finance, 25,* 383–417.

Fama, E., & French, K. (1992). The cross section of expected stock returns. *Journal of Finance, 47*(2), 427.

Foster, R., & Kaplan, S. (2001). *Creative destruction: Why companies that are built to last underperform the market-and how to successfully transform them.* New York: The Currency Press.

Graham, J., Lemmon, M., & Wolf, J. (2002). Does corporate diversification destroy value? *Journal of Finance, 57,* 695–720.

Harvard Business School. (2009). Alibaba's Taobao (A), HBS Case: 9-709-456, July 2009.

Hayek, F. (1945, August). The use of knowledge in society. *American Economic Review, 35,* 519–530.

Hotz, C. 2005. China's economic growth 1978–2025: What we know today about China's economic growth tomorrow. *Working Paper,* HKUST.

Hsieh, C.-T., & Klenow, P. (2009). Misallocation and manufacturing in China and India. *Quarterly Journal of Economics, 124,* 1403–1448.

Huang, Y. (1996). *Inflation and investment controls in China: The political economy of central-local relations during the reform era.* Cambridge: Cambridge University Press.

Huang, Y. (2010). *Capitalism with Chinese characteristics.* Cambridge: Cambridge University Press.

Ivey School of Management. (2013). Huawei enters the United States, Case W13306, July 2013.

Jensen, M. C. (1986). Agency costs of free cash flow, corporate finance, and take-overs. *American Economic Review, 76,* 323–329.

Jensen, M., & Meckling, W. (1976). Theory of the firm: Managerial behaviour, agency costs and ownership structure. *Journal of Financial Economics, 3*(4), 305.

Johnson, S., Kaufmann, D., & Shleifer, A. (1997). The unofficial economy in transition. *Brookings papers on economic activity,* fall (2), 159–239.

Johnson, S., La Porta, R., Lopez de Silanes, F., & Shleifer, A. (2000). Tunneling. *American Economic Review, 90,* 22–27.

Khanna, T., & Palepu, K. (2000). Is group affiliation profitable in emerging markets? An analysis of diversified Indian business groups. *Journal of Finance, 55*(2), 867–891.

Kornai, J. (1980). *The economics of shortage.* Amsterdam: North-Holland.

Kraemer, K., Linden, G., & Dedrick, J. (2011). Capturing value in global networks: Apple's iPad and iPhone. UC Irvine, *UC Berkeley and Syracuse working paper*.

Krugman, P. (1994). The myth of Asia's miracle. *Foreign Policy, 73*(6), 62–78.

Lamont, O. (1997). Cash flow and investment: Evidence from internal capital markets. *Journal of Finance, 52*, 57–82.

Lamont, O., & Polk, C. (2001). The diversification discount: Cash flows vs returns. *Journal of Finance, 56*, 1693–1721.

Landry, P. F. (2008). *Decentralized authoritarianism in China: The communist party's control of local elites in the post-mao era*. Cambridge: Cambridge University Press.

Lang, L., & Stulz, R. (1994). Tobin's q, corporate diversification, and firm value. *Journal of Political Economy, 102*, 1248–1280.

La Porta, R., Lopez de Silanes, F., & Shleifer, A. (1999). Corporate ownership around the world. *Journal of Finance, 54*, 471–517.

La Porta, R., Lopez de Silanes, F., Shleifer, A., & Vishny, R. W. (1997). Legal determinants of external finance. *Journal of Finance, 52*, 1131–1150.

La Porta, R., Lopez de Silanes, F., Shleifer, A., & Vishny, R. W. (1998). Law and finance. *Journal of Political Economy, 106*, 1112–1155.

La Porta, R., Lopez-de-Silanes, F., Shleifer, A., & Vishny, R. (2000). Agency problems and dividend policies around the world, *Journal of Finance, 55*, 1–33.

La Porta, R., Lopez de Silanes, F., Shleifer, A., & Vishny, R. W. (2002). Investor protection and corporate valuation. *Journal of Finance, 57*, 1147–1170.

Levine, R., & Laeven, L. (2007). Is there a diversification discount in financial conglomerates? *Journal of Financial Economics, 85*(2), 331–367.

Li, H., & Zhou, L.-A. (2005). Political turnover and economic performance: The incentive role of personnel control in China. *Journal of Public Economics, 89*(9–10), 1743–1762.

Liu, Q. (2006). Corporate governance in China: Current practices, economic effects, and institutional determinants. *CESifo Economic Studeis, 52*(2), 415–453.

Liu, Q., Lejot, P., & Arner, D. (2013). *Finance in Asia: Institutions, regulation and policy*. London: Routledge.

Liu, Q., & Lu, J. (2007). Corporate governance and earnings management: A tunneling perspective. *Journal of Corporate Finance, 13*, 881–906.

Liu, Q., & Qi, R. (2008). Stock trading and diversification discount. *Economics Letters, 98*, 35–40.

Liu, Q., & Siu, A. (2011). Institutions and corporate investment: Evidence from an investment implied return on capital in China. *Journal of Financial and Quantitative Analysis, 46*(6), 1831–1863.

Liu, Q., & Wang, X. (2015). Those born in the winter know how to weather the storm: An investigation of firms born in recession. *Guanghua School of Management working paper*.

Liu, Q., Zheng, Y., & Zhu, Y. (2012). The evolution and consequences of Chinese pyramids. *Peking University Guanghua School of Management Working Paper*.

Lu, D. (2015). Exceptional exporter performance? Evidence from Chinese manufacturing firms. *University of Rochester working paper*.

Lucas, R. (1990). Why doesn't capital flow from rich to poor countries? *American Economic Review, 80*(2), 92–96.

Malkiel, B. G. (2000). *A random walk down wall street*. New York: W.W. Norton & Company.

McKinsey Global Institute. (2015a). *The China effect on global innovation*. Washington: McKinsey Global Institute.

McKinsey Global Institute. (2015b). *The new global competition for corporate profit*. Washington: McKinsey Global Institute.

Micklethwait, J., & Wooldridge, A. (2003). The company: A short history of an evolutionary idea. *A Modern Library Chronicles Book*.

Nathan, A., & Gilley, B. (2002). *China's new rulers: The secret files*. New York: New York Review of Books.

Philippon, T. (2015). Has the US finance industry become less efficient? *American Economic Review, 105*(4), 1408–1438.

Pistor, K., & Xu, C. (2005). Governing stock market in transition economies: Lessons from China. *American Law and Economic Review, 7*(1), 184–210.

Plath, S. 1982. *The collected poems* (T. Hughs, ed.). London: HarperPerennial.

Porter, M. (1980). *Competitive strategy: Techniques for analyzing industries and competitors*. New York: Free Press.

Porter, M. (1985). *Competitive advantage: Creating and sustaining superior performance*. New York: Free Press.

Prasad, E., Rajan, R., & Subramanian, A. (2007). The paradox of capital. *Finance and Development, 44*(1), 16–19.

Qian, Y., & Xu, C. (1993). The M-form hierarchy and China's economic reform. *European Economic Review, 31*, 541–548.

Rajan, R. (2010). *Fault lines: How hidden fractures still threaten the world economy*. New Jersey: Princeton University Press.

Raynor, M. E., & Ahmed, M. (2013). Three rules for making a company truly great. *Harvard Business Review, 91*(4), 108–117.

Sharpe, W. (1964). Capital asset prices: A theory of market equilibrium under conditions of risk. *Journal of Finance, 19*(3), 425–442.

Shleifer, A., & Vishny, R. W. (1997). A survey of corporate governance. *Journal of Finance, 52*, 737–783.

Shleifer, A., & Vishny, R. (1998). *The grabbing hand: Government pathologies and their cures*. Cambridge: Harvard University Press.

Solow, R. (1956). A contribution to the theory of economic growth. *Quarterly Journal of Economics, 70*(1), 65–94.

Southern Weekends. (2013). The punishment on *Wanfu Biotechnology*, a joke! May 24.

Studwell, J. (2013). *How Asia works: Success and failure in the world's most dynamic region*. London: Profile Books.

Whited, T. (2001). Is it inefficient investment that causes the diversification discount? *Journal of Finance, 56*, 1667–1691.

Wiggins, R., & Ruefli, T. (2002). Competitive advantage: Temporal dynamics and the incidence and persistence of superior economic performance. *Organization Science, 13*(1), 81–105.

Wiggins, R., & Ruefli, T. (2005). Schumpeter's ghost: Is hyper-competition making the best of times shorter? *Strategic Management Journal, 26*, 887–911.

Wired Magazine. 2016. Lei Jun: It is time to copy China, Xiaomi's formula for success, by David Rowan, April Issue.

Xu, C. (2011). The fundamental institutions of China's reforms and development. *Journal of Economic Literature, 49*(4), 1076–1151.

Young, A. (2003). Gold onto base metals: Productivity growth in the People's Republic of China during the reform period. *Quarterly Journal of Economics, 111*(6), 1220–1261.

Zhu, X. (2012). Understanding China's growth: Past, present, and future. *Journal of Economic Perspectives, 26*(4), 103–124.

INDEX[1]

---

[1] Note: Page numbers followed by "n" denote notes.

© The Editor(s) (if applicable) and The Author(s) 2016   233
Q. Liu, *Corporate China 2.0*, DOI 10.1057/978-1-137-55089-7

Printed by Printforce, the Netherlands